Practical Problems

of a

Private Psychotherapy Practice

Practical Problems
of a
Private Psychotherapy Practice

Compiled and Edited by

GEORGE D. GOLDMAN, Ph.D.

Clinical Professor of Psychology
Supervisor of Psychotherapy and Director
Postdoctoral Psychotherapy Center
Institute of Advanced Psychological Studies
Adelphi University
Garden City, New York

and

GEORGE STRICKER, Ph.D.

Professor of Psychology and Assistant Director
Institute of Advanced Psychological Studies
Adelphi University
Garden City, New York

CHARLES C THOMAS · PUBLISHER
Springfield · Illinois · U.S.A.

Published and Distributed Throughout the World by

CHARLES C THOMAS • PUBLISHER

BANNERSTONE HOUSE

301-327 East Lawrence Avenue, Springfield, Illinois, U.S.A.

© *1972, by* CHARLES C THOMAS • PUBLISHER

ISBN 0-398-02296—8

Library of Congress Catalog Card Number: 71-187656

Printed in the United States of America

HH-11

CONTRIBUTORS

Tess Forrest, Ph.D., *Faculty, William Alanson White Institute; H.I.P. Queens-Nassau Mental Health Service; Private Practice, Great Neck, New York*

Haim G. Ginott, Ed.D., *Adjunct Professor of Psychology, Graduate School of Arts and Sciences, New York University; Clinical Professor of Psychology, Institute of Advanced Psychological Studies, Adelphi University, Garden City, New York; Former UNESCO Consultant in Child Guidance to the Government of Israel, Ministry of Education*

George D. Goldman, Ph.D., *Clinical Professor of Psychology, Supervisor of Psychotherapy; Director, Postdoctoral Psychotherapy Center, Institute of Advanced Psychological Studies, Adelphi University, Garden City, New York; Private Practice, New York, New York*

S. George Greenspan, C.P.A., *C.P.A., Winter, Greenspan & Company; Consultant, Manhattan College, New York, New York*

Florence Halpern, Ph.D., *Clinical Associate Professor, New York University School of Medicine, New York, New York*

George L. Jurow, Ph.D., LL.B., *Staff Psychologist, The Mental Health Consultation Center, New York City; Assistant Professor, Manhattan Community College of the City University of New York, New York, New York; Member, New York Bar*

Abraham Lurie, Ph.D., *Director of Social Work, Hillside Hospital, Glen Oaks, New York; Associate Professor of Social Work, Adelphi University, Garden City, New York*

William E. Mariano, LL.B., *Counsel, New York State Psychological Association, New York, New York; Private Practice, New York, New York*

George Nicklin, M.D., *Clinical Associate Professor of Psychiatry, New York University School of Medicine; Associate Attending Neuropsychiatrist, University Hospital; Associate Attending Neuropsychiatrist, Bellevue Psychiatric Hospital, New York, New York*

Irving Shelsky, Ph.D., *St. Charles Hospital, Port Jefferson, New York; Nassau County Cardiac Work Evaluation Unit, South Nassau*

Communities Hospital, Oceanside, New York; Private Practice, Smithtown, New York

Max Siegel, Ph.D., *Professor of Education, Brooklyn College of the City University of New Yark, New York, New York; Director, School Psychology Training Program, Brooklyn College, Brooklyn, New York; Clinical Professor of Psychology, Institute of Advanced Psychological Studies, Adelphi University, Garden City, New York; Private Practice, Brooklyn and Queens, New York*

Rose Spiegel, M.D., *Training Analyst, Supervisor and Fellow, William Alanson White Institute, New York, New York; Associate Psychiatrist, New York State Psychiatric Institute Fellow, American Academy of Psychoanalysts*

Thea C. Spyer, Ph.D., *Private Practice, New York, New York; Consultant, St. Vincent's Hospital of Westchester, Harrison, New York*

George Stricker, Ph.D., *Professor of Psychology and Assistant Director, Institute of Advanced Psychological Studies, Adelphi University, Garden City, New York; Clinical Psychologist, Queens-Nassau Mental Health Service; Private Practice, Great Neck, New York*

To our wives
BELLE *and* JOAN

INTRODUCTION

Most psychotherapists are trained in academic and clinical settings which prepare them for the professional responsibilities of private practice. Rarely, however, does this training include information about how to handle the myriad of practical details that are part and parcel of the day-to-day business of being a private therapist. Such details and practical matters are usually learned only by trial and error or consultation with more experienced colleagues. Neither are adequate solutions. The trial-and-error method is time consuming and unreliable, and what works for your colleagues may not always work for you.

For the past seven years, Dr. George D. Goldman, one of the editors of this book, has taught a course called, "The Practical Problems of a Private Therapeutic Practice" in the Postdoctroal Program at Adelphi University. It has been so well received by successive groups of students that it was decided to make the content of this course available to more people by expanding its nuclear ideas and incorporating them into a book. A multi-authored volume seemed the most appropriate format, since it would bring to readers the expertise of acknowledged leaders in each of the areas discussed. The editors owe a debt of gratitude to the foresight of the Administrative Committee of the Post-doctoral Program at Adelphi for including such a course in the curriculum, and particularly to its co-directors, Dr. Gordon F. Derner and Dr. Donald S. Milman.

In dealing with the practical issues of private practice, this book should be for the psychotherapist what a book on medical economics is to the physician, or practice management is to the dentist. This particular book, however, goes beyond the scope of most such books by including, where it is reasonable to do so, some speculation about the psychotherapeutic implications, from a psychoanalytic point of view, of the practical decision. Because of the orientation of the authors, clinical psychologists are most

likely to respond to its content, but the material is equally rel-
event to psychiatrists and social workers. Therapists who are
contemplating private practice or who have recently opened a
practice will profit most from this volume, though it can also
serve as a valuable reference for therapists of long standing.

The initial chapter, written by Dr. George D. Goldman, de-
scribes how one goes about setting up a private practice—from
finding appropriate office space to collecting fees. It is followed
by three chapters on the kinds of problems that arise in specialized practices. Child therapy is discussed by Dr. Haim Ginott,
group therapy by Dr. Max Siegel, and family therapy by Dr.
Tess Forrest. The next three chapters deal with specific problems
in private practice which call for special solutions. First there is
Dr. Rose Spiegel's paper entitled "Management of Crises in
Psychotherapy"; then Dr. George Nicklin's on the use of drugs
in private practice; and finally Dr. Abraham Lurie's chapter,
"The Decision to Hospitalize." The problem of ethics is common to all areas of private practice and is covered by Dr. Thea
Spyer in Chapter 8. Chapters 9 through 11 look at issues in
private practice which are other than the purely psychotherapeutic. These are Dr. Florence Halpern's chapter on the "Psychodiagnostic Practice," Dr. Irving Shelsky's on the special problems of working with the handicapped, and Dr. George Stricker's
chapter entitled "Research and Private Practice." The last two
chapters deal with general problems in the administration of a
private practice. First, there is William E. Mariano and Dr.
George Jurow's section on law followed by S. George Greenspan's
paper entitled "Accounting, Tax, Retirement, and Estate Aspects
of the Psychotherapist's Practice."

ACKNOWLEDGMENTS

The editors wish to thank Mrs. Leslie Meltzer for indexing the book and being generally helpful, Miss Barbara Anne Leavy for her editorial assistance, and Mrs. Marie Kehoe for contributing her typing and secretarial skills. Many thanks also to Miss Rhonda Warshaw for her general assistance and helpfulness with this publication and other related activities here at the Institute of Advanced Psychological Studies.

CONTENTS

xiii

Practical Problems

of a

Private Psychotherapy Practice

Chapter 1

THE ESTABLISHMENT OF A PRIVATE PRACTICE

George D. Goldman

With a modicum of apologizing, let us attack head-on a topic that many clinicians find uncomfortable and most training schools avoid—how to set up a private practice. All of us, both beginning and more advanced practitioners, struggle with the same questions. What are the advantages of private practice? The disadvantages? When should I consider opening up my own practice? Should it be part-time or full-time? Where should it be located? How do I get patients?

Once these questions have been answered and private practice is still indicated, there are the everyday details of how to run the store, household practicalities such as setting up an office, establishing fees, and billing, without which we cannot effectively do the larger professional things that we have spent so many years learning to do. My task in this chapter is to put all of this in some perspective without taking these problems either too seriously or too lightly.

PREREQUISITES

What Private Practice Requires of You

As a private practitioner, every decision you make is your own. No one is looking over your shoulder to advise or correct you. To be able to work independently and to deal effectively and professionally with this much responsibility without experiencing a disabling amount of anxiety, you need a high degree of personal maturity and self-confidence. Though one can get a good deal of theoretical knowledge and some solid practical experience in school, an M.D., a Ph.D. in clinical psychology, or a

3

M.S.W. in social work is not really enough. You should also have at least two or three years of hospital or clinical experience plus some postdoctoral training. Ideally, you should then enter private practice gradually, with another job to back you up financially. In this way, you can slowly evolve your practice and grow into it at your own pace.

By the time you are considering private practice you should have been exposed to most of the current theories of psychotherapy, and more than likely you will find yourself particularly attracted to one or two. Personally, I do not feel that a therapist should operate under any single theoretical framework, be it Freudian analysis, rational therapy, or behavior modification. This is not to say, of course, that you should not have your own organized system of beliefs by which you do therapy. Rather, your particular theoretical orientation to patients and their problems should arise through utilizing your unique talents and experiences in living, combined and integrated into a thorough and up-to-date knowledge of what is being done in the areas of psychotherapy that interest you. Flexibility is important, and your theories should be open to revision when challenged, either by new ideas or thought-provoking experiences with patients.

Not only does a private practitioner need to have confidence in his professional skills and abilities but he should also be very clear about the kinds of patients he can work with. It is an illusion to think that even the most competent and experienced therapist can work with anyone who comes to him for help. Certain kinds of problems may trigger so much anxiety in a therapist that he and the patient can not work together fruitfully. The patient would be better off with another therapist and the therapist, with a different patient.

This brings me to what I feel is a particularly important prerequisite for anyone who wishes to enter private practice. He must be more consciously aware of his assets and liabilities as a human being than others are; he must have a better, clearer understanding of himself than he would have been able to compromise on if he had never chosen to enter private practice and had continued working in either a hospital or clinic. This does not mean that a private practitioner has to be a superhuman, well-adjusted individual who has resolved all his conflicts. You simply have to know yourself well enough so that when working with patients you only minimally act out of your own pathology and then correct for it. It is my belief that anyone planning to enter private practice should have had their own experience as a patient for a sufficient amount of time to work out their major difficulties in life and, if necessary, continue treatment and/or analysis, or at least not discount the possibility of having to return to it later. To put it more precisely, being therapists mandates the need for therapy ourselves when we are to do anything but the most superficial of counseling.

For therapists who do not have an analytic orientation or who, for whatever the reason, do not feel the necessity for their own personal therapy, good supervision may be very helpful. Seeing a more experienced colleague of your own choosing and discussing your work with him will not only be one step in your striving for a continuing education but can help you get clearer on yourself and your patients. It could, for example, clarify where you are meaningfully in contact with their needs or where you may be relating to them out of some unfilled needs of your own. The end result of this supervisory experience could be faster change in your patients as well as greater insight into yourself as a person and a functioning professional.

I particularly stress this point because I believe that working with people necessitates a greater and more sincere commitment to your own personal growth than you might be able to get along with in another field. Helping people grow and change is the greatest responsibility, as well as, in my opinion, the greatest advantage, of being a therapist in private practice. Few experiences in life compare with watching and participating in this process. But it is impossible to validate your patient's attempts to resolve personal conflicts, to work toward becoming a more thoroughly *human* human being, if your orientation toward growth and change in your own life is one of despair and hopelessness. You must make a commitment, either on your own or with the help of therapy, to being alive and involved in the world, to grow personally and professionally all the time. The personal benefits of such a commitment are obvious. Professionally, it will enable you to relate more empathically to your patients. Of course it would be much easier and a good deal less painful to sit up in our analytic ivory towers and pass judgment on the lives of other people, without allowing ourselves to notice how much more similar than dissimilar we are to most of our patients and that our understanding of them goes beyond anything we have read in a textbook. Being a therapist allows you the constant opportunity to learn, both on a professional and personal level, from other people's experience. You would be cheating yourself of one of the greatest fringe benefits of your profession if you refused to acknowledge it.

Reaping the Advantages and Coping with the Disadvantages of Your Own Practice

While I feel that the advantages of going into private practice far outweight the disadvantages, I nevertheless would advise anyone interested in doing private therapy to give due consideration to both. I suspect you have already given some thought to the advantages of setting up your own practice, so let us review them together.

In addition to the endless opportunities to learn about other people and yourself, private practice brings with it greater income as well as the freedom to set up your own schedule, work the hours and days you want, choose the vacations you please, and decide who you want to work with and who you do not. But more importantly, it affords you the opportunity to creatively use your personal and professional talents to their fullest extent and to pursue your own ideas and beliefs in whatever way you think is most effective. This makes private practice very different from a hospital or clinic where your work is under careful scrutiny by supervisors not of your own choosing, whose opinions you may not respect, and who you may not even like personally. Also, when you are a private practitioner, patients choose you as their therapist and work with you because they like you and respect your abilities, not because they were assigned to you. Many therapists feel that this experience brings out the best in them. They can be looser, more relaxed, and more open with private patients than they could be with patients they see in a hospital or clinic.

But one can rarely gain additional freedom without incurring greater responsibility, and therapists in private practice are no exception. Some experience this greater responsibility as a challenge. For others, it can be a source of tremendous anxiety, particularly if they lack maturity and self-confidence. I cannot emphasize strongly enough that private practice should not be undertaken by someone fresh out of graduate school who has had little or no full-time experience working with patients. The personal and professional responsibilities of private practice are greater than most experienced therapists have ever previously encountered. For a novice, the disadvantages and subsequent discomforts of such responsibility will be multiplied.

Many of you planning to go into private psychoanalytic practice must also be prepared to handle a good deal of loneliness of a very unique variety. The loneliness I am talking about goes beyond working by yourself in an office without colleagues or a secretary. It is the very special loneliness of many psychoanalytically oriented therapists who, although they are with people hour after hour, day in and day out, are nonetheless alone. For them, the classically analytic therapist-patient relationship has no social reality; it is purely symbolic. It is the therapist's task to focus on the patient and his needs rather than to mutually interact with him. Most patients, except for those in the later phases of treatment, do not know and often do not want to know who you really are. You are the therapist, Dr. So and So, and whoever else they need you to be—not yourself. I am, of course, referring to the transference aspects of the therapeutic relationship which will often leave you with a strong need at the end of the day for someone who just knows who you are and cares how *you* feel.

This situation can be aggravated by the fact that, after a hard day's work, a therapist may go home to a family who has similar needs for understanding, when he is so needful of contact and understanding himself. Under these circumstances, communication between the therapist and his wife (or her husband) could be facilitated if the spouse is, or at least was, in therapy.

The unique loneliness of a full-time therapist in private practice is real and must be dealt with. Otherwise, you may inadvertently begin bribing your patients to somehow fulfill your needs for understanding and relatedness. There are many things you can do to lessen the loneliness and thus avoid exploiting your patients. Some therapists find it helpful to share an office with another colleague or two, with or without a secretary. A professional affiliation, such as teaching at a university or working in a clinic, can provide you with some meaningful social contact. Or perhaps you would like to supervise less-experienced colleagues as a way of adding some variety to your professional life.

While each of these suggestions would result in your making contact with other people, they can be engaged in only after "business hours." Furthermore, none really touch on the truly experiential loneliness of the full-time analytically oriented practitioner who sees relatedness with a patient as unreal and only a transference phenomenon. One way of handling this is to broaden one's concepts of transference. Despite the fact that much of the therapeutic process necessitates that the patient attach his early life reactions and feelings to the therapist, there is much real nontransference relating going on which, if the therapist chooses to be aware of it, can be a source of meaningful human interaction. Though you as a therapist are specifically there to relate to your patients' needs and not vice-versa, patients often interact sensitively with their therapist, recognizing them as real people who, like themselves, have real feelings and real needs. This can most certainly undercut the feelings of loneliness that some therapists experience in private practice.

A private therapy practice is a rather sedentary occupation in which you spend a good part of the day sitting in the same chair, in the same office. Most, if not all, of your work will involve only a tiny segment of the population, who tend to be better educated, more verbal, and wealthier than average. You will meet few blacks, fewer poor people, and only a modicum of the middle class. Thus you will have spent years perfecting professional skills which will benefit as few as twenty people in any one year. None of these factors are restrictions in and of themselves, but if you experience them as such, you should do something about it. For example, working in a university, hospital, or private clinic one day a week could allow you to give your talents and time to a more varied group of people. The loss of income is more than compensated for by the stimulation and satisfaction you will experience. To diversify your private practice and to make your skills available to more people for less money, you could also do group psychotherapy.

SETTING UP YOUR OFFICE

If, after carefully weighing the advantages and disadvantages of being a private practitioner, you still feel that this is the direction you want to go, the first step is to find a place to practice. When choosing an office location, there are several important factors you need to consider. Certainly, it should be near an urban center where there are sufficient numbers of people needing the services of a psychotherapist. If possible, your office should be accessible by public transportation so that whether or not a patient has a car will not be a determining factor in his selection of you as a therapist.

For many, the most controversial issue regarding where one should set up private practice is whether or not it should be set up at home. The advantages are obvious. You do not have to commute to work and thus have more free time to spend with your family, friends, or by yourself. You do not have to go through the trouble of finding a suitable office or laying out additional money for rent. Finally, there are many tax advantages to working at home which will be discussed in Chapter 13.

But in terms of how effectively you can work (especially in an analytic practice), it is my opinion that a therapist's office should not be in his home. For years, I have been conducting my practice in two offices, one at home in the suburbs and the other in a large nearby city. In the city, I am simply Dr. Goldman. But in my office at home, I am also my wife's husband and my kids' father. Besides, something is always happening there to distract me—a delivery, a repair, the dog barking, or minor emergencies.

It has been my experience that there is less interference with the transference phenomenon (the patient can more readily see you at this stage of his developmental process where he demands and needs you to be) if the realities of your home and family life minimally intrude upon him. Even if your theoretical orientation is not as analytic as my own or if your philosophy is that "everything is grist for the analytic mill," you would probably agree that family pressures can often make it difficult for a therapist—particularly one who is just starting out—to give his complete and undivided attention to his patients.

Once you have decided where to practice, the question is how much room you need. To a large extent, this is determined by how much room you actually have or how much you can afford. However, a therapist's office should minimally consist of a consultation room, a closet or rack for the patients' coats, and a separate bathroom just off the waiting room which is to be used only by patients and the therapist.

Furnishings for your waiting room should include chairs, adequate lighting (including reading lamps), a table with ash trays and magazines, and perhaps pictures and plants. The actual size of the room is not very important if you work only with individuals. However, if you see groups or families, for example, the waiting room must be sufficiently large to comfortably accommodate everyone. There should be soundproofing to block out conversations being carried on in the consultation room. Some therapists simply have double doors installed between the consultation and waiting rooms. Others use a radio or some kind of "white noise" machine to distort the voices.

As for the consultation room, many therapists contend that it should be completely neutral, devoid of pictures or artifacts which would "artificially" stimulate the patient to make associations rather than spontaneously reveal himself. Others, like myself, believe that an office, like any other room the therapist spends time in, should reflect his personality and personal interests. In my office, for example, there are bookcases, wall hangings, paintings (some of which were done by my patients and some by me), and momentoes from my travels. I also have some plants and I buy fresh flowers each week because they are beautiful, and hopeful, and alive, and I feel they add to the kind of lived-in atmosphere I feel the room should have.

Since both the therapist and his patients will be spending a good deal of time in the consultation room, it should, above all, be comfortably and warmly furnished. If the room is thoughtfully planned to meet both the therapist's and patient's alternating needs for proximity and distance, it can be of any size, though preferably no smaller than ten feet by ten feet. If the therapist needs a desk, he should have one, but I do not advise that he sit behind it when working with patients. It has been my practice to set up two large comfortable chairs—one for the patient and one for me—which are more or less alike in appearance. They should be no more than eight to ten feet apart, although for patients who need more emotional contact they can be moved closer together. A fairly necessary source of comfort and relaxation should be two hassocks, one for each chair. Tables should be placed near the chairs, and ashtrays and a box of tissues should be available on the table without the patient having to request them.

If the therapist's orientation is an analytic one, there should most certainly be a couch in addition to the two chairs already mentioned. The chairs allow for face-to-face contact during the initial sessions (presenting problems, history taking) when the therapeutic relationship is being established. The couch is used if and when both the patient and therapist feel the patient is ready for it. It then can serve the purpose of freeing the patient from the stereotype role playing he may get into in the face-to-face living-room-like situation offered by the chairs. With the therapist's chair behind the couch so that the patient does not have to see the therapist unless he wants to, many patients ramble and free associate more easily. Since there are no set social standards for talking to someone you cannot see, the thoughts that arise in the patient's mind tend to be more spontaneous. Furthermore, in face-to-face contact with the therapist, some patients make a habit of scanning the therapist's face, hands, and posture, looking for signs of approval or disapproval about what they are saying. Such patients often censor their thoughts and statements accordingly, whether or not any such signs are, in reality, apparent. On the other side of the dyad, I will only casually mention the therapist's needs for privacy. The couch alleviates these problems to a large degree.

Another essential piece of office equipment is a clock which should be very near or directly opposite the therapist and preferably where the therapist can unobtrusively see it and the patient cannot. Ideally, a telephone should be within easy reach of the therapist. Some therapists believe that a patient's sessions should not be interrupted by telephone calls, since, in their opinion, this is the patient's time and an uninterrupted atmosphere is most conducive to the regression believed necessary, particularly in the early stages of transference. If you wish, the phone company will install a telephone that can be temporarily turned off with the flick of a switch. But when it is switched off in your office, it must ring somewhere else—at your answering service, for example. Other therapists feel that as long as they do not talk for more than a minute or so, there is nothing wrong with answering the telephone during an analytic session.

Many therapists wonder whether or not they should have an answering service. I have found it to be a necessary business requisite and invaluable professionally. An answering service makes you more available to both colleagues and patients because someone knows where you can be reached or will at least take messages twenty-four hours a day, seven days a week. One filled consultation hour pays for the extra cost of the service.

Some people prefer a mechanical answering device in lieu of an answering service. Many of these mechanical devices have a special feature whereby you can call your office from anywhere and have all your recorded messages played back to you over the phone. These devices are, in the long-run, less expensive and perhaps also more efficient and foolproof than an answering service, and there is the additional advantage of having your own voice answering calls when you are not in your office. However, there are several drawbacks. Some people, for example, feel very uncomfortable about speaking into a tape recorder and consequently may think twice about leaving a message or even calling you. Secondly, even though it is your own voice, a recorded message is very impersonal. It gives the illusion that you are there and available when in fact you are not. Finally, an answering machine cannot make any decisions about an emergency. If someone must get through to you, the operator on duty at an answering service can tell them where you can be reached or, if nothing else, can use her own ingenuity in handling the situation. Incidentally, if you hire an answering service, you probably will be asked if there are any special instructions which should be given to the operator who takes your calls. It is certainly advisable to inform them that you are a psychotherapist and give them some idea of the kinds of daily situations as well as the occasional emergencies that may arise and how you want them to be handled. For example, you may or may not want patients calling you at night, at home, or on vacation. I try to emphasize how important it is for them to express kindness and consideration to the people who call me in a personal emergency.

HOW TO GET REFERRALS

Once you have set up your office, your initial success as a private practitioner depends on your getting patients, which means getting referrals. It is only after you have patients and begin utilizing your professional skills that you will be able to measure your real success as a therapist. But why should a colleague refer a patient to you rather than to someone else who is equally well-trained and qualified? I maintain that a therapist gets referrals because of some unique quality he has that makes him stand out in the mind of the person making the referral. Unfortunately, your uniqueness as a therapist may rarely be related to your professional integrity or competence. More often, it may simply be the geographical location of your office, what fee you charge, or as irrelevant as who you had lunch with yesterday and who he has lunch with tomorrow. How, then, can you maximize *your* chances of getting referrals?

Based on the practical experience you have had in either a hospital or clinic setting prior to setting up your own practice, you should have some ideas as to what kinds of patients you work with best. You may be particularly good with paranoids, borderline patients, or "acting out" adolescents. This is part of your uniqueness as a therapist, and it is important that you recognize it as part of your professional self-image and communicate it to your colleagues. Also, if you are doing some innovative work in the area of psychotherapy, another way of keeping your name alive in the minds of your colleagues is to write a paper on it and try to get it published in one of the professional journals or give a presentation at a conference. This can help establish your reputation as a professional and possibly an expert in your area of special interest.

Therapists who are beginning private practice often get referrals by charging a fee that is somewhat lower than the prevailing rate. An experienced therapist is at times hard-pressed to find someone who will take on patients who cannot afford his fee but who, all the same, need treatment. If he knows a respected colleague who is just starting out and who is charging a lower-than-average fee, this colleague might very well be the first to come to mind and more than likely will get the referral.

Another method that may help you to get referrals is to become specialized in a particular area of psychotherapy—child therapy, group work, or marriage counseling, for example. One of my colleagues inadvertently doubled the size of his private practice by doing volunteer work with a local group of divorced and separated parents. It started out as an interesting project and a meaningful way for him to utilize his spare time. Within a relatively short time, he become known to this group as a therapist who knew and understood their unique problems. As a result, whenever anyone came to this group looking for professional help, my colleague was heartily recommended.

Another way to handle the business of getting referrals is to become part of a small group of professionals who see each other regularly and know and respect each other's work. Meeting regularly for lunch, for example, to discuss patients and other professional and personal matters may prove to be both socially and professionally rewarding. An extension of this kind of activity is to become an active member in professional organizations both in terms of submitting papers and being active on various committees which will allow other people in the field to become acquainted with you and your work.

One potential source of referrals often overlooked is contact with your family doctor, dentist, lawyer, minister, etc., who are often asked to refer people to psychotherapists. Briefing these people on your qualifications and experience, and informing them that you are setting up your own practice may prove to be quite helpful in getting referrals.

If you have entered the field of psychotherapy via a doctoral program in psychology or if you are a medical doctor, it is to your advantage that you always introduce yourself as *Dr.* Smith or *Dr.* Brown in all your professional and social activities. If you are a social worker, let people know you are doing therapy.

Because there are so many factors involved, referrals are rarely ever tailor-made, and even on those occasions when the referring party is consciously trying to match a patient with a therapist, referrals are rarely ideal. If a therapist has been in supervision with another more experienced therapist, if he has undergone special training during which time a sizable number of people got to know him and respect his work, it may be possible for someone to have a somewhat tailor-made referral made to him. But many therapists do not have this type of experience or have lost contact with many former colleagues by the time they are ready to set up private practice. They must then rely on their previous reputation as a therapist in a hospital or clinic setting, or operate on the realization that if the people he knows are aware that he is going into private practice, they might, if asked, refer to him. I have tried to give you some idea about what, in my experience, really exists in terms of referrals—not necessarily the ideal or the theoretically best professional practice but what empirically has worked out as I observed it.

I have attempted to explain *why* you can expect to get referrals. Now the question is *how* to go about it. Obviously people have to know that you want referrals. This may sound banal, even ridiculous, but I have heard stories about therapists who set themselves up in a brand new private practice, sent out business cards, and then sat around wondering why no one called them for appointments. Did they send the announcements to people who really knew and respected them? You must let people know that you're looking for patients! Your business or announcement card only says that you have opened a private practice.

Unless you make it clear that you need patients, your colleagues may assume that your time is all "booked up."

One good way to handle the problem of getting referrals, particularly when you are just getting started in private practice, is to send a short note to those colleagues who you think would really care about the fact that you have set up practice and would probably be interested in sending you patients. Tell them where your practice will be located, what hours you plan to work, how they can reach you, and perhaps the kind of people you would like to work with. Also, try to make it a habit throughout your career as a psychotherapist to acknowledge referrals by a consultation report and thank-you note. Also, you might send reprints of articles you have published to anyone you think might be interested in your work. Not only will this enhance your reputation but it may get you some referrals by keeping people informed of where you are now.

One of the most fertile sources of referrals are your fellow students, faculty members, or colleagues in a clinical setting. These are people who have known you personally and professionally for a long time. It may seem to you that by asking for referrals you are asking your colleagues for a favor, but actually you are doing them a service by letting them know that a competent person like yourself has some free time. Do not be afraid to be specific: "I have some free hours in the evening," or "I'm trying to build up my daytime practice," or "I'm trying to set up a private practice and for the present I am willing to see people at fifteen to twenty dollars a session."

Some therapists make it a point to introduce themselves to other professionals in the vicinity of their office who may ultimately prove to be additional sources of referrals. For example, I recently moved into a new office in New York City. Soon I discovered that there are four physicians in the building, and I paid each of them a visit, introducing myself and telling them a little about my work. Then as appropriate situations arose with my patients, I began referring my patients who need medical consultation with someone in their specialities to them, and they also referred patients to me. Visiting clergy in the area can also be helpful. None of this advice should be confused with the unethical practice of soliciting patients, which means that you actually go to a person who you think needs treatment and tell him that you are a therapist and available to see him.

Setting up speaking engagements with professional groups, the PTA, churches, and synagogues is a good way to keep yourself before the public and build up potential referral sources. For therapists who are good speakers, this can be an effective way to let people know who you are, what you do, and what you believe in. The difficulty, of course, is running that thin line between doing a good professional job on the talk and in some way being seductive in trying to get people to like you and perhaps come to you as a therapist. Not only is this unethical, but you may appear to be promising potential patients something that your therapeutic orientation ultimately prevents you from following through on—friendship or relatedness of a more personal sort.

It is for this reason that I rarely take on as a patient someone I have known socially and who later asks me for a consultation. Of course, it depends on how much real contact I have had with the person, under what circumstances we met, how well they know me, and how involved their life would be with mine in the future. But generally I refer such people to someone else so that the transference can be free to go in any direction that the patient needs it to go.

Similarly, I make it a point not to take on husbands, wives, brothers, sisters, or close friends of patients I am currently working with. It is my opinion that each of my patients deserves his own therapist and should not have to feel that he is sharing me with someone else. Furthermore, I feel that such situations set up a kind of sibling rivalry that is very difficult to analyze as transference, because it is real. In addition, conflicts arise which become impossible to analyze and work with. In this situation, I can be neither sufficiently objective nor get cues from the patient which lead to correct timing of my interpretations when treating both parties at the same time and getting two sources of data.

I think that by taking on relatives or close friends of patients, a therapist creates more problems for the patient than he had when he first entered your office. For those therapists who do not agree with me on a theoretical level and who feel that "everything is grist for the analytic mill," I would suggest that before taking on such a patient, consider carefully what kinds of problems are likely to arise and how you will deal with them. How will the choice of taking on this new patient affect your treatment of the other patient? Are you potentially intensifying your patient's problems or helping him solve them?

RELATING TO COLLEAGUES AND OTHER PROFESSIONALS

When all your hard work begins to pay off and you start getting calls for consultations, how do you relate to the people who have referred patients to you? Some therapists blithely assume that a "thank you" at the end of the phone conversation during which they were informed of the referral is enough. Yet whoever referred the patient to you did so because he cares about the patient and feels that you have the professional competence and know-how to work with him. So, be professional as well as courteous and give the referring party a follow-up report.

When I get a referral I routinely send a very short note to the referring person, thanking him for the referral and informing him that I have set up a consultation with the patient. When the referring person is a fellow therapist, I send him another note soon after the consultation (with the patient's permission, of course) indicating the date the consultation was done, the patient's presenting problems, how often I intend to see the patient, and a short summary of my treatment plan. I then thank him again for the referral. I find this method a systematic, worthwhile means of communicating and establishing good relationships with fellow psychotherapists.

As for those relationships which may be somewhat more distant, like the doctors in my building for example, I let them know that the person is coming for consultation, and that unless my patient requests it, or they request it of me and my patient gives me permission, this will be our last contact about this patient. If, in private conversation, they start talking about the patient again, I politely remind them that I prefer to get the information from my patient, that I work better that way and generally find that it is best for the patient, too. For the most part, they accept it.

When starting with a new patient, I do not request a history from the previous therapist or referring party. I prefer that the patient and I work on his history together. A basic outline of his life history is generally obtained in the initial sessions, and the rest arises out of the day-in, day-out therapeutic interaction that evolves later. I feel that I connect more genuinely to the events in my patients' lives when I take my own histories. If I immerse myself in someone else's notes and interpretations, I find that I come to the sessions with certain preconceived ideas about the patient which often interfere with our thoughts and associations. Furthermore, if I am working from my own notes, my timing is better geared to my patient's capacity to understand and accept new insights; that is, I use my own perceptions of the patient to cue me in. If I know something about the patient, I only know it because in one way or another he told it to me. And when I know it, somewhere he is ready to know it too. But if there is something rolling around in my head other than what I have personally experienced with the patient, my whole cue system gets jammed. As I have already pointed out, this method works best for me, I do not advocate that every psychotherapist use it. In fact, for someone who is just going into private practice, it may be best to request the patient's history in the beginning. You may feel less anxious by having this structure to fall back on, or by simply knowing it is there.

When I am referring a patient to another colleague, and if I know he has some free time and feel he is a good choice for this particular patient, I generally give the patient only one name. However, if the patient requests more names or if I do not know whether or not a particular colleague is the ideal person or even has free time, I give the patient three names. I never send a history along unless it is requested. But I am more than willing to cooperate with a colleague's request for one as long as my patient signs a release asking for it. By the way, if you are referring a patient to another colleague, it is a good idea to telephone him in advance. This will give him time to look over his schedule to find out what hours he has available. It also allows you to give any necessary preliminary information to the potential therapist on pathology, occupation, education, etc. that would give him some basis for deciding whether this patient fits into his practice.

THE INITIAL INTERVIEW: COMMUNICATING
PRACTICAL INFORMATION

While I do not plan to go into all the details of the initial interview, there are certain practical details that should be dealt with in your first meeting with a newly referred patient. If beginning therapists know certain things in advance, it will avoid a lot of confusion later.

First, you need to find out if the person sitting in your office is in the right "store" and if he wants "to buy what you have to sell." That is, is he specifically looking for a psychotherapist—someone who "sells' knowledge of human beings in general, the kinds of conflicts they have, why they have them, and how they can get rid of them? If the answer is yes, then in some sense you have established a contract with the patient; he wants to change and you will help him.

Incidentally, if the patient brings up physical complaints during the initial interview or at any other time, I suggest that he see his family physician or internist. Then, with the patient's permission, I telephone the physician to discuss his findings.

In addition to whatever else the patient may wish to know or say in this first session, it is important that you clearly communicate the practical features of the contract. He should know how long the sessions will be, and that they will start at the assigned time and end 45 or 50 minutes later, whether he is late or not. On the other hand, if I start late, it is my policy to give my patients their full session. I also inform my new patients that they can have their set hour as long as they wish, provided they uphold their end of the contract and that they may call me in an emergency at any hour of any day. Regular calls should be made in the ten-minute break between hours.

Some therapists do not take short breaks between patients and prefer a longer break in the middle of the work day. If you intend to set up your schedule this way, your answering service can intercept calls, take messages, and inform callers that you will return the call on your free time.

If a patient cancels a session with less than 24 hours notice or if we both do not think that the reason for the cancellation is valid, it must be paid for anyway. I expect my patients to attend every session except when I go on vacation. I try to let them know several months in advance when I plan to take my vacation so they can plan theirs accordingly. If a patient takes his vacation at any other time, I consider it possible resistance to treatment and something to be talked about in therapy. Occasionally a patient has no choice about when he can take his vacation. For example, one of my patients worked for a company that took its vacation en masse at a certain time of the year. In such a situation, my patients are expected to make up their vacation time, and I do my best to fit them into my schedule at other times.

You may or may not agree with the terms of my contract. But whatever your terms, whatever contract you plan to make with your patients, you must communicate it to them directly and clearly in the first session.

As for fees, I have a standard fee which I occasionally lower if a patient cannot afford it. But I never lower it by more than five dollars per session because I know I feel uncomfortable working for less money, and this feeling would interfere in my relationship with the patient. No therapist should work for a fee lower than what he feels he is worth in terms of training, experience, and competence. These factors considered, he should gauge his fees according to his needs and the fees of his colleagues and should not discuss this over the phone prior to the patient's first appointment. On getting a transfer patient from another therapist, it is often expedient to not set a fee immediately and to say that for the first session the fee would be the same as his previous therapist charged.

Patients should be told in the first session when and how they will be billed. I bill the last week of each month and expect to be paid by the tenth of the following month. If a patient has not paid by then, I consider it resistance and a matter for discussion. I explain to my patients in the very beginning, in the initial session, that if an emergency arises and they cannot pay on time, I will not carry them longer than two months unless we have worked out a suitable arrangement. I try not to build up a backlog of debts. It is not good for me, and in the long run, it is bad for the patient as well.

HOW TO KEEP FILES AND TAKE NOTES

With each new patient, I start a file in which I keep a "contact sheet" or cumulative record of each contact (including telephone calls) that I've had with the patient which includes a one or two sentence summary of what transpired between us. This sheet can be an important source of information for writing up more detailed and up-to-date histories as well as resolving any conflicts about billing. The folder also contains the patient's history which I update from time to time and detailed accounts of his dreams which are a very important source of analytic material. Any correspondence I receive from patients is also kept in their files.

On the whole, keeping up-to-date and complete files on each of your patients is very helpful. It is important to remember, however, that in some states, psychotherapists are not protected against having their records subpoenaed. If you live in such a state, you might consider leaving out any confidential information and references to other people that you feel might be destructive to your patient or others.

Some therapists take detailed notes during analytic sessions which they later place in the patient's folder. I do not at this stage of my practice take notes during sessions because I feel it interferes with *my* ability to concentrate, and from the patient's point of view, it can be somewhat distracting. But I often make notes during breaks between sessions. My advice to you as a beginning therapist, however, is to take notes during sessions if for no other reason than to keep you from talking too much, and it can be an obvious aide to memory. Incidentally, I think it is essential that a therapist take breaks between patients. You not only need the rest, it gives you a chance to pull your thoughts about the previous session together and, if necessary, to make additional notes. You may need to go to the bathroom, get a drink of water, stretch, or even just be alone. It is also a good idea to use some of this time to prepare for your next patient either by simply sitting down and thinking about him or reviewing your notations from his last session.

As an essential piece of office equipment, I highly recommend a tape recorder, particularly one of the easy-to-use cassette types. It can be very helpful for making notations between sessions and can also be used to record sessions with individuals as well as groups (provided, of course, that you have their approval in advance). I often lend patients tapes of their sessions with me. Listening to themselves talk with me or in a group has proven to be a great source of insight for many of them and a way of intensifying the therapeutic experience under conditions of minimal threat in the privacy of their own home.

SELECTING THE RIGHT STATIONERY

Every therapist in private practice should have personalized stationery (8½ x 11 in. and/or 5 x 8 in.) with envelopes to match, business cards, and billheads indicating his name and degree, office address and zip code, and telephone number, including the area code.

When you set up private practice or relocate your office, business cards should be sent to colleagues and friends with a short personal note to let them know where you are practicing and how they can get in touch with you. A formal announcement card is an extravagance, since it is something strangers tend to ignore and friends do not need. In addition to the information mentioned above, your business cards should include only the phrase "By appointment" and possibly the particular kind of practice you are starting, i.e. adult psychology, child psychology, etc. Any additional information such as the schools you have attended or special honors you have received is, in my opinion, unnecessary and could even be ethically inappropriate.

On the billhead, however, a few additions may be helpful. Many therapists, for example, have "For Professional Services" printed at the left margin near the center of the page, and at the bottom they list the twelve months of the year and the numbers 1 to 31. For each session as the patient attends it, in any given month, the therapist checks one of these numbers, thereby indicating the date of the session. In this way, all your bills are made up and ready to be mailed at the end of each month. Furthermore, if any conflicts arise over how many sessions the patient actually attended, this particular kind of billhead can be used as a duplicate check against your appointment book. As a minimal record of your billing, you could keep a carbon copy of each bill. This can be done by slipping a piece of carbon paper between every two sheets of billhead, or you can have special pads of duplicate sheets, each with its own carbon, printed up. More detailed methods of record keeping are covered in Chapter 13.

ESTABLISHING YOUR FEE

Most therapists starting out in private practice tend to charge too little. Do not underestimate yourself. Find out how much colleagues with your level of training and experience are charging, and set your fee accordingly. In the New York City area, for example, private-practice therapy fees range from 10 to 75 dollars per session which I feel is a ridiculously wide range. Most medical therapists charge from 40 to 50 dollars per session, whereas most experienced nonmedical therapists charge 25 to 35 dollars per session. Set your fee, and then if you decide to take on a patient for less than your usual fee, make it clear in his first session what your regular fee is and that you are temporarily reducing it because of his present economic situation. Some agreement in advance when the fee is being set should then be made as to when the fee will be reevaluated and possibly changed.

When the cost of living goes up, therapists should not hesitate to change their fees to meet their increased expenses. Some therapists see the initial fee as a contract for the duration of treatment. With treatment taking as long as it does, this becomes unrealistic. In any discussion of fees, the patient is in a very disadvantageous bargaining position because of the transference. It therefore behooves the therapist to be aware of this and not unilaterally charge or change fees without discussing it with his patients and having them choose to change it. If worse comes to worse, when an old patient may not be able to afford your new fees, I would continue them at the old fee and certainly not refer him to a therapist whose fees are somewhat lower when he cannot afford your new fee. This is what you minimally owe him.

SOME PRACTICAL DETAILS OF BILLING

There are three basic ways to bill patients. The first is handing them the statement, the second is mailing it, and the third is having them take the responsibility of figuring their bill and paying it on their own.

For most therapists, billing each patient the last week of each month is the most convenient and least complicated procedure. Patients should be presented with the statement at the onset of the session. Since the initial interview they have known that they would be billed at the end of each month, and they also know when you expect to be paid. A less personal way of handling the situation is by mail. The advantage to this method is that all of the statements get out at the same time, but many therapists, including myself, feel it is too impersonal. It also involves the additional cost of postage.

On the surface at least, the last method whereby patients take the responsibility for payment on themselves appears to be the simplest. The patient knows that you expect to be paid on the first of the month. Since he also knows what his fee is and how many sessions he has had, he should figure out how much he owes you and bring a check at the beginning of the following month. This method necessitates a much greater sense of responsibility and involvement on the part of the patient and might be most effective for a long-term, mature person.

For personal reasons, some therapists find it necessary to bill more often than once a month, so they bill their patients either once a week or after each session. How often you bill is up to you, but keep in mind that there can be a good deal of acting out on both the patient's and the therapist's part around the issue of fees and billing. The therapist can play the benevolent "good parent," the nice guy, and indulge his patients' irresponsibility about money. The patient, on the other hand, can try to get the "bad parent" to give in to him either by lying about his income or not paying promptly. It is important that both therapist and patient be aware of these possibilities so that if they come up they can be analyzed and dealt with.

Occasionally you may have a patient whom you have terminated for nonpayment of bills and who still owes you money. This becomes particularly difficult when you are on a monthly billing system, since theoretically he would be reminded that he owes you money only once a month. In such a case I usually send the patient a letter of inquiry with the second or third statement. If I still do not receive payment, I telephone. As a last resort I send him a registered letter informing him that I am going to put the matter in the hands of my attorney. Finally, I call my attorney and let him handle it. Most people pay the bill long before this. In my years of practice, I have lost very little money as a result of unpaid bills. Collection services are not, in my opinion, a particularly good way for a therapist to collect unpaid bills, since some of their techniques are too harsh and punitive. However, one source of collection that every therapist should know about is Small Claims Court where you can take out a summons for the amount the patient owes you. This will be discussed more fully in Chapter 12.

In conclusion, for most therapists who have the prerequisite education, experience, and personal maturity, the advantages of going into private practice are many. You have the freedom to choose when and where you want to work as well as whom you would like to work with. Your practice can be as large or small as you wish. Working on your own, without supervision by people not of your own choosing, gives you the freedom to use your talents creatively. Since private practice means greater income, you will have the time to diversify your practice and maintain active contact with people in your field by working part-time in a university, hospital, or private clinic. And there are endless opportunities to teach or supervise less experienced colleagues.

It is important that your office is easily accessible to patients and set up so that it is a comfortable and relaxing place for you and your patients, since you will both be spending a good deal of time there. I have mentioned several ways to get referrals. You can start by making a list of all the people you know who respect your work and who are in a position to refer patients.

Then make sure you send each of them a note telling them whatever they need to know about your practice. This is, at the very least, a good beginning.

Before you see your first patient, you should give some thought to practical matters such as your fee, how and when you will bill patients, and how you will handle lateness, absenteeism, and non-payment of bills. You should also decide what kind of records you will keep on patients and then try to be consistent in keeping them up to date. If all these practical matters are properly dealt with and if you not only are competent but feel confident in your ability as a professional, your practice should have a better chance to run smoothly and successfully.

Chapter 2
THE PRIVATE PRACTICE OF CHILD THERAPY
HAIM G. GINOTT

The private practice of child therapy is more complicated than that of adult therapy. It makes greater demands on time and energy. There is no end to the work of a child therapist. He has to purchase play materials, replace broken toys, replenish supplies and rearrange the playroom before and after each session. Unlike in adult treatment, a child therapist has to answer inquiries from his patient's parents, teachers, guidance counselor, school psychologist and pediatrician. They are all generous with time. They appreciate lengthy free consultations and detailed written reports. You may see a child for three sessions and for the next six years receive requests for reports from guidance clinics, family agencies, public schools, and private practitioners. (A Xerox machine may be your best freind.)

ON THE PHONE

When a parent calls for an appointment, I offer a definite choice of times: "I can see you on Monday morning or Tuesday afternoon. Which is more convenient for you?" Decisiveness and clarity are helpful to the anxious and the confused. It is best to avoid conversations that inevitably become long: "Mrs. Smith, I am in conference now. At this time let us decide a convenient hour for our first appointment." Often, a parent will call and immediately plunge into the family's case history. I transcend my polite upbringing, stop the case report, and focus on finding a convenient time for the first session. Many initial contacts are never consummated because the therapist has shown impotence on the phone. He was too loquacious, too soft, and too vague. ("He sounded like a marshmallow," said one mother.) During the initial call, I do not answer questions about my theoretical orientation and philosophical bent. When asked, I admit that I have heard of Freud, Jung, Adler, and Sullivan, but I refuse to discuss them. Under investigation, I name only my profession, degree, and fee. Before hanging up, I repeat that the first session is *not* for the child, but for the mother. If both parents wish to come, they are welcome.

FIRST SESSION WITH MOTHER

A mother often brings the first session by saying, "There is so much to tell; I don't know where to start." My answer is, "Start at the end. What brought you here?" Some parents want to discuss their child's dynamics and to interpret his symptoms. I ask them to describe behavior, not to ascribe reasons. "I want to get a clear picture of your child. Tell me what he does, then we'll consider what it means."

Parents often ask questions best left unanswered: "How is therapy going to help my child?" "What does play therapy mean?" "What do you do in the playroom?" No attempt is made to answer such questions comprehensively. The parent is told that children use this hour to gain confidence, to achieve independence and to express feelings and thoughts in constructive ways. How it is accomplished is not told during the first fifty minutes. If parents continue to press for an answer, I say, "That's my specialty."

The therapist helps Mother solve one immediate problem; how to tell a child about pending therapy. Together they formulate a nonthreatening announcement: "We made arrangements for you to come to a playroom to play."

"Why?"

"Because it's good for children. It helps them to understand themselves better."

This brief statement is more helpful than long explanations which focus on symptoms such as: "You wet your bed, you bite your nails, and you are always in trouble in school. We can't help you. Maybe a psychologist can straighten you out. When you have a toothache you go to a dentist; when you need your tonsils out, you go to a surgeon; when you have mental problems, you go to a psychologist." Such explanations intensify the child's defenses and increase his resistance to therapy.

PREPARATION FOR SEPARATION

A mother plays an important role in her child's introduction to therapy. She should be told in detail what to do and what *not* to do during the child's first visit. "When you and Andy arrive, I will say: 'Andy and I are now going to the playroom.' You answer: 'Fine, I'll wait here.' This will allow your son to leave you without fear."

During the child's visit, it is best not to converse with his parents, before or after the session. Parents are told: "Please don't ask me, 'Can I see you for just a moment?' Your child may fear that his confidences are being betrayed. If you have something to report or discuss, leave a note or call on the phone." Parents are advised not to ask the child questions about the sessions. During therapy, a child needs to express negative feelings. He may refrain from doing so if he has to account for them later. If a child talks about the session on his own accord a parent can respond neutrally, "Oh, I see; so that's what happened." The aim is to convey to the child that the therapy hour is his private time. Parents may be shown the playroom. They need the opportunity to examine the materials, touch the toys, and see the room to which they will give up their child at least once a week.

Mothers of preschool children may need special preparation for separation. They are instructed in how to be helpful. "Your child may hold on to you, cry, and refuse to come to the playroom. Children are often afraid of unfamiliar people and places. If your child cries, say, 'It's a strange place, I know. It's scary, but I'll wait for you right here."

Dramatic scenes can happen in the waiting room between mother and child: symbiotic embraces, tearful glances, and heartbreaking good-bys. Mothers are asked to avoid such scenes. I often tell mothers the story of little Bruce who started walking to the playroom willingly until his mother commented: "I'm so surprised. I was sure he would cry." Immediately Bruce complied. He ran back to his mother weeping loudly. His mother than said, "You see, I told you he would cry."

FIRST SESSION WITH THE CHILD

When the child enters the playroom for the first time, he is not met with questions and long explanations. He is not bombarded with words. He is not asked, "Do you know why you are here?" (Implication: "You wouldn't be here if there weren't something wrong with you.") He is not told, "Your mother said you've got problems, and I want to help you." (Implication: "He is in cahoots with Mother. What else did she tell on me?") The therapist does not promise easy friendship, nor does he ask for instant trust. ("I am your friend; I wish you would tell me what bothers you.") A child does not come for treatment because he feels bothered; someone else thinks so—parent, teacher, or judge. The child does not continue to come to therapy because of his desire for mental health. He comes because of his relationship with the therapist. Therefore, errors in relationship may bring a quick end to therapy.

From the start, the therapist's approach is free of threatening implications. He does not begin the new relationship by spotlighting problematic conduct or symptoms. He knows from experience that children can change and grow without confessing loudly that they have problems. The therapist aims to convey to each child the unique nature of the therapeutic encounter. Essentially, the therapist would have liked to say, "In here you may feel free to express yourself fully, in words and in play, in your own time and in your own way. You will be accepted and respected regardless of what you may feel, think, say, or do." However, a child cannot understand such a complicated speech, and even if he did understand, he would not believe it. The meaning of therapy is conveyed by experience, not by explanation. At the start, the therapist can only inadequately state his basic attitude by saying: "You can play with those toys all you like during this hour." It takes time for a child to grasp the meaning of the message. Through experience slowly, he becomes aware that it signifies a new freedom to be what he is and to become what he can.

PROBLEMS IN THE PLAYROOM

What can a therapist expect during the first play session from resistive small children? He can anticipate crying, temper tantrums, continuous coughing, and feigned needs to go to the bathroom. To counteract the bathroom subterfuge, mothers should be asked to see to this prior to the session.

The therapist is emotionally active. He accepts the children's angry feelings; he understands their fear and indignation, and he voices their plight. "I know you are scared and want to go to Mommy right now . . . but we go when the time is up." The therapist may point to his watch to concretize the time limit. He reflects the child's anger at having to stay in the playroom against his will. But the limit is upheld, "We leave when the time is up."

HELPING THE WITHDRAWN CHILD

Most children enter the playroom willingly and take to the toys readily; they present no difficulty in establishing rapport and relationship. At times a child comes into the room without showing resistance. He does not weep, howl, or whine, but does not do anything else either; he just stands in a corner or sits staring into space. Inexperienced therapists get anxious in such silent situations and try to activate their young clients. Many strange things have been said to hesitant youngsters during the first few minutes in the playroom, "Don't you know what to do first? We have so many nice toys. You can play with any doll you want. We also have guns. Lots of children like to play with guns. Would you rather paint? We have all kinds of paints. Don't you like anything in here?"

A rapport-chasing therapist overwhelms the withdrawn child with his energetic efforts to initiate therapeutic movement. The child's withdrawal may be a defense against fear of his own aggressive impulses and consequent retaliation by others. The therapist's active approach threatens the child's main line of defense and drives him further into isolation. Even a friendly conversation may be frightening to the withdrawn child, since for him any social contact calls for a modicum of assertiveness which he cannot afford.

How should a therapist help a silent child? He should sit down comfortably, smile at the child, and say, "It's kind of hard to start," leaving with the child the responsibility to initiate the next step. The therapist should not persist in trying to inspire activity by subtle suggestions. Nor should he attempt to select the activities or set the pace of the child's play sessions. Passivity does not imply inactivity on the part of the therapist. The therapist must be alert to note the unspoken wishes of the silent child. The child's handling of the doorknob may be safely interpreted as, "You want to go out." A deep sigh and a rolling tear may be reflected as, "You want your Mommy." Perking up in response to a passing police car may be voiced as, "You heard the siren." A startled reaction to a sudden noise may be mirrored as, "It scared you."

RELATING TO SUBMISSIVE, CUTE, OR PROVOCATIVE CHILDREN

Children respond to the strange playroom and unfamiliar therapist with reactions typical of their past relationships. The submissive child, who habitually relates to adults with compliance, will try to ingratiate himself with the therapist: he will offer to clean up the room or draw pictures for the therapist. The dependent child, who has known love only when helpless, will continue to act cute and meek. The "wise guy," who has learned to exploit adults, will try to manipulate the therapist.

The therapist' reactions will vary according to the child's history. To the child's obsequious offer of help, the therapist responds with a neutral comment: "If you want to." His aim is to convey to the child that in this relationship there is no need to be ingratiating and self-effacing. The angelic child soon learns that cuteness is not welcomed, that more mature modes of relating are expected. Provocative children, who invite rejection and criticism, are shocked when the therapist consistently responds with calm acceptance. Their past experience has conditioned them to expect punishment, direction, and control from adults. The failure to elicit these familiar responses confuses them. The lack of censure is as unreal to them as would be a sudden removal of gravity. They attempt to verify their picture of adults by provoking anger. They commit acts that in the past brought them condemnation and control. They "accidently" spill mud on the floor, splash paint on the walls, break a bottle, or make deafening noises. The therapist must be able to bear, without excessive strain, this trying behavior. He may draw comfort from the knowledge that the testing of his permissiveness signifies the beginning of the therapeutic process.

PERMISSIVENESS AND LIMITS

The permissiveness of the therapist inevitably engenders regressive behavior in children. At this phase of treatment, regression is anticipated and permitted. However, it is neither encouraged or sanctioned. It is accepted as a necessary stage in the child's process of maturing. The therapist must be lucidly aware of what permissiveness is and what it is not. If he is restrictive, regression will be hampered and so will improvement. If he unwittingly supports regression, he will encourage endless infantile behavior.

Permissiveness does not mean the acceptance without restrictions of *all behavior,* destructive as it may be. Permissiveness means the acceptance without limits of all *symbolic behavior,* be it hostile, sexual, sadistic, or masochistic. All feelings, fantasies, thoughts, wishes, passions, dreams, and desires, regardless of their content, are accepted, respected, and allowed expression through words and play. Direct acting out of destructive behavior is not permitted. When it occurs, the therapist intervenes and directs it into symbolic outlets.

The unfullfillable nature of some urges makes the setting of limits on direct acting out unavoidable. Certain acts (murder, incest, stealing, vandalism) are absolutely forbidden in our society. They may not be performed in therapy either, except in effigy. Symbolic play enables children to channel even destructive and incestuous urges into harmless outlets.

A child with Oedipal problems may undress and explore a mother doll. Obviously he may not act so toward his mother or his therapist. A child who is angry with his therapist may not hit him. He may draw ugly pictures of him and shoot at them, or he may kick, throw, stab, or step on any doll that represents him. By setting limits, the therapist helps the child to express hostility safely. By encountering therapeutic limits, the child learns to distinguish between wishes and deeds. He learns that he may feel all his feelings but may not always act as he pleases. By preventing undesirable acts while accepting hostile feelings, the therapist reduces the child's guilt and increases his mastery of reality. The child learns that his impulses are not dangerous, that they do no harm, and therefore need not be so rigidly inhibited. By mastering a variety of symbolic outlets for aggression, the child learns to accept and control impulses, without excessive stress or guilt (Ginott, 1961, 1965, 1968a).

LIMITS ESSENTIAL TO EFFECTIVE THERAPY

A Time Limit

A time limit is necessary in child therapy. A play-therapy session usually lasts 45 or 50 minutes. The therapist tells the child of the time limit and toward the end of the session reminds him that he has only a few minutes left to play. The therapist will say, "There are only five minutes more before time is up." He will also give the child a one-minute reminder. At the end of the hour the therapist will get up and say, "Time is up for today." With young children he may add, "Now we go out." The therapist should adhere to the time limit consistently. The child gains security from the predictability of the therapy hour.

Toys May Not Be Taken Out of the Playroom

Sooner or later, children want to take toys home. They may want to borrow, exchange, or buy playroom toys. A limit should be set stating that "All the toys must stay in the playroom." Toys may not be taken home or to the waiting room or to the bathroom. If the child wants to show a specific toy to his mother, he may invite her to see it in the playroom at the end of the hour. However, children are allowed to take home any painting or clay sculpture made by them during the session. The limit on taking toys home pertains also to broken toys. They, too, may not be removed from the playroom by the child. The reason is obvious: too many toys would be broken. What is the rationale for not allowing children to take toys home? Besides obvious budgetary considerations, there is a therapeutic reason: the relationship between therapist and child should be based on emotional, not material sharing.

Breakage

Children are not permitted to break room equipment or expensive toys. They may not pierce the rubber clown with a sharp instrument. They may not break the window or throw sand in the air conditioner. Their wish will be recognized but a limit invoked. The therapist may say, for example, "Bozo is not for breaking. He is for punching. This wood is for breaking, if you want to," or "The air conditioner is not part of the play materials. It is part of the equipment of the room."

Physical Attacks Upon the Therapist

The literature shows consent about the necessity of prohibiting physical attacks on the therapist. The rationale for this prohibition is as follows: (a) it assures the physical safety of the therapists; (b) it saves the child from guilt, anxiety and the fear of retaliation; and (c) it allows the therapist to remain emotionally accepting of the child.

Some therapists (Slavson, 1952) allows young children of preschool age to attack them physically. They interpret to the children the reason for the attack. Other therapists modify this limit to state, "You may hit me a little, but you can't really hurt me."

The limit against hitting the therapist should not be modified under any circumstances. There is little therapeutic value in permitting a child to attack an adult. Effective therapy must be based on mutual respect, with the therapist never abdicating his adult role. Allowing a child to dominate the relationship anchors therapy outside the world of reality. Telling a child that he may "hit but not hurt" the therapist is asking him to make a too-fine distinction. Such a vague limit does not contribute to the security of the child or the therapist. The child is irresistibly challenged to test out the prohibition and establish the "just noticeable difference" between hitting playfully and hurting seriously.

When Should Limits Be Presented?

Some therapists list the limits at the onset of treatment. They fear that children may feel betrayed and disappointed if confronted with limits unexpectedly. Yet, it is best not to mention limits before the need for them arises. There is little advantage in starting therapy by invoking prohibitions on actions that may never occur. The listing of limits may serve as a challenge to aggressive children and as an action deterrent to submissive ones.

When Tommy, age eight, first entered the playroom, he was told by his therapist, "You may play with the toys any way you want to, but you may not hit me or break toys." Tommy became quite upset and he said, "Oh, no sir, I'd never think of hitting you." Tommy hardly touched a toy during the next few sessions.

The Techniques of Limit-Setting

Children feel safer when they know the boundaries of permissible action. Therefore, limits should be delineated in a manner that leaves no doubt in the child's mind what constitutes unacceptable conduct in the playroom. There is a clear distinction, for instance, between splashing and not splashing water on the therapist. A limit that states, "You may splash me as long as you don't wet me too much," is inviting a deluge of trouble. Such a vague statement leaves the child without a clear criterion for making decisions.

Limits should be stated in a friendly and firm manner. Children do not readily accept restrictions invoked haltingly. When presented clumsily, limits become a challenge to children, evoking a battle of wills and focusing therapy on restrictions rather than relationships.

Limits should be presented in a manner that minimizes the arousal of resentment in the children. The very process of limit-setting should convey a spirit of nonpunitive, helpful authority. There are different ways of phrasing specific limits. At times, the following four-step sequence may prove helpful: (a) the therapist recognizes the child's feelings or wishes and helps him to express them as they are; (b) he states clearly the limit of a specific act; (c) he points out other channels through which the feelings or wishes can be expressed; (d) he helps the child bring out feelings of resentment that are bound to arise when restrictions are invoked. Johnny, age nine, wanted to take a cap-gun home:

"I'm going to take this gun with me."

"It's easy to see, Johnny, that you like the cap-gun and would like to take it home."

"Yes, I would. Can I?"

"The rule of the playroom is that *all* the toys have to stay in here, but you may have this gun whenever you come to the playroom."

"I don't like the rule."

"You wish there weren't such a rule."

"I wish the rule was that you can take all the toys home."

"You would really like that rule?"

"Yeah, . . . but then you wouldn't have a playroom."

At times it is more effective to state the limit first and reflect feelings later. When a child is about to fire a dart gun or throw a block at him, the therapist might say—and he better speak quickly—"Not at me, at the toys." He will do well to point to the toys in order to distract the child from himself. He might then reflect the child's wish to shoot at him and perhaps suggest to the child some harmless ways of expressing anger (e.g. "You may draw my face on the blackboard and shoot at it, or you may write my name on Bobo and punch it.")

Limits should be phrased in a language that does not challenge a child's self-respect. Limits are heeded better when stated succinctly and impersonally. "Time is up for today" is more readily accepted than *"Your* time is up and you must leave now."

"Walls are not for painting" is accepted with less resistance than "You must not paint the walls." "Toys are not for breaking" is better received than "You may not break toys."

At times, limits may be set nonverbally. When a child "plays" the xylophone with a hammer, the therapist may hand him drumsticks and take away the hammer. This can be accomplished without a word, just with a smile. The child may not even be aware that a limit has been invoked. The therapist may even be thanked for providing the appropriate tools.

THE PHYSICAL SETTING

The physical setting is of utmost importance in child therapy. The room and the equipment influence the therapeutic process for better or for worse. A small room compels unwelcome proximity, causing frustration and irritation. In a cramped playroom, isolated children withdraw further into themselves, aggressive children attack others. A very large room is also counterindicated.

It invites wild running from aggressive children and permits withdrawn children to avoid contact with the therapist. A playroom should be neither too small nor too large. A room of 150 to 200 square feet is adequate for individual play therapy; and a room of 300 to 400 square feet is desirable for group-play therapy.

In planning a playroom, every effort should be made to minimize the possibility of physical injury to children. The windows should be small and shatterproof; the lights protected by wire mesh; the floor waterproof and unwaxed. The walls should be sturdy and readily repaintable; the furniture functional and strong. Office desks, stuffed chairs, telephone extensions and personal books have no place in the playroom. Their protection calls for the setting of too many limits and interference with the therapist's ability to maintain free-floating attention. The playroom should be soundproof to preserve confidentiality and to tone down noise.

A RATIONALE FOR TOY SELECTION

The kind of toys and materials found in the playroom is an important therapeutic variable. Yet in many private offices, the children's room looks like a junkyard with a bizarre assortment of toys of various vintages. New toys are amassed at random, on impulse. As Fraiberg (1954) states: "I suffer temptations in toy stores—and I have no difficulty in persuading myself that a certain doll is just what I need for a certain four-year-old who has been getting along just fine without it."

The literature on toy selection is contradictory. Arthur (1952) and Slavson (1952) advocate a playroom with many enticing toys, whereas Fraiberg (1954) thinks that therapy proceeds more effectively when the child is given only a few toys and is not absorbed in fancy materials and fascinating activities. There is no agreement about the value of specific materials, nor even about the necessity of having a special room set aside and furnished for child therapy.

Clearly, a consistent rationale is needed for the selection of materials that contribute maximally to the process of child treatment. A treatment toy should (a) facilitate the establishment of contact with the child, (b) evoke and encourage catharsis, (c) aid

in developing insight, (d) furnish opportunities for reality testing, and (e) provide media for sublimation.

Tools for the Therapeutic Relationship

A therapeutic relationship can be maintained only if the
therapist understands the child's communications. The assumption is that everything said or done by the child in the playroom
has meaning in his frame of reference. Yet it is not easy even
for experienced therapists to understand the child's play messages.
Questioning the child about the meaning of his play is worse than
futile; it results in resistance and silence. Appropriate toys make
it easier for the therapist to understand the child's play. Thus,
for example, children usually play out family scenes by using
dolls that represent mother, father, and siblings. In the absence
of such dolls, a child may symbolically play out family themes
by using big and little wooden blocks, but the exact meaning of
the message may escape the therapist. Banging two blocks together may represent spanking or intercourse or may merely be
a test of the therapist's tolerance for noise. Inserting a pencil
into a pencil sharpener may represent intercourse or it may mean
that the pencil needs sharpening. However, when a father doll
is put on top of a mother doll, the therapist has less room for
misinterpretation. For the child, pencil and doll may be equally
useful as a means of expression, but to the therapist they are not.
The presence of a doll family enables the child to assist the therapist in understanding the child without diminishing the fluidity
of his play or conversation. A playroom with selected toys is
more conducive to therapeutic communication than one filled
with odds and ends of junk.

Toys for Catharsis

The assumption that children project their emotional needs
on any play materials is only half true. It ignores the fact that
materials have behavior-propelling qualities of their own. Some
toys elicit the expression of children's needs and problems, whereas others limit them. By a wise choice of toys, the therapist
augments his power to catalyze and control the play sessions.
Materials determine directly the choice of activity and indirectly

a connected chain of potential events. An activity once started leads to a more or less predictable sequence of behavior. Thus, beyond finger painting lurk events that are likely to occur because of the nature of the materials and the activity. Finger painting is likely to stimulate children. In the course of painting, they will get some paint on themselves. They will want to clean up then and there. In the process, they will splash water on themselves, the floor and the therapist. Feelings will be heightened; there will be complaints, apologies, cautions.

Such a chain of events largely determines the character of the therapeutic relationship. It determines whether the therapist intervenes out of choice or necessity and whether he must provide liberty or limits. The anticipated sequence of actions and reactions can be utilized to increase the specificity of treatment plans for children with different needs and symptoms. Since a child's behavior is drastically affected by variation in activities and materials, these variables can be manipulated to regulate the degree of mildness or wildness of the session. Specific decisions will depend on each child's nuclear needs and on the therapeutic intent, which is to help children achieve a healthy balance between acting out and self-restraint.

Another misconception frequent among child therapists is the belief that all acting out has therapeutic value. While catharsis in children almost always involves motility and acting out, *per se,* they have no curative effects beyond pleasure and release. Acting out in children does not usually lead to self-evaluation, recognition of motivation and attempts to alter behavior. This phenomenon is especially evident in young children in whom a weak superego and strong narcissism make acting out just fun. Therefore acting out by young children has to be limited through therapeutic intervention (Ginott, 1959, 1961, 1965, 1968b). Acting out is of value only when it represents working out of the child's core difficulties. Knowing each child's central problems and providing relevant toys and tools is an important, though often a neglected, part of a therapist's responsibility.

A therapist should furnish materials that elicit acting out related to the child's problems and should avoid materials that evoke diffuse hyperactivity. Thus hyperkinetic, overactive, and brain-damaged children should not find finger paints or running water in the playroom. Such materials overstimulate them and invite smearing of each other and the walls. Although such behavior may be highly pleasurable for children, it is psychonoxious in effect, it leads to weakened inner controls and disorganization of personality. These children need materials and activities that will *focus* rather than *diffuse* their flow of energy. Pounding pegboards, building block houses, shooting rifles, driving nails, sawing wood or constructing boxes may give form and direction to the disorganized urges of these children. These activities expose the children to sustaining interests that call for concentration and coordination. In an atmosphere of wise encouragement, the children's frustration tolerance will be enhanced, enabling them to focus energies on projects and goals both in and out of the playroom.

Fearful children should find in the playroom materials that can be handled without the aid of tools: water, paint, sand, playdough, dolls, chalk, crayons, etc. Such materials will allow them to conceal what they do not want to reveal, and to do and undo acts without detection and embarrassment. They can use clay for sculpturing or scalping, sand for building or burying and paint for decorating or dirtying. The reversibility of the media enables children to change the identity of their symbolic revelations at will and makes it safe for them to explore their problems.

Materials for Insight

Toys do not contribute directly to the achievement of insight. This is only gained through growth in inner security. But toys do facilitate interpretations that help children become more aware of themselves and their relationships with significant people. It is through this awareness that insight is attained.

There will be occasions on which it is desirable to arrange the materials in the playroom so as to provoke a child's habitual mode of reaction. In general, one would not aimlessly repeat within the playroom the frustrations and deprivations that the child is encountering outside. But occasionally frustrating situations may be set up in order to enable children to gain insight into the dynamics of their behavior. When only one attractive gun is provided for three aggressive children, the probability is that conflict will occur. The children's heightened reactions in the conflict situation offer the therapist a chance to confront each child with his habitual, unfruitful, self-defeating modes of reaction and to suggest more effective ways of handling conflict.

Toys for Reality Testing

From the moment he enters treatment, the child tests the realities of the setting, the reaction of the therapist, the nature of the materials. The frustrations and satisfactions encountered in handling playroom materials and the sense of power acquired in mastering them have direct bearing on the child's ego and self-image. The ego is strengthened by realistic success, and both are damaged by repetitive failure. While young children need encounters with reality as part of their treatment, it must be arranged to suit the child's changing powers. It is essential that children who come to treatment with vast experience in defeat do not relive failure in the playroom. Too many playrooms contain complicated mechanical toys that are hard to wind, guns that are impossible to put together. Such play materials produce frustration and dependence and hinder the development of mastery and security. A playroom should contain materials of *graded* difficulty which allow each child, regardless of handicap, to achieve some measure of success. Frequently a child with a long history of failure will discover that he had more ability in handling materials than he has ever known. The consequent improvement in self-image may mark the beginning of therapeutic change.

MEDIA FOR SUBLIMATION

One of the aims of psychotherapy is to help children develop sublimations that are compatible with society's demands and expectations. Our culture does not give children much choice about relinquishing infantile gratifications. Children are forced to give up interest in primary processes as early as possible. They are forbidden to handle body products—even the desire to explore them is prohibited. This task is usually accomplished by punishment which leads to repression. Play therapy offers children opportunities to enjoy forbidden pleasure in substitute ways. Since

"A small child's imagination makes urine of every fluid and feces of every messy substance" (Balint, 1954), sand, water, paint and clay provide excellent means of sublimating urethreal and anal drives. No playroom for small children is complete or adequate without such materials. Enuretic children should be given paint and running water; encorpretic children, mud and brown clay. Firesetters should have cap guns, sparklers, and flashlights. All young children should find in the playroom miniature utensils for cooking and serving meals to sublimate oral needs, dolls that can be dressed and undressed to sublimate sexual needs, and punching bags, targets, and guns to sublimate aggresive drives. Each child should have the opportunity to express his needs *symbolically* in a great variety of ways according to his changing capacities. A child should be led to express anger by punching dolls and destroying clay figures, as well as by composing critical poems and writing murder mysteries. The lack of adequate outlets in the playroom may impede the emergence of more mature means of sublimation. The therapy setting must provide materials that allow growth in the repetory of self-expression.

A SETTING FOR OLDER CHILDREN (AGES 10 TO 13)

Dolls, baby bottles, and similar toys lose their therapeutic effectiveness for a preadolescent. They cease to serve as media for catharsis or as symbols for communication. On the contrary, such toys become psychonoxious. They induce resistance against self-disclosure. "The sight of 'baby' toy dissuades twelve-year-olds from speaking. They seem to feel that such toys are beneath them and that the playroom is not theirs" (Lebo, 1956). Some therapists allow preadolescents to choose between the playroom and the office. However, such a choice does not solve the problem. For neither play nor interviews are suitable therapeutic media for many preadolescents.

> They giggle themselves to death about the mere idea of sitting in one room with an adult and playing a table game while that adult desperately pretends that this is all there is to it. . . . They find it funny that they should try and remember how they felt about things and . . . be constantly expected to have worries or fears—two emotions they are most skillful at hiding from their

own self-perception, even if they do occur. Most of these young-sters seriously think the adult himself is crazy if he introduces such talk. . . . They naively enjoy the troubles they make and they would much rather bear the consequences of their troubles than talk about them. (Redl, undated)

The question remains: What treatment setting should be used for children who are too old for play therapy and too young for interview therapy?

Aggressive preadolescents usually engage in boisterous and destructive activities, while the therapeutic aim is to lead them to more focused and more modulated forms of expression. In-hibited youngsters prefer quiet and safe activities, while the therapeutic aim is to lead them to more vigorous forms of expres-sion. A therapy setting must therefore contain activities and materials conducive to development of controls in the overactive and of spontaneity in the overinhibited.

Traditional materials have proven more appropriate for in-hibited than for aggressive preadolescents. Painting, model-build-ing, woodwork, and similar activities provide fearful and with-drawn children with safe channels for communication. Aggres-sive youngsters, however, find it difficult to accept such activities as substitutes for direct acting-out. They fail to use the equip-ment for its purpose; they turn all tools into torpedoes and all materials into missiles. The solution lies in providing these youngsters with absorbing substitutes for aggression, the setting should contain, in addition to traditional materials and activities, also equipment for safe and respectable expression of direct ag-gression such as facilities for fire setting and wood burning and modern communication devices.

FIRE IN THERAPY

Fire is a most therapeutic agent for aggressive preadolescents. It holds a magic fascination for them. They can spend hours absorbed in lighting matches, making fires and burning wood. In the process, they burn up a great deal of hostility which ordi-narily is directed against parents, siblings, teachers, and society.

At the end of a therapy session, Andy's mother said to her ten-year-old son, "What are you burning there? I bet you have burned your brother and sister and me and Daddy."

"Oh, never Daddy!" exclaimed Andy.

Safety is, of course, a prime consideration. The wood is burned in an enamel basin, half filled with water, and set on a large asbestos pad. A pail of water is nearby in case of emergency. The youngster sits at the basin, feeding the fire on the floating piece of wood. Fire-making is limited to the basin. The rule of the room is, "Fire over water." Only wood and small candles are for burning. For safety's sake, paper, plastic and other quickly consumed materials are banned from the fire. The therapist oversees the fire at all times. While the fire is on, he does not leave the room even for a moment. The box of matches stays in his possession at all times, and no child is allowed to take a match out of the room. The therapist is keenly aware that the price of fireplay is eternal vigilance.

From the first session on, the therapist establishes himself as a giving person. He holds the matches and the (birthday) candles and hands them out one at a time on request. The children react with utter disbelief. Whenever they ask for a match or for a candle, the therapist graciously complies. Never before have they encountered such a responsive adult, and they are bewildered. They take many sessions to test the therapist until they are convinced of his friendliness and strength.

One eleven-year-old boy was overheard saying to his father, "You won't believe it, but he let me use a million matches."

Fire can be beneficially used by most children: the aggressive, and the fearful, the gifted and the slow, the social and the silent. The aggressive ones use the fire daringly. They hold the lit match in their hands until it is consumed, and their wood burning becomes a bonfire. Often, the fire stimulates them to express their hostile fantasies.

Sexually inadequate boys may especially benefit from fire play. The symbolic meaning of the activity is not lost on these children. Like music, it talks to the unconscious. They encounter an adult male who allows them to use a big match with a red top that lights up when rubbed. Dramatically, many boys choose to light the match on the zipper of their fly. Symbolically, they are granted potency, and they sense it.

In sum, fire-play is readily available, inexpensive, captivating in process, and therapeutic in effect. Yet, few therapists make use of it. The reluctance may stem from realistic fear of possible dangers or from personal discomforts and restrictions. However, under proper safeguards, fire-play is a most valuable therapeutic tool. It attracts the withdrawn and the insulated, it appeals to the sexually inadequate and it offers the belligerent the most absorbing substitute for direct aggression that a therapy-setting can provide.

MODERN COMMUNICATION DEVICES

A tape recorder, a walkie-talkie, and a typewriter have a useful function in therapy with preadolescents. They directly encourage conversation and communication. Few youngsters can resist the temptation of broadcasting over a walkie-talkie, recording on a tape or typing on a typewriter. It is easier for a therapist to make contact, even with resistant children, when they need his help in activating these facinating devices.

The very presence of this type of equipment reflects permissiveness. Such gadgets are usually associated in children's experience with parental restrictions and punishment. Many children have been scolded for tampering with mother's typewriter, fooling with brother's transistor radio, or playing with father's tape recorder. The availability of these machines for their own use communicates loud and clear the permissiveness of the setting and the tolerance of the therapist. I can still recall the look of amazement on the face of a preadolescent, the son of a writer, who exclaimed in disbelief, "What! A typewriter for children?"

The communication devices allow preadolescents to experiment in safety; they can type or tape infantile and hostile wishes at one moment and erase them the next. They discover that they can express forbidden fantasies without dooming themselves or destroying others.

SOME COMMON-SENSE DON'TS

1. *No Smoking.* A therapist should not smoke in the playroom. He should not demonstrate to children undesirable behavior. Some children come from homes in which smoking is prohibited. The therapist should not introduce unnecessary con-

flicts of values. Also, the symbolic meaning of holding a cigarette or cigar in the mouth should not be overlooked. And perhaps the main reason against smoking is that during therapy, the therapist should not be occupied nor preoccupied with his own pleasure.

2. *No Tuxedoes.* Napoleon is credited with the saying that he who goes into battle should not wear his best pants. This advice pertains also to child therapists. A play therapist should not wear his best suit in the playroom. The preoccupation with keeping clothes clean will interfere with his active attention and listening.

3. *No Gifts.* Some children bring along an arsenal of chocolates, chewing gum, and candy and offer it generously to the therapist. It is advisable not to accept gifts from children, especially during the first sessions. The therapist may say, "Thank you, but you keep it." If the child offers his painting or clay work to the therapist, the therapist should acknowledge it by saying neutrally, "You want me to have it." He will then let the child put the painting wherever he wants, in the therapist's hands, out on the table, or in the closet.

4. *No Autobiography.* Infrequently the therapist will encounter children who try to interview him directly, as though taking his case history. They do not hesitate to ask many personal questions of the most intimate nature. It is not necessary for the therapist to give the children a detailed autobiography. The therapist will reflect the fact that the child wonders about him and wants to get to know him better.

WHO CLEANS UP THE PLAYROOM?

It is inadvisable to make the child clean up the playroom at the end of the play hour. Such a demand may inhibit the child's free play. It may also give the rebellious child an opportunity to dirty the walls, the furniture, and the therapist's clothes, all in the name of careful cleaning. Another disadvantage is that it puts the therapist in a role of a judge who evaluates the child's clean-up performance . The therapist himself does not clean the playroom during the session, except to remove dangerous objects. If a bottle is broken accidentally, the therapist

...er is to be of assistance to the therapist who is ...
...oup practice and perhaps to the therapist who ...
...ucting groups privately and may wish to reexam...
...g on. Colleagues in agency or institutional setti...
...se, wish to review what they are doing in light ...

...ME DEFINITIONS AND DELIMITATIONS

...ter has described elsewhere (Siegel, 1968) the prob-
...antics which are so pervasive in this field. Titular
...ns are tiresome if they serve only xenophobic pur-
...contribute little to a genuine understanding of what
...ng. Whatever it may be called, group psychotherapy
...e meeting of individuals on a volitional basis in order
...help in dealing with personal problems in living. A
...dience, a parent-teachers meeting, a college class, in
...s, would not be regarded as a group. No collection of
...s can be called a group, and what they do together
...called therapy, unless they assemble on a voluntary,
...basis for help of some kind in their lives. Those con-
...y be facing vocational, educational, or familial crises;
...be isolated, lonely people who wish to get closer to
...otherwise change their characteristic modes of behaving
...ng; they may be physically well or ill; they may be of
...ducation or possessors of graduate degrees; they may be
...nale, homosexual, bisexual, or asexual. Whatever and
...they are, they do not become a therapy group unless
...help, assemble regularly, and have a leader who is the

...in the limits of this structure, I feel that no real purpose
... in attempting to differentiate sharply among group
...alysis, group psychotherapy, group counseling, group
..., group discussion, group education, group orientation,
...like on some kind of continuum of decreasing depth and
... This is not to say that services of a clearly advisory
...re to be considered as phychotherapy. They are not, of
...any more than are classroom or instructional situations,
...their possible psychotherapeutic side effects. Similarly,

---

may comment, "The bottle broke," then proceed to remove the broken glass or sweep the floor.

A therapist in full-time practice of child treatment needs domestic help. He should not clean up the room session after session. He can be much more therapeutic if he knows that someone else will sweep the floors and tackle the toys. It is not easy to keep the room in order. The playroom must be rearranged before each appointment so that the activities of children will not be influenced by the arrangements of preceding sessions. The playroom is a miniature world to the child. To symbolize that the world can be orderly, it must be neat (in the beginning of each session), with the floor swept, broken toys removed, paints and clay in working order, and the nursing bottles sterilized and refilled. This job requires a helper. The therapist should be able to rest in the interlude between sessions and meditate about life outside the playroom.

REFERENCES

Arthur, H.: A comparison of the techniques employed in psychotherapy and psychoanalysis of children. *American Journal of Orthopsychiatry,* 22:484-498, 1952.

Balint, A.: *The Early Years of Life.* New York, Basic Books, 1954.

Fraiberg, S. H.: *Psychoanalytic Principles in Casework With Children.* New York, Family Service Association of America, 1954.

Ginott, H. G.: The theory and practice of "therapeutic intervention" in child treatment. *Journal of Consulting Psychology, 23*:160-166, 1959.

Ginott, H. G.: *Group Psychotherapy with Children.* New York, McGraw-Hill, 1961.

Ginott, H. G.: Interpretations and child therapy. In Hammer, E. F. (Ed.): *Use of Interpretation in Treatment.* New York, Grune and Stratton, 1968a.

Ginott, H. G.: Innovations in group psychotherapy with pre-adolescents. In Gazda, G. M. (Ed.): *Innovations to Group Psychotherapy and Counseling.* Springfield, Thomas, 1968b.

Lebo, D.: Age and suitability for non-directive play therapy. *Journal of Genetic Psychology, 89*:231-238, 1956.

Redl, F.: *Preadolescents—What Makes Them Tick?* New York, The
    Child Study Association of America, not dated.
Slavson, S. R.: *Child Psychotherapy,* New York, Columbia University
    Press, 1952.

**SPECIAL PF
PSYCHOTE**

In accordance with the thru
is restricted to problems in t
therapy. Needless to say, coll
child-care institutions, child
hygiene clinics, social agencie
labor unions, industry, settlen
bilitation programs, and per
today utilizing group psychot
of choice. That group psycho
method of treatment in the m
be questioned. Indeed, the ex
its counterparts (by whatever ti
and become pervasive in con
watching and systematic study.
being employed not only to de
problems, generally, but also to
give up smoking, gambling, or
find an "ideal" mate and for othe
mention. This chapter deals onl
group therapy, as has been noted
lems are being presented.

No effort is made within the li
depth with the history, nature a
therapy. The reader is referred fo
sive literature reflected in the Refe
cially, in this connection, to Durl
Mullan and Rosenbaum (1962), Ro
Rosenbaum (1965), and Wolf and

of this chapt
ginning a g
already cond
what is goir
may, of cou
this materia

SO

The wr
lems of ser
identificatio
poses and
we are doi
involves th
to obtain
theater au
these term
individual
cannot be
systematic
cerned m
they may
others or
and feeli
limited e
male, fer
whoever
they seek
therapist
With
is servec
psychoar
guidanc
and the
intensit
nature
course,
despite

the therapy group may well be educational, as a byproduct or side effect, but its primary purpose is the helping one, along interpersonal and intrapsychic lines.

INDIVIDUAL AND GROUP PSYCHOTHERAPY: SOME PARALLELS

In many respects, the individual and the group psychotherapist have much in common and may be one and the same. Ethics, law, confidentiality, personality, training, and related factors are clearly the same, in certain ways. For example, the therapist has no differing set of ethical responsibilities in the individual or the group situation. Without exception, everything applying to individual psychotherapy in this realm applies equally to group work. Thus it is assumed that therapists will hold inviolate the confidences of patients; it is assumed that therapists will insure that adequate medical examination has been completed on every patient; it is assumed that a competent evaluation has been conducted, in addition, to include psychological testing and any other procedure that may be indicated.

Along other lines, it would be assumed that no group therapist would undertake to treat children or young adolescents without specific group training and experience with this population. This would, of course, be equally true of the individual therapist. Just as we expect individual therapists to have experienced personal psychotherapy, so would we expect group therapists to have experienced group psychotherapy and, in both instances, as therapeutic experiences. In the area of training, the parallels would continue. The group therapist should have specific course work, supervision, and other didactic training and experience in group psychotherapy just as the individual therapist obtains specific training and experience (see, for example, Chapter 15 in Mullan and Rosenbaum, 1960; also Chapter 8 in MacLennan and Felsenfeld, 1968). On the other hand, it must be emphasized that training and experience as an individual psychotherapist do *not* establish competence as a group therapist.

There are other obvious parallels, such as the need for an adequate, soundproofed office setting, the handling of telephone interruptions, the use of clinical data for research purposes, the management of fees and billing, absences, lateness, and other critical considerations in any psychotherapeutic encounter. Many of these, however, merit separate elaboration in the group setting, despite the apparent relatedness of individual work.

THE OFFICE

While every therapist requires an office in which to work, the group therapist must make special provisions which go beyond the one-to-one relationship. A room should be available which can seat about ten people in a circular kind of face-to-face arrangement. There should be no furniture or other barriers to this circle, so that a desk is frequently an unnecessary encumbrance, unless it is really out of the way. The room should not be so large as to give the group too diffuse a feeling with excessive room to roam. The intimacy and cohesiveness of the group are actually reinforced by a relatively small room (e.g. 150 to 200 square feet). Where this is available, a separate group-therapy room may be used, as against the usual consultation room. Since most therapists do not have this facility, conversion of the office to a group setting is often necessary. This means chairs, sofas, ashtrays and the like should be so arranged as to permit all members of the group to be able to see each other and the therapist. With a relatively small therapy room, I discarded my desk years ago as an essentially vestigial item.

Adolescents can usually be worked with in the same office as adults. If group therapy is being conducted with children, the separate playroom usually used for play therapy should be available. The playroom, just as the group therapy room for adolescents and adults, should neither be too small and confining nor too large. Ginott (1961) recommends a room of 300 to 400 square feet for group play-therapy, as against 150 to 200 square feet for individual play-therapy. In the case of activity-group therapy, a much large area is necessary (about 600 square feet) according to Slavson (1943).

Some therapists prefer that the telephone not be in the group therapy room. Individual practices vary with regard to the telephone and its use. These include removing the phone from the receiver, having the answering service pick up the calls, or answering directly. Most therapists are consistent in both individual and group practice and should do what is most comfortable for them. I answer directly, keeping the contact to the barest minimum but insuring that if there is any emergency involving the patients in the room, the message can be conveyed.

Ventilation and soundproofing are particularly important in the group room. The use of fans, exhausts, air conditioners, and sometimes music is recommended, according to the individual setting. Wherever possible, adequate ventilation and safeguarding of privacy should not be at the expense of the group in terms of distraction and interference. No secretary, nurse, or assistant should be in the office when groups meet unless the physical set-up is such as to maintain without question the intimacy and privacy of the transference relationship.

ADMINISTRATIVE ARRANGEMENTS

Groups generally meet for 90 minutes on a schedule established by the therapist. Frequency ranges from one to three group sessions weekly with one alternate meeting or a variation thereof, sometimes called "coordinated meeting" (Kadis and Markowitz, 1958). Perhaps the only consistency offered by the literature is the agreement on 90-minute group sessions. Controversy continues regarding the use of alternate or coordinated meetings, though the impression of the writer is that a significant trend in the direction of agreement on the value of alternate sessions is observable.

Practical and theoretical considerations seem to play critical roles in the determination of time schedules. Therapists who practice "combined therapy," in which group and individual hours are continued concomitantly, tend more often to have groups meet once weekly. Therapists who work with patients either in group or individually, but not both, tend to meet their groups twice weekly for ninety minutes most commonly. These decisions relate specifically to one's theoretical position regarding combined therapy, which is treated more extensively elsewhere in this chapter, as is the alternate or coordinated meeting.

In private practice, the practical considerations which loom largest are those involving hours which fit the schedules of most patients. Evening hours beginning at 5:30 or 6:00 P.M. seem to be best for adults, as are Saturday hours. Depending on the location of the therapist, mid-day hours are often posible. College-age groups can be scheduled during day hours, depending on academic programs. Adolescents of high-school age are generally best seen during the late afternoons, again depending on school programs. Adolescent group hours are more subject to change than are other age groups, since high school and college programs vary from semester to semester. The writer, for example, has found the hours of 3:00 or 4:00 P.M. to work out quite well for adolescent groups and 5:45 P.M. for adult groups.

Play-therapy groups for children may be scheduled during ordinary school hours out of practical considerations, and most often school authorities will cooperate on this score. Nevertheless, it is the writer's experience that children should be seen outside of school hours wherever possible. This avoids undue parental anxiety, helps to avoid the stigma all too often associated with leaving school early and appearing to be "different," and realistically helps the child to keep up with his school work. There are only a limited number of hours in the week after 3:00 P.M., however, and once again flexibility must be the guideline.

FEES

In private practice, fees are a significant part of the therapeutic process. This is no different, essentially, in group or individual psychotherapy. This is how the therapist earns his living, whatever the modality or specialty. Problems of transference and countertransference will present themselves, as may be expected, whether individually or in group. The group setting, however, frequently makes it more possible for many patients to raise questions regarding fees or otherwise attack the therapist for his greed, wealth, or whatever. The group situation, additionally, makes it uniquely possible for the therapist to determine fees on a kind of sliding scale basis and also to raise, lower, defer, or even waive fees.

All too often, the literature of group psychotherapy pays but scant attention to the problem of fees. Equally often, in the opinion of the writer, the manner in which fees are handled influences the process of therapy, the structure of the group, and indeed the success or failure of treatment. Each therapist must, of course, make his own determination regarding fees. Each therapist must establish for himself principles and procedures in a professional design for living within which he can be most comfortable. There certainly can be little basis for right or wrong so long as the therapist is clear on what he is doing and so long as countertransference problems are not obscuring his visibility.

Some workers in the field advocate a basic rate for most patients, with an understanding that deviations from this rate are to be discussed privately with the analyst and not mentioned in group (Wolf and Schwartz, 1962). Others consider what their time is worth, divide the amount among the group members on some graduated fee basis and then encourage all patients to discuss openly all aspects relating to fees (Mullan and Rosenbaum, 1962).

I believe that fees should be established individually with each patient, based on the times, circumstances, locale, ability to pay, and every other personal consideration that may emerge. Thus, fees generally tend to run higher in large metropolitan areas like New York City, Los Angeles, Chicago, or Philadelphia than in more rural parts of the country. Costs of living are higher also in such areas, so that a balance is essentially maintained. I disagree vigorously with the point of view of Wolf and Schwartz (1962) insofar as open discussion in group of fees is concerned. Any arrangement which precludes complete and open sharing of attitudes and feelings can only be destructive to the group process, in my opinion. The position of Mullan and Rosenbaum is most strongly supported, therefore.

In general, fees for group therapy tend to run approximately half of those for individual therapy. The range of fees in private practice around the United States is from seven dollars and fifty cents to 25 dollars per group session, with a closer range of 10 to 20 dollars per session in the large urban centers. Needless to say, there are many variations. Most therapists seem to leave the manner of payment up to the patient, who may prefer to pay weekly, monthly, or whatever. Many therapists bill their patients once a month, though there is evidence of great variability here, once again. Whatever one's theoretical position may be with regard to fees, one should apply no differently to the group therapy situation. If one feels, therefore, that payment is the patient's responsibility, without billing, then this is the way to proceed with groups. If one feels that bills should be directed only to the patient and not to the spouse, parent, bank, or whoever may be paying the bills, then the group situation should not change anything. With children and young adolescents, however, the writer believes that bills should be sent to the responsible adult figure.

A constant problem in all private practice is that of the absentee in connection with payment of fees. This is especially sensitive in group work, which actually provides us with a vehicle that makes possible greater flexibility with fees. In general, the writer believes that unattended group sessions should be charged to the patient except in most unusual circumstances. There can really be no "cancellation" of a group appointment, since the therapist is not in a position to bring in another patient for one or more group sessions. Unusual circumstances, therefore, warranting waiving of the fee should be kept to the barest minimum, such as hospitalization, accident, or severe injury. The therapist should not permit himself to be placed in the position of making a judgment as to whether a cold is severe enough to justify absence. In the long run, no great hardship is worked on any patient financially, and the therapeutic process is enhanced, if hours are paid for almost without exception. *Whatever* is done, however, should be analyzed in the group with no holds barred and nothing withheld.

Vacation periods sometimes present a problem with regard to fees. The writer does not charge fees for sessions missed because of usual vacations during the summer or other holiday periods. Fees are charged, however, if a group session is missed because the patient elects to take a long weekend. The essential humaneness of the therapist must be the guiding criterion, along with flexibility, consistency, and a minimum of countertransference. Money is a significant problem to people in contemporary society, whatever one's financial strata. The handling of fees in open discussion can play a critical role in the group process, in the group relationships, and in the working through of resistance, transference, and countertransference problems.

SIZE AND GROUP COMPOSITION

Most workers in the field agree that the optimal number of adolescents or adults in a group is from six to ten, with a mean of seven or eight. Fewer than six or seven reduces possibilities for interaction and activity within the group, and with the inevitable occasional absentee, this interaction is reduced even further. More than ten tends to dilute the individuality of each patient, immobilizes some and threatens others with a classroom rather than a family kind of setting. Wolf and Schwartz (1962) caution against any rigid view of an ideal number for any group, but they prefer eight as the optimal number, as do Slavson (1964), Goldfarb (1953), and others. The caution recommended by Wolf and Schwartz, bearing clearly in mind the dynamics of the particular patients in any group and their motivations and activity, is strongly endorsed by the writer.

In the case of children, the writer would agree with Ginott (1961) that the number of children in a play-therapy group should not exceed five. More than this number makes it excessively difficult for the therapist to keep up with the shifting activities that may be expected with children. Ginott goes on to recommend that beginning therapists start with groups of three. In my experience, this is the kind of recommendation that produced more anxiety than security in beginners. Groups of three will all too often become individual, not group, therapy, what with illness, holidays, parental resistance, and the like. Furthermore, with too small a group, the therapist tends to develop an excessive stake or investment in each child and runs an increased risk of countertransference problems. The beginner has enough of this problem without compounding it.

With children up to the age of latency or the juvenile era, and with those in middle adolescence and older, mixed groups are preferable. There is little controversy in the literature insofar as including boys and girls in children's groups and males and females in adolescent and adult groups are concerned. There is general agreement that with the preadolescent latency groups, mixed groups tend to produce a male and a female subgroup, each in different worlds. The writer's experience would extend this point to early adolescence (approximately twelve to fourteen), where mixed groups do not really permit a group cohesiveness to develop. With middle and older adolescents, as well as with adults of all ages, the writer prefers to work with four males and four females wherever possible.

The principle of flexibility rather than rigidity must again obtain in the matter of group composition. There is a markedly significant difference between an immature, naive, depressed sixteen-year-old and a sophisticated, obsessive-compulsive, driven youngster of the same age. The former might do better in a group of early adolescents, and the latter in a college-age group. Similarly, a group of eight adults, all 30 years of age, would not necessarily be a homogeneous group. The variability and dynamics of each would make this clear.

The vast majority of group therapists generally seem to prefer heterogeneous groups insofar as age, personality dynamics, intelligence, marital status, symptomatology, education, vocation, race, culture, social strata, health, and any other factors are concerned. This would apply especially to groups beyond those of beginning-college age. The writer would agree with Mullan and Rosenbaum (1962), who urge "total heterogeneity" in group membership. In this manner, the unique individuality of each patient is emphasized.

Many attempts have been made empirically to establish criteria and standards for group suitability. Leopold (1957) has indicated the following requirements: that the patient (a) has contact with reality, (b) can be related to interpersonally, (c) has sufficient flexibility so that he may reduce or heighten intragroup tensions, and (d) can serve at times as a catalyst for the group. Patients who show destructive, impulse-motivated, antisocial behavior; who are in a constant state of acute anxiety; who cannot be reached by other group members because of constant chaotic behavior or who paralyze group interaction over an extended period of time should probably not be placed in a private group. In certain institutional settings, these considerations may, of course, not necessarily obtain. For example, homogeneous groups of drug addicts, criminals, or psychotic hospital patients, because of the very nature of their deep pathology, do often work well with limited therapeutic goals. In private practice, I feel such groups are contraindicated.

In general, it seems best not to include relatives, friends, or even acquaintances within the same group. Needless complications are avoided by adhering to this guideline. Married couples, however, would not be excluded. Many group therapists include husbands and wives within their groups, and others conduct married-couple groups. The writer has tended more often, based on clinical experience, to have husbands in one group and wives in another, all groups being *totally* heterogeneous. There is no contraindication, however, to having a married couple in a group, providing that the group does not become a marriage counselor, arbitrating and mediating.

THE ALTERNATE SESSION

The alternate session is a meeting of the group without the therapist, established in order to carry forward the group process, to separate patients from parental-authority dependency, to lessen restraints and help release feelings otherwise repressed. Such meetings are regularly scheduled, involve the whole group and usually take place in the homes of respective group members. These sessions, according to Kadis (1956), help patients to achieve ever-increasing freedom of expression and ego strength in the struggle for separateness.

From the time that Wolf first introduced the concept of the alternate session in 1938 (Wolf and Schwartz, 1962) opposition has been most vigorous. Heated debates continue in the literature around the values in and advantages of group meetings without the therapist. Those opposed to the concept of the alternate session insist that such meetings stimulate acting out, obscure the analysis of the transference reactions evoked in the group sessions, and otherwise retard the therapeutic movement (Slavson, 1956).

A variation of the alternate session, as originally introduced by Wolf, is the premeeting or postmeeting session, occurring immediately before and/or after regularly scheduled group-therapy sessions. Kadis (1963) has suggested the term "coordinated meetings" to include all meetings of the group without the therapist, though she makes clear her preference for the alternate session as the most desirable form of coordinated meeting. The premeeting of groups is much like a warm-up, paving the way for the actual group session, and usually takes place in the office of the therapist. Postmeetings, providing for a release in tension built up during the regular group session, may take place in the therapist's office, at members' homes, at a restaurant, or at any other place convenient to the group.

Whatever the kind and wherever the place, the essential ingredient in the coordinated meeting is the group as a total group without the therapist. Subgroups should be strongly discouraged. The emotions stirred up among group members should be analyzed by the whole group at regular sessions, and the spontaneous social gathering of several group members tends to be conducive to acting out transference resistances (Kadis, 1963).

In private practice, practical considerations once again influence the kind of alternate or coordinated meeting that is arranged. The group may, because of realistic limitations in travel, schedule, work, residence, etc., simply not be able to arrive at a time that all can make for an alternate session. The analyst must exercise great care here to work through group resistances involving passive dependency and difficulty in coping with problems of separateness. I am convinced of the value of alternate sessions, and in each of the groups where this is feasible, I encourage a premeeting and postmeeting as an extension of the alternate-session idea. For example, two of my groups continue for two or three hours after my departure at 7:15 P.M., the end of the regular group session.

One caution regarding alternate or coordinated meetings should be observed. This procedure cannot be used effectively with children or young adolescents, in my experience. From about the age of 18 and up, no problem is encountered with the acting out and need for supervision of the children and young adolescents involved.

COMBINED THERAPY

Another area of controversy among group therapists is the

value of combined therapy, sometimes referred to in the literature as concomitant or concurrent therapy. Combined therapy is the concurrent use of individual and group sessions during the course of treatment. There are vigorous opponents and critics of combined therapy (Wolf and Schwartz, 1962), but it seems clear that the vast majority of group psychotherapists combine group with individual therapy in varying degree (Kadis and Markowitz, 1958). Arguments against combined therapy tend to focus upon the therapeutic property of the group, with individual sessions viewed as an expression of resistance to the group process. The arguments noted above are indeed sometimes very valid, and it is crucial that the therapist retain the freedom and flexibility to adjust schedules to patient needs. The evidence suggests that relatively few therapists subscribe to the point of view expressed by Wolf and Schwartz, and I find it difficult to believe that the large number of therapists who practice combined therapy are therefore experiencing serious countertransference problems.

In practice, I usually *add* group psychotherapy to the individual therapeutic experience. The patient who is being seen twice weekly in psychotherapy, for example, and who seems ready to join a group is then seen in group as an *addition* to the treatment program. When the therapeutic process has reached the point that multiple transferences with peer as well as parental figures can be worked through, and when these sibling and parent prototypes are being confronted in group, the individual hours can be reduced gradually, with the group becoming the main or focal point.

OPEN OR CLOSED GROUPS

Open, or continuous, groups are those in which new members are added as old members leave. In this sense, the group is self-perpetuating and does not disband at any time. Closed groups are those which begin and end as a unit with no new members admitted during the life of the group. While both open or closed groups are feasible either in private or in institutional practice, there is a tendency for open groups to be more prevalent in private work. Intensive treatment settings, which approximate the private office setting most closely, will often have open groups.

Schools, colleges, and social agencies more often conduct closed groups, as a function of time schedules, academic programs, and the like. Except for the initiation of a new group, where the members begin as a unit, the writer recommends the open or continuous group to the private practitioner.

The nature and goals of psychotherapy inevitably influence the matter of open or closed groups. Intensive psychotherapy, continuing for over 200 group sessions and involving significant personality change for each group member, is usually conducted in open groups. Less intensive groups, which are often more homogeneous in various respects and are relatively short-lived (under 200 sessions), are usually closed groups (Mullan and Rosenbaum, 1962).

ORGANIZING A NEW GROUP

While open groups tend to be self-perpetuating, as noted above, there are times that a therapist faces the organization of a new group. This is most applicable, of course, to the beginning group therapist. The literature offers very little consistency of opinion with regard to the preparatory period. Some therapists have one or two interviews, and proceed to organize a group. Others work with patients for 30 or more hours until a clear impression of the patient has emerged and a relationship with the therapist has been established. The variability which exists in this respect is all to the good. Transition to a group can be very anxiety-provoking, and the therapist should take all the preparatory time necessary to insure that the patient meets the requirements reported earlier in this chapter by Leopold (1957).

A new group should not be organized with fewer than seven or eight patients. Too small a beginning group runs the same risks as described by the writer under the heading "Size and Group Composition" but, in addition, introduces the danger of an inexperienced group therapist investing too much in any single patient. With four or five patients, the loss of a group member becomes too threatening to the therapist, whose professional security system is reinforced by a good, solid, well-prepared nucleus.

When the prospective group members have been prepared adequately, the first group session may be scheduled. Normally, the group can be relied upon to get itself moving following introductions on a first-name basis. While each patient has heard about the group process during the preparatory phase, it may help to deal with some group "ground rules" at the outset. For example, the matter of confidentiality, ever troubling to most patients, is best laid right on the group table. Every group member must understand that if he breaches the confidence of any other patient he may be dropped from treatment. Other administrative details may be reviewed at this first session (e.g. time, lateness, procedures in the group, etc.), but it is wisest to plunge directly into the business at hand and avoid chit chat. Thus the group can be introduced directly to the "go-around," in which each member indicates briefly why he or she is in therapy, or in which each member reacts to the therapist or another patient in the group. A generally safe starting point in any group is the anxiety experienced by each patient at the outset. Patients can be asked to report a recent dream or anything else they may wish to discuss. Once again, adequate individual preparation begins to pay dividends in the first and early group sessions.

PREPARING FOR THE GROUP

As indicated above, it is essential that the therapist get to know the patient and establish a genuine relationship. Actual preparation for admission to an ongoing group is an individual therapist variable. Most therapists try to give the prospective group member an idea of what the group is like and how it operates. The therapist makes clear that he will not reveal to the group, without the patient's agreement, anything which has been discussed during the individual hours. Agreement must be reached on the maintenance of the strictest level of confidentiality for the protection of all concerned. Since people have a tendency to discuss things that go on in group, I take great pains to make clear that *no* violation of confidence can be tolerated. This means that husbands are not to tell wives who are not in the group about other group members; the material brought forth in group is inviolate.

Some therapists refer the patient to reading resources relating to group therapy. Others have extended discussions regarding the many questions posed by the ever-anxious prospective group analysand. Durkin (1964) suggests that most preliminary explanation is futile; that the sessions themselves must be the explanation. I have found that some orientation by the therapist is reassuring, some reading helpful, and have even shared with patients a published report of my own experience as a patient in group psychotherapy (Siegel, 1965 (a)). Nevertheless, I agree with Durkin that no explanation can really make clear what group process is like. The experience itself is vital and becomes the explanation.

TERMINATION

No significant problem exists in closed groups with regard to termination. When a time limit has been set in advance, patient responsibility is minimal. When decisions regarding termination are relegated to the therapist, the group member is deprived of his essential responsibility for his own life. The more intensive the group experience, the more painful and conflicting is the decision to terminate. It is as if one is leaving his family, where he has been made to feel he belongs, where he has been nurtured, where he has been able to interact freely, strip bare shame and facade and otherwise experience the truth. Yet, it is this very family, in the group process, which makes termination easier to achieve. In a sense, the goal of all psychotherapy is termination, a breaking of symbiotic patterns and the development of sufficient ego strength to exercise one's positive resources independently.

As in all therapies, inappropriate terminations must be guarded against. In intensive analytic groups, such false terminations are less likely. Authentic termination will generally not be impulsive and sudden, will not receive a negative group response and will not present seemingly spurious reasons for leaving. The patient who is really ready for termination will respect the judgment of his therapist and of his group. Such a patient is no longer acting out negative feelings to parents, is no longer seeing parent figures as good or bad and has arrived at a point of mutual respect with reference to parents, therapist, the group and the world.

Some workers consider a decision to terminate as irrevocable.

Others prefer to keep the door open, should the necessity arise, both to the group and to the therapist. In my experience, the rigidity and inflexibility of irrevocability seems to keep some patients in treatment who might otherwise have terminated. During recent years, I have tended increasingly in the direction of flexibility, and the open-door policy to patients seems to be the essentially more human and rewarding one. Together we have dealt with the ingredients of living: fear, anxiety, hate, love, anger, resentment, birth, death, illness, accident, aggression, sex (homosexual and heterosexual), money, identity, power, jobs, prestige, status, and so on and on. Together termination is planned and becomes not the end but the beginning of a life in what we might term the ultimate group—the world in which we live.

REFERENCES

Armentrout, W. W.: Group counseling: misnomer of consequence? Letter to the editor. *Journal of Counseling Psychology, 5*(1):71-72, 1958.

Bach, G. R.: *Intensive Group Psychotherapy.* New York, Ronald Press, 1954.

Bach, G. R.: The marathon group: intensive practice of intimate interaction. *Psychology Reports, 18*:995-1002, 1966.

Bennett, M. E.: *Guidance and Counseling in Groups,* 2nd ed. New York, McGraw-Hill, 1963.

Bilovsky, D., McMasters, W., Shorr, J. E., and Singer, S. L.: Individual and group counseling. *Personnel Guidance Journal, 31*:363-365, 1953.

Broedel, J., Ohlsen, M., Proff, F., and Southard, C.: The effects of group counseling on gifted underachieving adolescents. *Journal of Counseling Psychology, 7*(3):163-170, 1960.

Burrow, T.: The group method of analysis. *Psychoanalytic Review, 14*(3):268-280, 1927.

Calia, V. F.: A group guidance program in action. *Junior College Journal, 27*:437-442, 1957.

Cohn, B., Ohlsen, M., and Proff, F.: Roles played by adolescents in an unproductive counseling group. *Personnel Guidance Journal, 38*:724-731, 1960.

Corsini, R. J.: Historic background of group psychotherapy: a critique. *Group Psychotherapy, 3*:213-219, 1955.

Dickenson, W. A. and Truax, C. B.: Group counseling with college underachievers. *Personnel Guidance Journal, 44*:243-247, 1966.

Dilley, N. E.: Group counseling for student teachers. *Educational Administration Supervision, 39*(4):193-200, 1953.

Dreese, M.: Group guidance and group therapy. *Review of Educational Research, 27*(2):219-228, 1957.

Dreikurs, R. and Corsini, R. J.: Twenty years of group psychotherapy. *American Journal of Psychiatry, 110*:567-575, 1954.

Durkin, H.: *The Group in Depth.* New York, International University Press, 1964.

Eiserer, P. E.: Group psychotherapy. *Journal of the National Association of Deans of Women, 19*(3):113-122, 1956.

Ford, D. H.: Group and individual counseling in modifying behavior. *Personnel Guidance Journal, 40*:770-773, 1962.

Foulkes, S. H. and Anthony, E. J.: *Group Psychotherapy.* London, Penguin Books, 1957.

Freud, S.: *Group Psychology and the Analysis of the Ego.* London, Hogarth Press, 1948.

Fromm-Reichmann, F.: *Principles of Intensive Psychotherapy.* Chicago, University of Chicago Press, 1950.

Ginott, H. G.: *Group Psychotherapy with Children: The Theory and Practice of Play-Therapy.* New York, McGraw-Hill, 1961.

Glanz, E. C.: *Groups in Guidance; the Dynamics of Groups and the Application of Groups in Guidance.* Boston, Allyn and Bacon, 1962.

Goldfarb, W.: Principles of group psychotherapy. *American Journal of Psychotherapy, 7*:418-432, 1953.

Gorlow, L., Hoch, E. L., and Telschow, E. F.: *The Nature of Non-Directive Group Psychotherapy.* New York, Columbia University Press, 1952.

Grier, D. J.: *Orienting Students Through Group Counseling.* New York, Teachers College, Columbia University, 1950.

Hare, A. P.: *Handbook of Small Group Research.* New York, Free Press, 1962.

Hewer, V. H.: Group counseling, individual counseling, and a college class in vocation, *Personnel Guidance Journal, 37*:660-665, 1959.

Hoppock, R.: *Group Guidance: Principles, Techniques, and Evaluation.* New York, McGraw-Hill, 1949.

Kadis, A. L. and Markowitz, M.: Group Psychotherapy. In Abt, L. E.

and Riess, B. F. (Eds.): *Progress in Clinical Psychology*. New York, Grune and Stratton, 1958, vol. 5, pp. 154-183.

Kadis, A. L.: The alternate meeting in group psychotherapy. *American Journal of Psychotherapy, 10*:275-291, 1956.

Kadis, A. L.: Co-ordinated meetings in group psychotherapy. In Rosenbaum, M. and Berger, M. M. (Eds.): *Group Psychotherapy and Group Function: Selected Readings*. New York, Basic Books, 1963, pp. 437-448.

Kadis, A. L. and Winick, C. (Eds.): *Group Psychotherapy Today*. New York, S. Karger, 1965.

Kelsey, C. E., Jr.: Group counseling: an annotated bibliography, *Journal of Psychoglogical Studies, 11*:84-92, 1960.

Kemp, C. G.: *Perspective on the Group Process: a Foundation for Counseling with Groups*. Boston, Houghton-Mifflin, 1964.

Klapman, J. W.: *Group Psychotherapy, Theory and Practice*. New York, Grune and Stratton, 1946.

Lawrence, R. M. and Kiell, N.: Group guidance with college students. *International Journal of Group Psychotherapy, 11*:78-87, 1961.

Leopold, H.: Selection of patients for group psychotherapy. *American Journal of Psychotherapy, 11*:134-637, 1957.

Lifton, W. M.: *Working With Groups: Group Processes and Individual Growth*. New York, Wiley, 1961.

Lubin, B. and Lubin, A. W.: *Group Psychotherapy: a Bibliography of the Literature From 1956 Through 1964*. East Lansing, Michigan State University Press, 1966.

MacLennan, B. W. and Felsenfeld, N.: *Group Counseling and Psychotherapy With Adolescents*. New York, Columbia University Press, 1968.

Moreno, J. L.: *The First Book on Group Psychotherapy*. New York, Beacon, 1957.

Moreno, J. L. (Ed.): *The International Handbook of Group Psychotherapy*. New York, Philosophical Library, 1966.

Mullan, H. and Rosenbaum, M.: *Group Psychotherapy*. New York, Free Press, 1962.

Poser, E. G.: Group therapy in Canada: a national survey. *Journal of the Canadian Psychiatry Association, 11*(1):20-25, 1966.

Powdermaker, F. and Frank, J. D.: *Group Psychotherapy*. Cambridge, Mass., Harvard University Press, 1953.

Raines, M. R.: Helping college freshmen identify problems through a case conference. *Personnel Guidance Journal, 34*:417-419, 1956.

Redl, F.: Psychoanalysis and group therapy: a developmental point of view, *American Journal of Orthopsychiatry, 33*:135-148, 1963.

Rinn, J. L.: Group guidance: two processes, *Personnel Guidance Journal, 39*:591-594, 1961.

Rosenbaum, M.: Group psychotherapy and psychodrama. In Wolman, B. B. (Ed.): *Handbook of Clinical Psychology.* New York, McGraw-Hill, 1965, pp. 1254-1274.

Rosenbaum, M. and Berger, M. M. (Eds.): *Group Psychotherapy and Group Function: Selected Readings.* New York, Basic Books, 1963.

Satir, V.: *Conjoint Family Therapy.* Palo Alto, California, Science and Behavior Books, 1964.

Siegel, M.: Group orientation and placement counseling, *Personnel Guidance Journal, 38*:659-660, 1960.

Siegel, M.: Recent experience of a therapist as a patient in group psychotherapy. In Kadis, A. L. and Winick, C. (Eds.): *Group Psychotherapy Today.* New York, Karger, 1965a.

Siegel, M.: Group psychotherapy with gifted underachieving college students. *Community Mental Health Journal, 1*(2):188-194, 1965b.

Siegel, M.: Group techniques in education, counseling and psychotherapy. In Siegel, M. (Ed.): *The Counseling of College Students.* New York, Free Press, 1968, pp. 99-113.

Slavson, S. R.: *An Introduction to Group Therapy.* New York, Commonwealth Fund and Harvard University Press, 1943.

Slavson, S. R.: The nature and treatment of acting out in group psychotherapy. *International Journal of Group Psychotherapy, 6*:3-26, 1956a.

Slavson, S. R.: *The Fields of Group Psychotherapy.* New York, International Universities Press, 1956b.

Slavson, S. R.: *A Textbook in Analytic Group Psychotherapy.* New York, International Universities Press, 1964.

Spotnitz, H.: *The Couch and the Circle.* New York, Knopf, 1961.

Warters, J.: *Group Guidance Principles and Practices.* New York, McGraw-Hill, 1960.

Willey, R. DeV. and Strong, W. M.: *Group Procedures in Guidance.* New York, Harper, 1957.

Wolf, A.: The psychoanalysis of groups. In Rosenbaum, M. and Berger, M. (Eds.): *Group Psychotherapy and Group Function.* New York, Basic Books, 1963, pp. 273-327.

Wolf, A. and Schwartz, E. K.: *Psychoanalysis in Groups.* New York, Grune and Stratton, 1962.

Chapter 4

SPECIAL PROBLEMS IN FAMILY
PSYCHOTHERAPY PRACTICE

Tess Forrest

Family therapy is defined as the treatment of the interaction of the family group as an integrated social unit that shares an identity and whose individual members influence and are influenced by the intrafamilial processes and patterns. Family diagnosis is evaluation centering on the dynamic interactional processes of the family as a system or organization.

The rationale for family therapy and family diagnosis rests on a number of interlocking assumptions. One is that the family is the socializing milieu in which the individual develops the personality, character, and behavior that represent his most adaptational solutions in the pursuit of satisfaction and security. The second assumption is that the interpersonal family environment is a complex of individual personalities, dynamically and functionally interrelated to secure from each other the vital necessities of emotional, social, and biological life. The third assumption is that the family group, the total interpersonal field, substantially influences and is affected by the operation of any part. The family group's unique configuration and distinctive homeostatic balance is determined by and determines the configuration and homeostatic balance of each integral member. Last is that pathology in any constituent unit is as much a symptom of failure of the group operation as it is an expression of individual personal distress. Individual behavior, sound or pathological, is an adaptive attempt to maintain homeostatic balance both in the individual and within the group.

TRAINING FOR THE PRACTICE OF FAMILY THERAPY

Despite the encouraging results with family therapy reported by community clinics and hospitals, private therapists who practice the family treatment modality remain a minority. There are several reasons for this, but not the least among them is the unfortunate combination of the complexity of the procedure and the insufficiency of training facilities.

Family therapy is, in my experience, the most difficult and demanding of all modalities of psychotherapeutic treatment. The family therapist working with the family confronts the intrapsychic and the interpersonal dynamics of each individual family member and the intrafamilial dynamics, all in active operation. In session with an individual patient, the psychotherapist can dispassionately study his patient's reports of his past and present life experiences and can regulate the emotional climate to be most conducive to the therapeutic enterprise. Although the group therapist meets more urgent stress and demands for immediate interaction in an environment where emotional forces are less subject to his control, he can, with relative security, depend on the completion of each session to bring the group members a respite from each other. Only the family therapist must work in the force and heat of the ongoing family interactional system with sufficient speed and effectiveness to guard against possible destructive disruption of the family unit which must continue its life together between sessions without the therapist.

To develop expertise in family therapy, additional training beyond psychoanalytic and therapeutic study of the individual is needed. There is a specific theory of family dynamics whose subject matter is more and different than the sum of the dynamics of the individual members. Indeed, there is a growing realization that dimensions are added when individual dynamics are viewed in relation to the family system with which it maintains a homeostatic balance. For the therapist who wishes to practice family therapy, the initial roadblock is the dearth of training facilities for private practitioners. At the present time, no major psychoanalytic training institute or postdoctoral training program offers intensive training in this modality. While the clinician may acquire experience and technical knowledge by working in one of the better family-treatment clinics, this demands a lengthy bulk of time because the main focus in most treatment installations is on the rendering of service rather than on the training of the therapist. The need for training centers cannot be exaggerated, and this hiatus in training facilities makes it an almost insurmountable problem for the individual therapist in private practice to secure the training he would desire to practice family therapy. Until adequate training programs are offered by psychoanalytic institutes, postdoctoral training programs, community agencies or professional organizations, the therapist may have to content himself with accumulating direct experience with family therapy under private supervision of an experienced family therapist.

Assuming the requisite degree of expertise in the skills of family treatment, the family therapist in private practice still faces many complex problems. This chapter will address itself to some of the most immediate questions encountered in the family psychotherapy practice. How are time and fees established? When is family diagnosis indicated? For whom is family therapy indicated? When are family sessions useful adjuncts to individual psychotherapy sessions? When is family therapy countraindicated? How is family therapy initiated? What members are included in family therapy? Does family therapy permit sessions with individual members or with subgroup? At what age are children included in family therapy? How does one elicit and utilize family secrets? When is divorce and when is marital therapy indicated?

TIME AND FEES

The time required for family sessions, if all members are to be heard, is usually one and a half hours. For marital sessions, one hour may be sufficient. A family session is twice as long as an individual session, while a marital session is one third longer, if we consider the average individual session to be 45 minutes. If the added demands of this treatment modality on the therapist are not considered, a fee schedule may be based simply on expended time, using the fee scale of the individual session as base. The added cost of the family session for the family budget is balanced by the decreased number of sessions required. While some families need two sessions a week, family practice generally finds one session a week adequate. One advantage of family therapy is that the therapeutic process initiated in the session by the therapist is likely to continue at home with one or another family member embracing the therapist's role.

A major difficulty in the practice of family therapy is the scheduling of family-therapy sessions. It is obviously more difficult to arrange appointments with a group whose members are of different ages and have different commitments, such as school children and working fathers. In most cases, only the late afternoon and early evening hours are feasible for family sessions. However, in view of the added hardship of family therapy sessions on the therapist, it suits his need as well for his practice of family therapy to be limited to only part of his total practice, usually the latter part of the day. The comparatively less demanding, individual work can then take up the earlier hours of the day when children and fathers are not available.

FAMILY DIAGNOSIS

Ackerman (1958) has pointed out that family diagnosis and family treatment are two sides of the same coin. The therapeutic process itself is necessary for comprehensive and systematic evaluation, and conversely, the clarification of the dynamic meaning of observable interaction is itself therapeutic for the patients. However, this is not to be interpreted as implying that there is no place for a single or several family evaluative interviews along with individual treatment. On the contrary, since Ackerman and Sobel (1950) over a decade ago demonstrated the feasibility of arriving at an understanding of the child by studying the family, the valuable insights that accrue to the adult patient and the therapist from evaluative marital or family interviews have been reported (Ackerman and Sobel, 1950; Bowen, 1966; Forrest, 1968), and Szalita (1963-1964) has recommended that such interviews be included as a routine procedure in the early weeks of individual therapy. Troublesome familial interactional patterns that are observable but out of the patient's awareness are useful information immediately available to the therapist in the family session. For the group therapist, as well as the individual therapist, an evaluative family session aids in defining with whom the patient is identified and the precise role in the family system the individual plays that the therapist would wish to avoid reinforcing in the therapeutic encounter.

Actually, with patients of any age, when there is doubt as to the choice of therapeutic method most suitable for the identified patient, a family diagnostic interview is indicated. The therapist then seeks such vital information pertaining to the nuclear family as: how the family as a social system handles its life problems, the type and depth of the dyadic and multiple relationships within the group, the strengths and limitations of the individual members, their roles in the system, and how much and what kind of help family members other than the identified patient require. If the problems of the identified patient are clearly symptomatic of defects in the family social system, and if there are positive family ties, adequate ego strength, anxiety about and motivation to establish a meaningful relationship with each other, family therapy may be the most appropriate therapeutic modality. The evaluative observation of the transactional system orients the therapist to the kind of therapeutic interventions the patient and the family need, be it in individual therapy, marital therapy, family therapy or some combination thereof. Wittingly or unwittingly, the therapist affects the family of every patient he treats if his treatment changes the patient's interpersonal perceptions and behavior. It is helpful for the individual patient as well as the family if the therapist is aware of the impact the therapy makes on the family group, if the therapist alleviates the family's anxiety about the changes he might effect (Szalita, 1963-1964) and if the direction and goals of the treatment are validated by those who ultimately live with them.

CHOICE OF FAMILY THERAPY

Because family therapy is a treatment modality that has only been developed during the past decade, the patients and problems most effectively treated with this technique have not yet been fully ascertained. Nevertheless, inferences may be drawn from pertinent experimental data, clinical experiences and psychoanalytic theory as to the conditions under which family therapy may be recommended, either as the preferred treatment modality or as adjunctive to individual therapy.

ADULTS

Studies of schizophrenic patients have delineated peculiar and specific family interactions and communication patterns (Ackerman, 1958; Bateson, Jackson, Haley, and Wickland, 1956; Bowen, 1959; Lidz, Fleck, and Cornelison, 1965; Wynne, et al, 1958) that prevent individuation, invalidate personal experience, confuse, isolate and enmesh the patient. Statistical studies reveal that the patient's relationship to the family is the single most significant correlate determining the course of illness and that schizophrenic patients improved when the parents were emotionally close, while all management methods were unsuccessful when the parents were emotionally divorced (Bowen, 1959). These observations of the deviant way the parental relationship uses the schizophrenic patient point to the parental and family unit as the pathogenic root that requires therapeutic intervention with schizophrenic patients. Indeed, Bowen (1965) finds that "clinical results in dealing with the family projection process (characteristic of schizophrenogic families) are best in outpatient work and private practice."

There are, however, some major problems that the private practitioner must anticipate and cope with if he is to do family therapy with the schizophrenic patient. The discrepancies between the apparent and real group relations and communications and the chaotic or mystifying presentation of their lives and problems may weaken the therapist's reality testing and snare him in the family paralysis. The family's profound fear of change that prompts them to rigidly maintain the family homeostasis (Friedman, 1965) and exclude environmental intervention may manifest itself in the inability to collaborate on a decision or take action together (Lidz, Fleck, and Cornelison, 1965) to arrive together consistently at the therapist's office. Friedman *et al.* (1965) met these problems with encouraging results by having co-therapy teams conduct family treatment in home visits with schizophrenic patients. Such solutions as co-therapy teams and home visits, though difficult for the private therapist to arrange, may be necessary in the early stages of treatment until enough progress has been made for the family to consistently visit the therapist's office together and until one therapist can get sufficient foothold on the family system.

Another procedure successfully utilized by Szalita (1968) is to conduct family interviews adjunctive to individual therapy. By convening family sessions of the whole group or subgroups, as the course of therapy indicates, the therapist of the schizophrenic patient may directly learn about and influence the intrafamilial interactions that lead to conflict and difficulty.

With severely depressed married patients whose current lifestyle operates to maintain the pathological sense of deprivation and grief, it has been my clinical experience that a combination of marital therapy and individual therapy is especially effective and at times essential (1969A). The depressive patient is often bound in a symbiotic relationship with his marital partner, and he gives overt expression to the depression that the marital partner shares but camouflages with blandness and detachment. The symbosis serves to maintain the isolation, deprivation and sense of loss experienced by both partners but expressed by only one. The extreme dependency of the couple makes expression of any need or of anger at frustration of needs a threat which neither partner risks. Instead, a covert battle is waged for the care both crave and each refuses to give, a battle disguised by the helpless self-reproach of the identified patient and detached "helpfulness' of the marital partner. This covert struggle is what the depressive symptoms mask. During one or two individual sessions a week, the therapist can allow the transference relationship to develop to sufficient depth to give him leverage in the marital sessions. The individual sessions also allow the therapist to meet some of the index patient's needs for emotional nurturance and the patient to work through some of his feelings of frustration and loss. In the weekly marital session, the therapist can directly observe and interpret the interactional pattern of mutual isolation and avoidance, denial and frustration of needs, covert rage, and retaliatory operations and their secondary gains. The combination of individual and joint sessions enables the therapist to help the patient and his mate to touch and join and also to separate and individuate. The presence of the therapist attenuates the feelings of each partner that he is threatened with abandonment as well as his fears of uncontrolled aggression. The therapist both catalyzes and controls overt expression of the frustrated needs and helpless rage. By example and support, the therapist initiates and fosters a dialogue and an emotional exchange that relate the marital pair in a positive complementary relationship that assuages their fear of loss and satisfies their need for human relatedness.

Interpreting the Oedipus complex as a shared psychosocial family pattern of fixed dyadic primary-dependency relationships (Forrest, 1968) suggests family therapy as suitable for a patient whose Oedipal problems severely handicap the possibility of adequate family functioning. Characteristic symptoms are a symbiotic marital relationship and resistance to fulfilling the parental role in relation to the children. Family therapy is utilized to help the marital partners resolve their individual problems that are the pathogenic root of the family disfunction. Whether the treatment unit be the marital partners alone or the total family depends on how the marital configuration is structured to maintain the pathological marital relationship. If the symbiotic marital relationship excludes the children, it is helpful to include them in the sessions as a wedge into the marital fusion and as a prophylactic measure. If the marital partners defend against their intense dependency needs by affective isolation of each other and use the children as a barrier to marital intimacy or exploit the children for the emotional gratification the partners fail to provide each other, then the marital pair alone is the more suitable treatment unit. Therapy may then proceed directly to the problem of the partners' alienation from each other without interference from the children that the parents provoke.

When a severe transference neurosis may be anticipated from the clinical impression of the individual patient, discretion may be the better part of valor, and family therapy in which the transference may be neutralized may be the most prudent and pragmatic therapeutic modality. Rather than risk family diffusion and fragmentation by regressive acting-out in individual therapy, family sessions may utilize the weight of the transference to shift the balance of intrafamilial forces in a healthier and more cohesive direction. Using the leverage that the transference provides him, the therapist may help the family replace pathogenic patterns with productive ones.

With patients who manifest overt relational symptoms such as sadomasochistic acting-out, or implicit relational symptoms such as alcoholism or gambling, family or marital therapy for the pathologic unit may be tried. In conjoint sessions, the immediate stimulus and the reinforcement of the mutual acting-out may be identified and counteracted by equalizing responsibility, reducing guilt, and fostering more gratifying modes of relating.

Emotional problems that arise in response to natural family life crises such as birth, death, separation of adolescents from the family and marriage of children may most efficiently be resolved with family therapy. These natural life crises disturb an existing family equilibrium and require recalibration of a family system that may be adequate for less stressful periods. It is a mistake to underestimate the usefulness of therapeutic intervention with a limited goal such as clarifying the reasons for the vulnerability to the particular stress, exploring alternative methods of coping with the crisis, establishing a new basis for homeostatic balance and then leaving the family to utilize their own resources to continue the process of growth and change.

YOUNG ADULTS AND ADOLESCENTS

A major task of the young adult that is prerequisite to his full individuation and autonomy is the development of a realistic perception of his parents. Barnett (1968), viewing the dependency problems of the adolescent as primarily cognitive in nature, considers a syntactic appraisal of the parents and family identity essential to their resolution. Alexander (1963) finds family therapy highly effective with patients eighteen to twenty who have difficulty with the transition from high school to college, and he considers, "this technique ideally suited to problems relating to symbiosis, separation and the emergence of identity." Family therapy sessions afford the opportunity for a confrontation with interpersonal reality.

On the other hand, since the adolescent needs to find his own identity and separate himself from his family, he might better be assisted towards these ends by experiencing a firm relationship with an adult whose major concern it is to help him determine his own direction, thus benefiting from the reassuring conviction that separation from the family will not cast him adrift in an isolated sea.

Because the development of individual identity is inseparable from the ability to identify accurately the significance and nature of the family, and because the freedom to separate from significant others depends so heavily on the confidence of unity with them, the identity and separation problems of adolescents may require a flexible combination of individual and family therapy. In the family therapy session, the adolescent may differentiate himself from the parental images, idealized or punitive, that he has introjected and then move more freely to individual identity formation. A brief example is the case of a sixteen-year-old girl who was deeply troubled through months of individual therapy, without clues as to the roots of her constant dissatisfaction, self-criticalness and relentless contempt for others which made life by herself or with others continually miserable. In the first family session, her father, on entering, walked directly to a picture on the wall and straightened it. The girl's relieved laughter at the memory of her identical behavior in her first session signaled her realization of her self-defeating identification and marked a new sense of freedom to individuate herself that this realization granted her.

Rebellious acting-out is often motivated by a need for individuation or prompted by unconscious parental conflict and provocation, and may be reduced by family sessions that block displacement of conflict, sharpen the focus of individual personalities, and reveal the dynamic interplay within the family.

The unyielding grip of the family on the adolescent when the parents share and aggravate his separation anxiety may be released in family therapy as the parents are helped with their identity problems and with the anxiety precipitated by the need for a changing parental role. When the adolescence of the child is concurrent with approaching middle age in the parents, all family members may need support from each other to move forward, lest fear of change turn to panic that blocks movement. Family therapy sessions may help the family alter existing patterns by relieving the underlying anxieties that equate separation with abandonment and by initiating a family dialogue in which the members learn to give and receive gratification through the quality of understanding intimacy rather than through the quantity of dependent care. By helping the parents find in the marital relationship compensatory satisfaction for the increasing absence of the adolescent, much of the pressure and ambivalence is reduced in the separation problems of the adolescent.

CHILDREN

In the treatment of children where alterations in the marital and familial dynamics help free the child from the pathological family constellation and create a more viable social matrix for his natural growth, family therapy is recommended as a treatment of choice for most disorders. Helping the parents to be good parents together is clearly preferable to having the therapist replace them as the "good parents." Therapy can be a cohesive force. The child is protected from the stigma of bearing alone the family defect as the group together share and work on their common difficulties. It is reasonable to infer from psychoanalytic theory that, particularly in the treatment of the child who is yet undifferentiated and unindividuated from the family group, the family is the most effective point for therapeutic intervention. The child's self-concept and behavior reflect the parental appraisal of him and of themselves and his dynamic meaning and purpose in their interrelated organization, and these can be promptly understood and affected in family therapy. Corrective influence on the total family may be brought to bear specifically on the emotional experiences and interpersonal pressures that produce the child's illness, as they emerge in the family sessions.

It has been the experience of community clinics using family therapy that such a variety of childhood disorders as learning problems, behavior problems and phobias are alleviated in the course of family therapy as the family confronts and works through such problems as marital conflict, extramarital affairs, inadequate parental and sexual role functioning (Forrest, 1969B), and parental submission to domination by grandparents. Community outpatient clinics, using family therapy for the treatment of children, report similar positive results with even short-term contacts, success Kaffman (1962) attributes to the clarification of family conflicts and to the removal of disorganizing stress situations and pervading anxiety.

When individual treatment is considered more appropriate for the child, therapeutic aims may be furthered and consolidated by adjunctive family interviews. Vital information may be secured about the pathological family processes to which the child is adapting and contributing, and therapeutic intervention may promote structural and functional changes that are conducive to the child's, as well as the entire family's, growth.

When the child is the identified patient, the family therapist searches for the following vital information. He observes the family level of anxiety and the emotional climate to which the child is exposed and what and how the child contributes in his interaction with his parents. He specifically notes which transactions raise or lower the anxiety levels. He defines the meaning and use of the child in the marital relationship, uncovering what displacement of conflict there is from the marital partners to the child and what satisfactions are sought from the child that the parents lack in the marital relationship. Conversely, he specifies the child's effect on the parental relationship, revealing when and how the child promotes marital conflict and whether the child omnipotently plays an adult role in the parents' default.

The therapist evaluates the parents' appraisals of the child, including the degree of distortion, projection, and identification that exists in each parent's perception and how these transferences to the child are acted out in the group transaction and in the child's self-concept. He explicates what roles, attitudes, expectations, and taboos are molding the child, which potentialities are fostered and which are repressed. He determines the degree of internal role consistency, comparing family roles and norms with actual performance and potentialities and assessing the compatibility of family norms with societal norms to which the child must adapt.

CONTRAINDICATIONS OF FAMILY THERAPY

Because family therapy is a treatment modality that is new to even the most experienced practitioners, little can be said with any degree of certainty about the contraindications of family therapy. It is still too early to determine whether failure may be attributed to the relative inexperience of the practitioner or to the modality. For contraindications of family treatment, we must look to the experience offered us by the pioneers in this field. Ackerman (1958) indicates that when severe pathology is accompanied by an unmanageable amount of hostility, family therapy is contraindicated. Then reparative attention might best be focused on saving those members that one can. Illness that is deeply entrenched in the mind of an individual who barricades himself from family impact may more likely be reached and probed in individual therapy, with family therapy an adjunct when indicated. Where disintegration of the family group has progressed beyond repair, and fruitless efforts at cohesion would discourage even the individuals who are potentially good therapeutic risks, individual therapy is more expedient. In families where the malignant member is a hopelessly dominant force, therapeutic efforts are usually doomed. Family therapy with parents who are deeply dishonest is also unlikely to succeed.

Sometimes family therapy may be contraindicated initially until therapeutic efforts may counteract the disruptive forces and mitigate the circumstances. For example, a number of individual sessions with the most dominant member, in which the therapist may foster a positive transference, may align the dominant member with the therapist and give the therapist more leverage in the family group. It is suggested, therefore, that although contraindications need not be regarded as immutable and definitive and may be modified by special efforts and experimentation, they nevertheless should be regarded with health respect.

FAMILY TREATMENT UNIT

While the unit of treatment in family therapy has been expanded by Speck (1967) to large social networks and narrowed by Bowen (1966) to family-oriented individual treatment, the major focus of conjoint family therapy is the nuclear family that lives together. Significant extended family members, particularly grandparents or relatives centrally involved in the conflicts, may usefully be invited to sessions (Beatman, 1967) as the course of treatment indicates but are not centrally defined patients. Of the nuclear family members, children under eight who are not identified patients may be omitted from sessions, but only after they have participated in at least the evaluative interviews for their part in the family system, and the effect of the family system on them should be observed by the therapist and clarified with the family. For purposes of family evaluation, the inclusion of even tots or infants may be invaluable. Which parent holds the infant and how he is held can reveal much about the social roles and sexual identification of the parents and how the parental roles are enacted. The very young may offer the most intuitive cues about the causes of the underlying family conflict, as did the four-year-old who observed that the family unhappiness was not "because Daddy is strict," as the five older children claimed, but rather "because Mommy hasn't enough milk for all of us."

There is a difference of opinion on whether the entire family should always be seen together for each session or whether subgroup sessions may be permitted or even requested. The guiding principle recommended by the author is that the group composition be structured by the therapist in accordance with the therapeutic needs and goals. Absences of expected family members should be explored with the members present to try to work through the family resistance that the absence may serve. When subgroup or individual sessions are arranged, the therapist may avoid being drawn into alliances that are inimitable to the family interest and side-step manipulations by individual members if he establishes the practice that he reserves the prerogative, of using his discretion to decide whether or not to share with the whole family group any confidences entrusted to him by any part of the family.

THE INITIATION OF FAMILY THERAPY

From the first conjoint family therapy session, the focus of treatment is on the interpersonal interactions. The basic assumption, that all individual behavior has interpersonal meaning, is utilized to explicate and validate with the family members how each individual actively effects and responds to the intrafamilial transactions that culminate in the characteristic family patterns that are troublesome.

The initial statement of the presenting problem is typically a displaced scapegoating of one member that the family identifies as the patient. Nevertheless, how the statement is formulated, by whom and about whom, may be diagnostically useful to the therapist, and he can proceed with the therapeutic investigation by inviting each member to respond to the statement, careful to elicit the expression of feelings and perceptions of each member. Group operations and interactions, rather than individual problems, are the primary focus, and these are illuminated by the therapist as they emerge in the discussion. The data obtained in the discussion and the interactions accompanying it may be sifted by the therapist for implicit statements of unfulfilled individual and family needs and the underlying sources of conflict. The therapist may then present these to the family group to establish consensual validation of the family problems that beset them.

In the course of treatment, mutual communication, contact, and attention is encouraged. Such destructive group interactions as scapegoating, displacements and denials are intercepted and counteracted by direct action of the therapist and by clarification of their dynamic meaning. While the therapist may make explicit and clarifying statement of the covert conflict he observes, he carefully works to reduce the member's anxiety and helps control their hostility so that constructive solutions may be sought.

In evaluating and treating the family social system, the therapist should bear in mind normative family structure and functioning, using this ideal as an orientation point, not as an arbitrary imposition on the family. The instrumental authority and leadership role of the father (Forrest, 1966; Forrest, 1967) and the nurturance role of the mother, which are essential for effective social system operation, may be guidelines for determining system defects and may suggest direction for corrective intervention. Inadequate role functioning (Forrest, 1969B) is observed and discussed, the roots of the problem explored and individual and group resources noted and mobilized for new patterns of operation. All members are encouraged to cooperate in reorganizing the system so that it can fulfill its proper functions.

Over and above the analytic work of the sessions, therapeutic value is derived from having the family experience whatever desirable social patterns transpire in the conduct of the dialogue. It is not unusual that a family session is the first time that the family members reveal themselves or listen to each other. Adequate structure and process for making decisions might be introduced in the session. Ackerman (1958, 1966) recommends helping the family to find new solutions to conflict and teaching them more appropriate problem-solving techniques, and his work may be consulted for more detailed discussion of treatment procedure. In short, some of the social skills needed for effective group functioning may be taught and practiced as part of the therapeutic process.

FAMILY MOTIVATION

It is more the exception than the rule for the family group to present itself as sharing a problem. More typically, one member is considered to be "the problem" or is identified as "having problems," a perception he may or may not share. Consequently, defining the difficulty as a shared family problem is requisite for motivation of the family treatment as well as for clarification of the therapeutic goals. When the therapist is convinced that family therapy is the preferred treatment, he can implement his decision by refusing individual treatment to the identified patient, thus blocking the scapegoating operation by the family that has identified an individual member as the problem. The extrusion of the individual from the family and exoneration of the family's sense of responsibility which individual treatment risks is avoided as the family is forced to continue its involvement and discomfort with the troubling difficulty (Bowen, 1965). The prime task of the family session is to define the problem in terms of family interactions in which all members are involved and responsible. Toward this end, the index patient is encouraged and supported to resist the scapegoating operation as the therapist asks questions designed to elicit his perception of how the other family members contribute to the problems and invites him to express his feelings about being considered the major trouble in the family. The identified patient is thus often helpful in promoting family motivation. The therapist using this procedure must be cautious to avoid the trap of then scapegoating another family member and must carefully guide the group toward a realization of the responsibility each member has for his part in the intrafamilial interactions. Not infrequently, one member may fill the family healer role (Ackerman, 1958) in that his perceptions of the difficulties may distribute the causes of the problems more accurately and equitably than did the initial presenter.

Careful, thorough, and probing examination often manages to uncover more central problems, especially marital problems, than are initially suggested by the family. The relationship of these underlying conflicts and crucial problems to the symptomatic difficulties that trouble the family should be clarified in order for the family to be motivated for treatment. Finally, it is essential that the therapist makes contact with each family member, hears and responds to the feelings and needs of each individual, and offers hope of improvement for all of the family if motivation for family treatment is to be an authentic expression of each member. Family therapy can be considered to be launched when the problems are defined as family problems to which each member contributes and towards whose solution each member is responsibly working.

THE SILENT MEMBER

Though the family therapist observes and responds to the nonverbal as well as verbal communication of all the family members, a consistently silent member may present a particularly trying therapeutic problem since he threatens to remain enigmatic in his meaning, role, and relationship to the group. From the beginning, it is helpful to establish the fact that all behavior is communicative and exerts active effect, regardless of how silent or passive it may appear. With all due regard for the individual's rights to privacy and autonomy, it is nevertheless essential for the therapist to clarify what is being communicated by the silence of any group member. It is also important to explicate how the silence is interpreted by the other members, how they respond to the silent communication, and how the silent member receives their response. When the silence is truly an expression of a need for privacy, a validation of the legitimacy of this need may be useful for the entire group.

PRIVACY AND SECRETS

Privacy is not only a right but a necessity to the development of individual autonomy, and as such, it is to be guarded, particularly in the young and vulnerable, from undue invasion. It is also an essential element in preserving marital intimacy, and when it serves that purpose, it warrants protection from family invasion. The family therapist is inevitably confronted with the task of discerning when claims for privacy are authentic and legitimate and when they are resistances to therapeutic intervention. Some claims for privacy are designed to thinly disguise family secrets which all members share, consciously or unconsciously, but few acknowledge with each other or with outsiders. When the therapist senses that important family interactions are being concealed, more direct probing might be indicated through individual or subgroup meetings that might more likely yield the vital data. When he is given entry to the secret, the therapist must reserve for himself the decision regarding the overt sharing of the secret with all the family. If he is convinced that the secret is in fact no secret but is rather a guilty conspiracy to maintain some pathological intrafamilial pattern, he has no alternative but to frankly present the material to the entire family and to elicit from them the meaning and effect of the secreted phenomenon. Typical examples of such family secrets are addiction and incest, which, if allowed to continue, place a burden of pretended ignorance and indifference on some family members and guilty acting-out on others, with impenetrable barriers to family honesty and intimacy. The immediate pain of confronting these traumas is usually well compensated by improved communication and revitalized reparative processes which lead toward healthier interpersonal patterns and solution.

On the other hand, there are some secrets that the therapist may consider are in the family interest to maintain. For example, an adulterous relationship, if it is a genuine secret that is not shared, in some cases may best be handled as a matter of privacy. Since there is little to be gained by inflicting the pain of betrayal on one or all of the family members, and because personal responsibility may be fostered by the secret, the therapist may decide to preserve such a secret if he is convinced that the acting-out behavior will cease.

MAJOR FAMILY DECISIONS AND CRISES

The family often enters treatment under great emotional stress, with intense pressure to make a decision that has crucial implications for its future life. Such vital questions as whether to terminate an unwanted pregnancy or whether to continue a marriage are not infrequent in the course of family treatment as well as in individual therapy. The responsibility for making decisions cannot be permitted to leave the family. However, the therapist can help the family arrive at a decision. He can clarify with them the underlying conflicts about the range of possible solutions. Their fantasies of the anticipated consequences of the alternatives may be examined, and the family may be helped to distinguish pathological fears from realistic conceivable results. Differences in preferences may be mediated, and compromise solutions may be considered. The therapist's own value system should be clearly distinguished in his own mind from the patient's, and while it may be applied to expand the family's repertoire of conceivable possibilities, it should not be imposed on the family. Rather, the family's value system may be explicated and inconsistencies resolved. Fears of responsibility for making decisions, for taking action and contending with changes may be acknowledged, and the individual members should be encouraged to accept the tensions, anxieties and risks attendant upon confronting major issues and making significant decisions.

WHAT MAKES FAMILY THERAPY WORK

Interpersonal systems have a way of operating in a self-perpetuating system, unquestioned by the system members. The very introduction of a strange observer to the group calls the attention of the members to their modus vivendi. Needless to say, the family therapist does more than that to illuminate for the family their interactional patterns and to explicate their underlying operational assumptions. He raises pertinent questions, he draws inferences and points up implications from nonverbal as well as verbal communications, he provokes dormant covert interpersonal conflicts to overt expression that might lead to resolution (Ackerman, 1958). He provides a protective environment in which more fearful members may express themselves. His acceptance of the feelings of the family members encourages honesty and openness and serves as a model for each member to each other. His presence assures the group of control and neutralization of destructive impulses and practices. He reduces guilt and equalizes responsibility. He establishes lines of communication, explores their impact, and illustrates the differences between the intention of the sender and the perception of the receiver (Szalita, 1968). The clarification of perceptions and statements of issues for all members at once diminishes confusion and sets the stage for constructive action. Most important, as Ackerman puts it, "Through his use of self, the therapist injects something new into the emotional life of the family; new kinds of emotion and new kinds of perceptions of family relations, pointing toward the resolution of conflict, greater need satisfactions, and the discovery of levels of intimacy, sharing, support and identity that open the way to new growth" (Ackerman, 1958).

SUMMARY

Family therapy and family diagnosis offer a new dimension to the technical modalities available to the psychotherapist and to the theoretical understanding of the problems brought to our attention. This chapter attempts an overview of some of the problems involved in the use of family therapy in psychotherapeutic practice. Indications for its use in the treatment of adults, adolescents and children are discussed, and some of its methods of application are described. Family therapy, as a treatment of choice or as an adjunct to individual therapy has had clinical results that warrant its inclusion as one treatment modality in the repertoire of the experienced psychotherapist. Its theoretical perspective is considered essential to expand our understanding of all clinical practice.

REFERENCES

Ackerman, N. W. and Sobel, R.: Family diagnosis: an appraisal to the pre-school child. *American Journal of Orthopsychiatry, 15*: 744-753, 1950.

Ackerman, N. W.: *The Psychodynamics of Family Life.* New York, Basic Books, 1958.

Ackerman, N. W.: *Treating the Troubled Family.* New York, Basic Books, 1966.

Alexander, I. E.: Family therapy. *Marriage and Family Living, 25*: 146-154, May, 1963.

Barnett, J.: *The Resolution of Dependency Conflicts in the Young Adult.* Gottingen, Germany, International Forum for Psychoanalysis, in Press, 1968.

Beatman, F. L.: Intergenerational aspects of family therapy. In Ackerman, N. W., Beatman, F. L., and Sherman, S. N. (Eds.): New York, Family Service Association of America, 1967, pp. 29-38.

Bateson, G., Jackson, D. D., Haley, J., and Wickland, J. W.: Toward a theory of schizophrenia, *Behavioral Science, 1*:251-264, 1956.

Bell, J. E.: Family group therapy: a new method of treatment for older children, adolescents, and their parents. *Public Health Monographs, 64*:1-52, 1961.

Bowen, M.: A family concept of schizophrenia. In Jackson, D. D. (Ed.): *The Etiology of Schizophrenia.* New York, Basic Books, 1959.

Bowen, M.: The use of family theory in unusual practice. *Comprehensive Psychiatry, 8*:...., Oct., 1966.

Bowen, M.: Therapy in hospital and private practice. In Bozzormenyi-Nagy, I. and Framo, J. L. (Eds.): In *Intensive Family Therapy.* New York, Harper and Row, 1965, p. 232.

Forrest, T.: Family interviews to help adolescents and their parents. Presented at the Eastern Psychological Association, Philadelphia, 1963, unpublished.

Forrest, T.: Paternal roots of female character development. *Contemporary Psychoanalysis, 3*:21-38, Fall, 1966.

Forrest, T.: Paternal roots of male character development. *The Psychoanalytic Review, 54*:277-295, Summer, 1967.

Forrest, T.: The family dynamics of the oedipus drama. *Contemporary Psychoanalysis, 4*:138-160, Spring, 1968.

Forrest, T.: The combined use of marital and individual therapy in depression. *Contemporary Psychoanalysis, 6*:76-83, Fall, 1969A.

Forrest, T.: Treatment of the father in family therapy. *Family Process, 8*:106-118, March, 1969B.

Friedman, A. S. *et al.: Psychotherapy for the Whole Family.* New York, Springer, 1965.

Jackson, D. D.: The question of family homeotosis. *Psychiatric Quarterly Supplement, 31*:79-90, 1957.

Kaffman, M.: Short term family therapy. *Family Process, 2*:216-234, Sept., 1962.

Lidz, T., Fleck, S., and Cornelison, A.: *Schizophrenia and the Family.* New York, International University Press, 1965.

Speck, R.: Panel on family therapy. New York, Annual Meeting of Council of Psychoanalytic Psychologists, 1967.

Speck, R.: Psychotherapy of the social network of a schizophrenic family. *Family Process, 6*:208-294, 1967.

Szalita, A.: Course in family dynamics for the individual therapist. William Alanson White Psychoanalytic Institute, 1963-1964.

Szalita, A: Combined use of family interviews and individual therapy in schizophrenia. *American Journal of Psychotherapy, 22*:419-430, July, 1968.

Wynne, L. C. *et al.*: Pseudo-mutuality in the family relationships of schizophrenics. *Psychiatry, 21*:205-220, 1958.

Chapter 5

MANAGEMENT OF CRISES IN PSYCHOTHERAPY

Rose Spiegel

CHARACTERISTICS OF CRISIS
Occurrence of Crises

The psychotherapist, particularly one who accepts a diversity of patients, can hardly escape or prevent crises from arising within his practice (nor, be it said, in his own life). Crises often precipitate the engagement in therapy in the first place.

Their variety is legion. Some are linked to the gross emergencies precipitated by individuals with severe psychopathology—who are psychotic, alcoholic, or psychopathic, or are givin to "acting out." The crises may involve the violence of suicide, homicide, or other physical aggression inflicted on others. Crisis situations may arise in career, marriage and other relationships involving sexuality. Still others may involve interaction with society and the law, whether related to offenses arising from infringements as from delinquency or, where the principle and social action of the individual run counter to the dominant culture or local subculture, being consciously a matter of concern with principle. There may be intrapsychic crises involving the threat of inner disruption, which seemingly are self-contained and not precipitated by contemporaneous situations. There are crises occurring in the course of psychotherapy or analysis, involving a number of aspects of therapeutic interaction, including termination of the whole endeavor. Crises may involve somatic changes and physical ailments, the patient's or a near one's, either as demands for decisions for action or because of the emotional responses.

The crisis experience may be a pseudoemergency which nonetheless threatens the patient's health or career, or the welfare of the marital partner or children.

93

Nor should we overlook the crises involving the various stations of maturation, indeed beginning with birth and moving through the child's separation for school, and continuing with the impact of adolescence, interpersonal sexual experience, childbearing, the parent's crisis of separation from the child, middle-aging, aging and dying. Most are linked with what have been termed identity crises. The crises at stations of maturation all involve the human progression in living and are to be considered normal turbulence but, as implied in the intrinsic meaning of "crisis," may have an unfavorable outcome. Nor do we as therapists get called in to cope with all of these critical points.

In contrast to such crises as the above, including the pseudo-crisis and emergencies, occasionally the reverse occurs—the denial of the presence of the critical situation, whether by patient or therapist.

In all of these categories of crisis, the person who is its storm center may be the patient himself or he may be acting upon the one who is the patient we are treating, and the latter thereby is subject to a crisis within his world, set up like a secondary fire and which may have a different configuration, meaning, and menace from that of the activator's. Nor is all this to be taken as pertaining only to problems originating in the patient's world, for events in the therapist's life, as well as crises and perturbations in his psyche, may reverberate in the psyche of his patient.

The impact of the crises from the storm-center person is not only a matter of one individual's experience but may stress a whole family and challenge the functioning both of the family as a unit and of its individual members. The professional who copes with these, whether social worker, family therapist, or individual therapist, has the difficult task of focusing in behalf of the person who is our responsibility and who is presenting his view of the crisis, whatever role he may have in it, and also of retaining sensitivity to what is involved for the other participants in the crisis situation.

The tone so far in this discussion has been as of a relatively tidy world consisting of the therapist, the patient, and at times the patient's family. However, events and atmospheres from outside this enclosed world press in on us. Crisis situations occur in the larger scene of living, as a crisis of the culture and society, which stir us all in our emotions and beliefs, and at points confront our lawmakers.

At this particular time in history, we as individuals, as members of the community and citizens of the world, share the confrontation along with many who come to us as patients, and we have no warrant for a prior wisdom; some of our patients have more than we and also greater courage for assertiveness. How we respond as persons affects our focused role as practitioners of a skill. We are called on at the least for the inner activity of recognizing the relation between our individual values and these large issues, and the outcome of this complex process colors our responses to the patient in a crisis of social encounter.

The present-day patterns of revolt by late adolescents and youths set up crises on the social scene and also reflect existing social and family crises. In addition, the outer crises and the intrapsychic crises of these young people are in intricate interaction and reverberation. Certainly their inner turmoil and their comportment on the social scene are to be respected as struggles involving integrity and as identity crises for which the word "normal" or "pathologic" seems only ineptly descriptive, though what may be occurring in the person is "sick" in the clinical sense. Some of these young people come to therapy, others should but cannot or choose not to, identifying therapists with the world they are protesting against. Often it is the parents or other relatives who come to us experiencing this complex crisis of the young person as crisis in their own terms.

Where the social crises are of the magnitude and character as of the invasion of a country, we in the United States can only imagine what the experience is and how the psychotherapist can help in coping with the inner crisis in himself and patients, in their holding on to a sense of structure and meaningfulness in life.

What Characterizes Crises in General and Crises in Psychotherapy?

Resolving a crisis involves snatching "the thistle of security from the nettles of danger." Clearly what comes through as the common element in all crises is the mounting tension involving a situation, the result of whose resolution is obscure, doubtful, and of grave import. What disinguishes the crises that are approachable by psychotherapy is the element that *choice* is available to an important protagonist in the crisis. Choice in the larger range of crises outside the purview of psychotherapy is often possible but not in the same predominance—often it is the opposite, that the striking characteristic is suspense involving an outcome outside the choice of most of the individuals affected. Another element in the experience of crisis is of transitoriness, that it must have one resolution or other, for better or worse; that if the crisis is sustained, the experience becomes that of an impasse that one is powerless against or drearily inured to.

In psychotherapy, crises are not necessarily co-extensive with psychiatric emergencies. Crisis may precede the emergency at a time when choice is called for but neither the choice nor the ensuant result is yet clear or established; in the emergency, however, the desirable choice for action, difficult though it may be, is far more clearly delineated. This distinction is illustrated in one therapist's experience with a patient who came initially on the brink of an acute schizophrenic break when it seemed possible to help her pull back by psychotherapy and medication but at the next visit several days later, had been completely taken over by the acute psychosis with physical danger to herself. In the first interview, a crisis involving a threatened psychotic break appeared to be within the range of office psychotherapy; in the second, there existed a psychiatric emergency with a patient in disruption who had lost ego strength and was in concrete danger. The psychiatric emergency offered the clear indication that the safety of hospitalization was called for. Obviously, the distinction between crisis and emergency cannot be rigidly maintained, since coping with emergency can be experienced as a crisis because action is called for, but at least a working rule of thumb is offered here.

Crisis is often accompanied by characteristic feeling states which feed back into the tension of the crisis. The experience of tension and restlessness is very vivid and distinctive and not identical with the anxiety also present. The range is very wide and will surely not be completely stated here—for some individuals it is an anticipatory despair or confusion; for some even elation in mobilizing resources, real or fantasized, for coping. Perhaps the most usual mood is of concentrated interest in the crisis, making all other concerns appear trivial or colorless. For some persons there is a profound push to escape awareness of the crisis, to minimize it or ignore its reality entirely, with a flight into pseudoserenity or distraction by other interests. A sense of frustration, sometimes of helplessness, of a longing to be helped, of not being able to communicate the desperation—these are among the emotional evocations. There are, however, some other persons who experience that they communicate most effectively through the desperation of crisis. Clearly it is important for the therapist to recognize what the characteristic mode of response is in the participants in a crisis, not the least being recognition of his own mode.

The elements in the crisis situation are often not easily sorted out, and an important function of psychotherapy is clarification and a recognition that clarification is a process that is time-bound. Often this clarification, by factoring the crisis into its elements, shrinks the sense of crisis and makes it more soluble and less overwhelming.

Over the years, among the responses by therapists to whom I have put the question, What is crisis in psychotherapy?, I single out the following as capturing its spirit: "Any situation that the therapist experiences as a demand for direct intervention instead of working through, as in the usual way in therapy; maybe when the therapist is on the spot"; "Someone has to be anxious"; "What it is not is an *impasse*"; to which the rejoinder was that the *impasse* might be considered a crisis in reverse, that it should be turned into recognition that it is actually an unrecognized or denied crisis. It was suggested that one of the prerequisites is that the crisis be acute, sudden, surprising, without occurring when a patient is becoming aware of something in his life, even though he is anxious. Borrowing from biology, it was suggested that a crisis is a threat to homeostasis. Again and again the sense was that something has to be done.

A useful working concept in conceiving of crisis and in mobilizing one's resources in coping is what the writer terms *the moving parts in a crisis.* These are as follows:

1. The situation or condition considered by the individual, his family, or other observant but less-participant individual, as the crisis.
2. The personality and resources, psychologic and practical, of the person in the crisis situation; his emotional reaction to the crisis.
3. The personality of the therapist and his role, including his social authority, in helping cope with the crisis; his collaboration with members of other professions.
4. The resources which may be called on outside of the patient to help cope with the crisis and which range from family or friends to social agencies, including those directly representing the law.
5. The recognition, or its lack, of the existence of the crisis, whether by the central person concerned, significant persons in his life, the therapist, or social agencies.

FUNCTIONING OF PSYCHOTHERAPIST IN CRISES

The psychoanalyst, in particular, has been trained to the listerner's role, with emphasis on nonintervention which, in our world of officious and authoritarian personalities, is essential to the patient's finding himself. There are two hazards to this stance, however. One is the translation of every event into talk, with the analyst directed solely toward the intrapsychic, with the direction to the outer world being minimized and the necessity for personal action by the patient underestimated or misunderstood; the other is the haziness of his authority role as analyst.

Our obfuscation about our authority role makes for a vast confusion about appropriate action and adds to the stresses of our professional lives. We are generally not clear about our powers and responsibility in the eyes of the law, nor about the role assigned explicitly or tactily by the patient and his family concerned in the critical situation, nor do we work through, as individuals, our own views about being an authority figure.

Though crises and anxiety overlap, the handling of crises realistically in the outer world and analytically in the inner world is not necessarily a direct derivative of what is generally his own "didactic analysis" of his own anxiety. Indeed, his own life may have been relatively serene and not particularly preparatory in experience for the crises of his patients. All of these limitations of recognition and conception may be experienced only inarticulately, with a sense of stress, powerlessness, and oppression.

The challenge to the therapist is to resolve the crisis both in practical terms and in the character problem of the patient. The former depends also on having a working knowledge of the collateral professional services that bear on the situation and on having criteria as to the point at which it is more appropriate for other social forces to take over.

Besides the external elements involving the functioning of the therapist, there are, of course, those which are based on his essential personality, the forces within which determine his response to the varied stresses of crisis in others or in himself and which involve countertransference.

The therapist has his own susceptibility to crisis—that arising from his professional life and another from the personal. The thrapist, not surprisingly, himself undergoes a crisis experience when the course of therapy is threatened by disruption or termination or when the patient is involved in destructive acting out or suicide. Concerning termination of therapy which the therapist considers ill-advised, he has a sense of failure in having his efforts recognized, a feeling of futility, and an inability to communicate persuasively. At times, the loss of the patient means also loss in income and fear of loss of prestige but most oppressive of all is the depressive element in the shrinkage of self-esteem. When a patient is teetering on the edge of a suicidal crisis, the therapist himself experiences anxiety and intrapsychic crisis. There are occasions when the crisis in therapy or the therapist's tension and problem in countertransference can only be resolved by a change in therapists, and we all need to achieve the fortitude both to sustain a patient's terminating therapy against our rational—or irrational—wish, and to recommend termination or a change.

When the therapist is faced with serious illness or a major disruptive life situation involving his own person or a dear one, he may experience the neurotic material of his patient with inner impatience as trivial and empathize less with the underlying suffering. The patient whose therapist is suffering from an illness that requires termination of treatment or change to another is confronted with a complexity of emotions that require therapeutic assistance, partly by the therapist whose condition sets up the loss and partly by his successor who can help by virtue of not being the participant undergoing the private suffering. Of course, patients vary enormously in their response to such a crisis—ranging from reproach and resentment of the therapist as though these events are his personal failure; a reliving of previous grievous loss; a feeling of love and protectiveness for the therapist; to a withdrawal and denial of the importance of the therapist and his life situation. At another extreme are joyous events in the therapist's life—marriage, pregnancy (particularly for women therapists)—which generally are a matter of public information sooner or later. It seems to me that the timing of sharing this information with patients as well as others falls within the individual therapist's prerogative. It is hoped that his or her sense of security can bear both the sharing and the variety of responses that patients present—delight for the therapist, an apprehension of displacement, fantasies about the pregnancy, puzzlement, shyness about touching on someone else's private experience—and then working through whatever is indicated in a particular patient's response.

For some patients, what are actually minor interruptions in the schedule of psychotherapy, such as the therapist's vacation or an impromptu change, evoke a crisis of despair, resentment, depression, or acting out. These feelings turn out to be based on early experiences of actual or threatened abandonment by a parent or other significant person. Attempting to forestall the crisis for someone with this psychodynamic by informing him quite early of an anticipated vacation and also specifying a covering therapist for that time often mitigates surprisingly little of the distress the first time but rather requires patient and fairly prolonged working through of the underlying traumatic relationships and reaction formations for the anticipatory depressive response to be averted.

We have here considered the psychotherapist in crisis situations, beginning with some characteristics and predilections of his role; then the role of his particular personality and style of responding to crisis; next his own critical life-situations, joyous or tragic, and how patients respond to them; and lastly, how some patents respond with crisis to the therapist's routine but prolonged absences, as vacations. We turn now to consideration of specific crisis situations confronting patients; in particular, psychosis, marital difficulties, and suicide.

SOME MAJOR CRISES IN PSYCHOTHERAPY

Crises Involving Psychoses

The most pressing alternatives confronting the therapist for decision in the management of psychotic crises are whether this particular patient can be helped in treatment outside of a hospital, or is hospitalization necessary? A number of issues fan out around these alternatives. These are the clinical criteria for hospitalization; the patient's resources financially and in his human milieu; the therapist's, the patient's, the family's attitude, respectively, toward hospitalization; the therapist's access to knowledge about what different hospitals offer; the therapist's knowledge of the formal legal procedures involved in hospitalization; the therapist's attitude toward calling in emergency help from other professionals; the relation of the therapist to the family of the psychotic patient.

The diagnostic label, such as schizophrenic reaction, depression, alcoholism, does not of itself declare the presence of a psychotic crisis nor the necessity for hospitalization. There is no substitute for appraisal of the actual clinical condition and the life situation of the individual patient in providing the rationale for the mode and milieu of treatment and for the particular role family may helpfully play. The same critical clinical condition in someone who has a cushioning of responsible family and financial resources, and in another who lacks these, is often solved by different types of therapeutic environment and even modality of treatment—for instance, where the family is willing and able to afford provision of a highly protected environment at home for a suicidal patient, and where this resource simply is not available. And we have been made familiar by Hollingshead and Redlich (1958), and by Grey (1966) and others, of the variation in treatment which is linked to sociologic differences in patients.

Patients in Psychotic Crisis in Extramural Therapy

The patient on the edge of psychosis and having enough ego strength and self-awareness of his disequilibrium may seek professional help in his crisis. Another, perhaps in the course of therapy, may present indications that are highly suggestive of an impending break—such as experiences with hallucination, bizarre delusions not yet dominating the entire psychic scene—which the therapist rather than the patient recognizes. Here the crisis may involve the fortunate outcome of the therapeutic collaboration without recourse to hospitalization.

One important dynamic, but not the only one, for a favorable outcome in extramural treatment is the patient's trust and rapport with the therapist. When these are solid enough, the patient is able to share with the therapist his fears for himself and others, even to the extent, in my experience, of asking for hospitalization in coping with his violent impulses or delusional panic. These patients have been able to inform me of their passing doubts about me but as though these were ego-alien, while other patients, with similar clinical pictures but without this trust, have not been treatable by me. Such trust and rapport from the patient call for an extreme adaptability of the therapist outside the conventional confines of a daily schedule.

The balance point in the psychotic crisis calling for the patient's being in the safety of the hospital centers on the classical criterion of gross destruction to himself or others. Where there is threat to life or to the physical integrity of the patient or others, where there is threat of arson or of other serious damage to the physical milieu, hospitalization is warranted. The psychotic individual may be running amok in an anguish of panic, without, at that time, indication of such gross destructiveness, but still need the support of the hospital for his own feeling of security and for the therapeutic resources available.

There are some patients in crisis who may be helped considerably by day hospital care, there receiving enough support to enable them to be based in their own homes. These are among the new modes of community help for selected patients in crisis.

The therapist's decision concerning hospitalization depends not only on the clinical condition of the patient and his resources but also on his own knowledge about and attitude toward hospitalization. Does he have access to information about what is offered by residential and by day hospitals in his community? Does he know of the differences in the social climate in the world of different hospitals and of the therapeutic modalities stressed? Does he know of the accessibility of different hospitals to emergency admission? This would seem like obvious information but is not as easily arrived at as would seem, for how various institutions differ is not in any handy compendium of information, though the brochures many private ones send out are often lengthily descriptive.

The practical knowledge about hospitalization includes also that of the proper legal procedures for commitment, voluntary or involuntary, which reflect also the patient's rights in the admitting process to the hospital and in the duration of his stay.

In some crisis situations involving the psychotic patient, in which there is violence or danger to himself or others or grossly to the environment, outside help is required, such as provided by the police, who are authorized by law and (in my experience in New York) are trained and competent in coping with the disordered patient. The psychotherapist needs to remember that there are some situations involving patients which are outside his professional functioning and the implicit roles assigned to him by society and that there are other professionals, of religion (priests, ministers, rabbis) and of legal authority who have their role developed through the years of helping in crises. The therapist's attitude concerning hospitalization affects the smoothness of the proceedings. Does the hospitalization signify to him (and perhaps also to patient and family) a failure of his therapeutic efforts? Does it signify a disaster?

The function of hospitalization is not necessarily limited to serving as a haven in a storm of crisis or a haven for the family's surcease from the patient. But the hospital, depending on its philosophy, may provide opportunity for growth in the patient's relation to others as individuals and as members of a community. Such hospitals, concerned with providing a whole milieu, possess many characteristics of the outside world, including some irrational ones, but with an integrating force from the efforts of the staff at self-understanding and understanding of interaction with patients, which helps in preparing the patient afresh for living in the more random outside world.

There are some occasions when the therapist finds himself involved with the family of the psychotic patient—another exception to the course in usual psychotherapy. He may find inescapable the recognition of the family's contribution to the psychotic crisis, be it from parents or from marital partner. With one young woman in an acute schizophrenic reaction with terror concerning suicide and with delusions as well as terror about being killed, there was a kernel of reality that played into her symptomatology. This was her husband's hobby of guns and his insistence of having knives under the mattress at night and such whimsy as keeping pistols in the bureau among her undergarments. His behavior, which struck me as bizarre, was not amenable to any discussion in depth or any modification through the interview in which this was disclosed. It had become necessary for his wife to be hospitalized, and he was then referred to the male psychiatrist who supervised her in-hospital therapy.

The family may need help in their morale concerning their sense of guilt focused on the hospitalization and their technical role in it, or of shame about the anticipated stigmatization.

In general, as implied in the above-cited experience, it is preferable that any work in depth with the family, apart from shared interviews with the patient, should be referred to another professional.

In all these situations in which the therapist is involved in coping with psychotic crisis, confidentiality should be respected. There is a line between referring to the open symptomatology which is, so to speak, in the public domain and for which hospitalization is required, and disclosing personal information from the interviews.

CRISES INVOLVING MARRIAGE

Though the subject of such crises presents a vast terrain of its own, some points are appropriate for discussion here. A most important one concerns the role and the authority of the analyst over the patient's change in marital state. Crises involving change of marital state occur in the lives of persons regardless of whether or not decisions taken for action detract from the analytic process (which is so variously conceptualized). The patient's working through of such a crisis may culminate in a decision outwardly or inwardly disapproved of by the therapist. The situation, then, may at some point be a crisis for the therapist as well as for the direct protagonists and confront him with the necessity of deciding whether or not to continue with the patient. This kind of critical issue seems to me particularly frequent with the patient's decision to marry.

There are a number of tacit assumptions on which is based the therapist's authority over decisions concerning the patient's entering on marriage. These are a threat to the analytic process by the change in direction of libido, the validity of his appraisal as to the resolution of neurotic conflicts and the attainment of maturity and readiness for marriage, and a high reliability of his forecasts as to the soundness of the marriage. And in addition to these quite rational-appearing assumptions is one which I consider moot, namely a more intrinsic assumption of professional authority as being axiomatic.

To consider these in more detail, there is more and more the trend to marry before the attainment of "readiness" and to work toward growth and maturity as a shared goal in marriage rather than in the single state, which is quite contrary to the former social-economic (as well as analytic) prerequisite for marriage that many of us have taken for granted—so subject are we analysts, as well as our fellow mortals, to the impact of mores in our own upbringing. Though, hopefully, we have achieved expertise in having educated hunches, if not always reliable prognostications, experiences such as the following are not extraordinary. Two patients decide on marriage abruptly, despite counsel by their two therapists for more consideration, and there ensues a basically devoted, loving relationship in spite of some turbulence. But there are other instances in which marriage is counselled against and the analyst's worst apprehensions are fulfilled. The ardent relationship swiftly becomes demanding and intolerable, moving on from crisis to divorce after an abortive attempt at psychotherapeutic joint interviews.

Often the new marriage calls for time out from analysis—converse to the dictum that a new marriage drains libido from therapy. Here, it is the analysis which drains "libido" from the new marriage. There is the wish to have the new stage in intimacy remain private, away from submission to another's vision, much more so where the patient's personality problem has been the inability to sustain an intimacy. In some new marriages, the husband more often than the wife resents her communication with the analyst as a reflection on his fully encompassing her emotional needs.

Where, then, does the analyst's authority come in? What are his options for decision and movement in the therapeutic enterprise? Certainly if his appraisal is that with the marriage, therapy in fact has come to a termination or a pause, or if he experiences his own countertransference as insolubly interfering with his professional functioning with the patient, then indeed their endeavor should be given up. If the therapist and the patient have explicitly set up a quasicontractual understanding about the requirement that the analysis should have been completed before marriage is entered on, the issue has a built-in answer if they so wish it. However, it is my view that the person in analysis retains the right as well as possesses the inherent power to make decisions about marriage and divorce. Though it is the function of the therapist to help in reaching these decisions, he is most unwise to work himself into a corner in which he has such an investment in his control that he pits himself against the patient and experiences an affront or a fall in self-esteem if the patient's behavior runs counter to his opinion. He, on his side, of course, retains the right and power to terminate the professional relationship. Any decisions of this kind should be made on the elements in the particular case.

Another enormous range of crises consists of those which

threaten the life of the marriage. The unifying principle to my mind that determines the likelihood of a marriage being viable in the face of a threat of disruption is the presence of the basic, though perhaps hidden, desire to maintain the marriage, despite the presenting annoyance, impatience, harrassment, rage, difficulties in communication, and/or infidelity. Then at least one member will be the more understanding and available for change and tolerance, and in such critical situations, I have felt that I have been permitted to be helpful. On the other hand, where there is a basic, often covert, directedness away from the marriage by one of the partners, no compromise, no amount of change made by the other, no allowance for time for process in therapy nor effort by the therapist is acceptable, and the relationship moves to dissolution. In these marriages, I experienced that in spite of the ostensible gestures of co-operation in coming for the individual and the joint sessions, the time put in was used as part of a measured progression, as in a Greek play, in which the conclusion is foregone but the ritualized steps must be gone through.

The hostility occurring in the intimacy and mutual knowledge of vulnerability in a marriage can have such potency of destructiveness that the most therapeutic service possible is to help in the recognition of the implacable hurtfulness and in the disengagement from the bind.

Some technical details about interviews have been indicated above. Certainly, confidentiality of what is said in the individual sessions should be maintained, though often the same material spontaneously is disclosed in joint interviews.

In working with the crises that threaten the continuation of a marriage, the role of the therapist is complex—he can help in the partners achieving an authentic constructive decision which, however, is not necessarily the storybook happy ending.

SUICIDAL CRISES

Suicide presents the psychotherapist with the most formidable emergency, one which evokes emotional reverberations in himself and which particularly call for self-understanding. We are then faced with core problems that we all have at least glimpsed in ourselves. These are such profound questions as Freud attempted to answer in his formulation of the "death instinct." We are confronted not only by our tug of identification but by mystification and denial of this psychic reality; we may experience rage or disappointment in the actor-victim or with those who have contributed some impetus to his attempt or his final act. If the suicidal attempt occurs in the course of therapy, the therapist often experiences a sense of futility and of guilt about his own competence and effectiveness.

Suicidal crises have increased in number and have been more urgently recognized in the last ten years, with a wide range of professionals now engaged in the enterprise of recognizing, understanding, treating, and salvaging the suicidal persons and coping with the contributing factors. Suicide has been subject to a complexity of cultural attitudes varying through known millenia from approval to indifference and to condemnation. Those social values which make the individual vulnerable to a sense of failure, worthlessness, and abandonment give subtle but powerful impetus to the suicidal resolution of some dilemma in living. Recent cross-cultural studies on suicide, notably Hendin's *Suicide in Scandinavia* (1966), have drawn attention to such pressures.

The philosophic position which considers a "right" to suicide as within the individual's privilege, the ultimate act of choice and free will, and the converse—when the individual does not avail himself of this privilege—as an active choice of affirmation of life lends itself to grave misunderstanding when the attempt is made to equate it literally with psychotherapeutic thinking and practice. This metaphysical consideration, when taken outside its own context, is most often used by the would-be suicide as an intellectualized rationalization for a disturbed orientation to life (Grey, 1966). Surely it is not within the function of a therapist to accept such a suicidal vote as a principle overruling his own sense of obligation to meet the crisis. Experience with individuals who had supported a suicidal attempt with this ideology (or rationalization) shows that with the passage of time, this belief-system becomes ego-alien and the affirmative involvement with living is resumed.

It is part of the therapeutic enterprise to ascertain what the suicidal attempt means to the particular patient, what its communicative import is. The view that indication of a suicidal move is a "cry for help," in Stengel's phrase, has encouraged individuals actively and explicitly to turn for help in the throes of their inner struggle, whether to a therapist or friend, or to a formal agency such as a suicide-prevention center.

Besides the outright calls for help, persons who are suicidal may leave a trail of clues such as the outright threat, statement, or note not only to some significant person in their lives but also to physicians, particularly those in general practice *(Medical World News,* 1967).

Such clues, whose relevance certainly is not limited to physicians, are references to dying, a feeling of "wanting to end it all" or of life being unbearable attributed to the discomfort from fairly prosaic physical symptoms—headache, "colds," insomnia— voiced with an affect of depression, hopelessness, or despair. Such psychosomatic manifestations may be associated with an unfortunate life situation of loss—perhaps of relationship by parting or death, money, or career. Loneliness, perhaps associated with aging in a person with limited inner resources, may be the basic soil for the turn to self-destruction. Specific inquiry should be made of the person about his mood and about preoccupation with death or the wish to "end it all," and also whether a recent loss or disappointment had been sustained. These inquiries serve the purpose both of acquainting the professional and of helping the patient become aware and share his awareness with the professional.

Reluctance has been experienced about such inquiry, with the concern that it might activate a potential suicide. Though of course no rigid dogmatic statement is intended here, the inference from reported experience is that it is the lack of inquiry that played in with the suicide—that the message was missed. One practical and important detail about unwittingly playing in with a suicidal drive is the following. Since some suicidal persons methodically accumulate, perhaps by request for medication, drugs that are to be used suicidally, the prescribing physician should be on the alert about this possibility.

One contingency in the treatment of a depressive patient,

which is the concern of physician, psychiatrist, and family, is the covert return of a suicidal impulse during a time of symptomatic relief (Lesse, 1965). Particularly to be watched with alertness is a release from a severe depression into a mood of seeming serenity and equanimity, as though all the difficulties in the world have vanished. This may occur four to six weeks after hospitalization with intensive antidepressant drug therapy. Such a change in mood without the working through by means of psychotherapy, it has been found, may herald a clear decision, beyond conflict, to carry out the final act. It is particularly tragic when the suicide occurs on a home visit, as it does at times, while the patient is apparently in a convalescent phase of hospitalization.

Among the fallacies that have been exposed are the notions that the suicidal individual is necessarily psychotic and that a declaration of the suicidal wish or the enactment of repeated attempts means that the decisive or final act will not be committed (Schneidman and Faberow, 1957). Suicides have occurred in the gamut of psychiatric diagnosis, including the apparently normal.

Occurrence in Children and Adolescents

Consideration of suicidal crises must include those of adolescents and children. The incidence is startlingly high. Suicide is the second greatest cause of death among our college students (*New York Times,* 1969). However, the high incidence of suicide among young people is a worldwide phenomenon. It has been noted that boys have more tendency to use violent methods than girls. In Sweden, the girls gave as the preponderant immediate reason "love problems" and next, "family problems"; while of 30 boys in military service who had attempted suicide, 17 attributed the decisive cause for the act to being in military service (Bergstrand, 1962).

In a Maryland group of middle-class adolescent patients seen in private practice following attempted or threatened suicide, the increase of this crisis in this socioeconomic group was attributed to the emotional stress from the adult pressure at home and at school. Their families were constantly "moving to a better neighborhood, with failure ever to sink roots anywhere" (Glaser, 1966).

For these young people, helping them to a realistic appraisal of family pressures and to cultivation of their own inner resources was most promising. In this study, the external precipitating factors contributing varied stresses seemed most important. The good students with the higher subjective goals for achievement were particularly hard hit. These factors implicated in the suicidal attempts of these young people are reminiscent of Hendin's conclusions that one element in the high rate of suicide attempts in Sweden is correlated with the great importance attached there to achievement and ambition.

A report from Creedmoor Hospital in New York on 60 adolescents who had made suicidal attempts indicated that most were from the low socioeconomic groups. The distribution was as follows one half black, one fourth white, and one fourth Puerto Rican. This contrasts with the distribution in American adults, in whom reported suicides among blacks occur in the smallest number in proportion to population. In the adolescents reported, the most striking manifest psychopathology involved hallucinations in 50 of these young people, and in 30 the suicidal behavior was clearly influenced by hallucinations. "Voices were action voices, with a bad voice telling him to fight, run away, steal, kill someone or, as important in this study, kill himself" (Winn, 1966).

Toolan (1962) has long emphasized that depression and suicidal attempts in the young have been overlooked and occur particularly in association with the disruptive stress from a chaotic home situation, with generally most impact on the first-born. Depressive reactions were noted to be more frequent in youngsters over age 12, and schizophrenic reactions predominated in the younger ones.

Suicidal moves occur also in exaggeration of adolescent turmoil and involved problems of male identification for boys and concern of the girls with rape or pregnancy, whether or not they were promiscuous sexually (Schneer, 1960).

Suicidal attempts in children as young as three years of age have been reported following the anguish of the loss by death of a beloved one—sibling, parent. Some of the suicidal attempts by young boys have actually resulted in their death. Children, too, make suicidal gestures or threats which may be a focused attempt to make an aloof or hostile parent understanding and loving, often with an escalation of misbehavior through the years that evokes an escalation of hostility and rejection but at least is attention. The child may be acting out the mother's unconscious wish for his nonexistence, with pseudoaccidental episodes preceding overt suicidal acts (Schrut, 1964). Fuller discussions of such misfortunes are outside the range of this chapter, though their consideration is warranted here in the survey of the predispositions and precipitants to suicide and the wide age span of the incidence. Their treatment would most likely fall within the purview of the child psychiatrist.

On the other hand, though late adolescents have their particular vulnerabilities that may make their suicidal problems call for more specialized patterns, coping with their crises are more likely to call upon the endeavors of the psychotherapist who is treating adults.

The suicidal attempts of adolescents may be precipitated by an intense sense of alienation from other peers; by a disrupted love affair or a love affair that is more than can be coped with emotionally; by a pregnancy; by a misdeed whose exposure involves disgrace and punishment, whether by his society or parents; by a failure in school (perhaps only in his own eyes); or by despair at parental separation or divorce. The suicidal drive may have been activated by a bad "trip" from psychedelic drugs.

The suicidal attempt may occur in the adolescent in the feeling state of an acute and anguished depression or of feeling detached and alienated from all humankind and without any awareness of pain, rage, cold purposiveness, elation, or hallucinatory excitement. Disruption of the family may be brought about by serious parental quarrels, alcoholism, poverty, financial pressure and aspirations, separation or divorce, remarriage, placement of the child away from home, or changes in the family environment contributing to a feeling of rootlessness. All these elements enter into a lack of communcation with parents, a sense of being rejected, and at times of shame vis-à-vis the world, and have been found to be prominent in the background of the suicidal adolescents (Teicher, 1966). Let it be said at this point, in anticipation of the fuller discussion of the management of suicidal patients in general, that the adolescent's opening up of communication with the psychotherapist, of his sharing such experiences as have been detailed here, of itself builds a sense of relatedness, of hope in living and in solving difficulties, and offers a bulwark against repetition.

Psychodynamics of the Suicidal Variants

Understanding the psychodynamics of the suicidal act is far from meeting the law of parsimony. We are faced with such awesome problems as What are the common elements that subsume the suicide attempts in the wide span of ages? What are the disparate characteristics? In coping both with the acute crisis and the prevention of its recurrence, we had best keep in the foreground the unique constellation of problems of the particular person and sustain in our background thinking the amassed experience and studies of other observers. Furthermore, we need to use as a consistent approach, as best we can, regard for what precipitated the attempt and for what the problems in personality and in living predisposed to it. This understanding, where we can attain it, offers promise for communicating affirmatively with the suicidal person and at times with those persons significant to him who are either a supportive resource or, on the contrary, are reinforcing the suicidal drive.

The patterns of precipitants for suicidal attempts bear considerable correlation to the kinds of stress to which the person in subjected and vulnerable to at different epochs in life as well as to personality and environmental resources to withstand these. Some of the precipitant patterns spelled out for children and adolescents may be recognized with little disguise throughout the different ages of man. These are the loss of love; inordinate shame, blame, or guilt; uprootedness; and the strong sense of failure. More clearly, the impedimenta of the passage of time are severe or incurable illness, loss of one's contemporaries, the sense of worthlessness from enforced cultural obsolescence, and the loneliness and the shrinking world of the aging. All of these are assaults on the personality and the sense of living meaningfully and hopefully.

These precipitants put one in mind of the depressions, with

their relation to loss of love, whether of a person, an ideal, or material emoluments; or the sense of being loved and accepted by that vague but powerful entity, society.

With these suicidally prone individuals who may have made actual attempts, some of the therapeutic efforts need be directed to the elements entering into the depression and also, under appropriate circumstances, having social agencies step into the endeavor to replenish the environmental lack. However, there are many persons with suicidal syndromes—as of threat, gesture, and attempt—who fall outside the above-described unfortunate individuals and who may or may not turn to psychotherapy. (Whether or not the person turns to psychotherapy is meaningful, not only in terms of sociological determinants for therapy but also in terms of the stake involved in the suicidal syndromes. Some examples are suicidal gestures by reluctant soldiers or suicides of public figures out of a failure of relationship to their particular society.)

In the suicidal threat, gesture, or even attempt, are involved such elements as the token assuagement of the deeper drive toward death, the communication of despair to someone who is obdurate or who is responsive only when, as it were, blood is drawn. The communication of despair by the suicidal move when words fail may be a pattern not at all pertinent to the contemporary scene but that had been effective in outer reality in the intrafamily relationship of childhood and then may be acted out with the therapist, either as the pattern of communication in depth of emotion, in the transference, or on the transferential assumption that this surrogate parent plays the same parental game.

I have had the supervisory experience in which the patient was making suicidal threats to the analyst, after a long entrenchment of the analyst in noncommittal silence and the frantic appeals of the patient for some answer in explicit words to his troubling queries. These frantic appeals and declarations of unbearable anguish for which suicide would give peace subsided when the analyst moved into communication with the patient, dealing both with the questions explicitly and with the patient's intolerance of silence, and then matters of the analogous parental behavior were opened up. I therefore suggest that, since some such actual or transferentially fantasied impasse of communication and of crisis may be occurring in psychotherapy and be outside the awareness of one or other participant, when a suicidal move is made by a patient in the course of psychotherapy, inquiry be directed to the therapist-patient interaction, disconcerting though it may be at times to the therapist.

A patient, even at the commencement of therapy with a new therapist, may make and inform him of a suicidal move. With one such patient, this first suicidal move had a multiplicity of meaning. First, it was part of long-standing psychopathology for which therapy was sought; second, it served as test for the therapist's concern; third, it provided an answer to curiosity about the analyst's resourcefulness. These motivations are easily covered by the term "manipulative"; however, if left at that, the meaning of, and basis for, the move remain undetermined. With this patient, for instance, the testing of the therapist by setting up a crisis was transferentially related to the blandness of the mother, which was impenetrable to any physical illness or crisis occurring in the children or husband.

From the discussion of suicide, it must be apparent that the trend of opinion concerning the underlying psychodynamics is that these cannot be reduced to the simple formula declared by Freud in *Mourning and Melancholia,* in which he suggested that the introjected sadistic ambivalence of the melancholiac is the essential psychodynamic; that "We have long known that no neurotic harbours thoughts of suicide which are not murderous impulses against others re-directed against himself." Hendin (1966) and Meerloo (1962), in their extensive researches and reflections on suicide, have each included such varied psychodynamics as the suicidal person's fantasy of achieving a reunion with the beloved in death and the suicidal person's sense of inner deadness which makes life meaningless with actual death—then, a recognition of the death-in-life.

The therapist (or whoever in the suicidal person's environs has some perceptivity and power to intervene) finds it hard at times to distinguish between the suicidal threat, the gesture, and the intended act; and indeed may be confronted by the act, reversible or irreversible, on its way to finality, if outside intervention is not available or effective. Coping with these varieties differs enormously in activist terms, ranging from the completed irrevocable act to the act in process which calls for intervention with life-saving measures, to the suicidal impulse which is within the range of psychotherapeutic exploration and does not call at all for activist intervention. That is, the suicidal syndromes include the range from emergencies to crises.

The suicidal threat, gesture, and incomplete attempt have been so much impressed on us as having manipulative significance that I believe we have swung to an extreme of irritation and suspicion at its assumed presence which interferes with working through the meanings constructively of what the psychodynamics are in the particular person, for always more is involved than manipulation. In these and other suicidal syndromes, our first concern is with the severity of his intention to suicide, for a seemingly playful but macabre game of suicide, judging from the Russian-roulette type of taking chances with having the suicidal move intercepted, contains a high potential for an irreversible act, or may, with pressure from some interaction, stop being the seeming manipulation and become an undisguised intended act. A co-equal concern is getting a sense of what Schneidman (1968) has termed *"the lethality of the patient,"* which is, "the probability of a specific individual's killing himself (i.e. ending up dead) in the immediate future (today, tomorrow, the next day—not next month)." As will be seen, these two formulations are related but not identical.

Including these criteria helps in the practical appraisal of whether we are up against an actual crisis involving life and death, and whether the patient must be protected from himself by resources involving knowledgeable attendants provided either by the family or by social agencies, particularly, but not limited to, the hospital.

In thinking of suicidal crises, what inevitably comes to mind are those extremes, rare in the usual clinical practice, in which the actor-victim is seemingly deliberating about the final step into oblivion, holding a large audience and would-be rescuers at bay, as he stands poised to jump from rooftop or bridge. These instances usually fall into the purview of social authorities such as police, firemen, priests and ministers, who, with physical heroism and the mobilization of all their psychological resources, attempt an all-out onslaught on the suicidal drama. The protagonist who is snatched from death requires and often enters upon a period of psychiatric treatment. Here lethality and intentionality were maximal and reinforcing in their summation.

Less starkly dramatic persons in whom the suicidal drive is backed by the ego, who have structured a rigid, rationalizing ideology for the act, which may blaze into emergency at some point in psychotherapy precipitated by a change in life-situation, present the most extreme challenge. Coping with their destructive efforts calls for maximum alertness, ingenuity, and protective measures on the part of the psychotherapist, family, and attendant staff.

One essential reminder about coping with suicidal crises, no less than with the other crises, concerns the role of the therapist's awareness of his own particular style, trust in his intuitions and recognition of his own limitations, especially in treating a particular patient in a particular crisis.

REFERENCES

Bergstrand, C. G. and Otto, U.: In *Acta Pediatrics, 51/1*:17, cited by World Wide Abstracts, April, 1962.

Farber, L. H.: Despair and the life of suicide. In *The Ways of the Will*. London, Basic Books, 1966.

Glaser, K., M.D.: Cited in *Medical Tribune,* August 17, 1966, p. 1.

Grey, A.: Social class and the psychiatric patient: a study in composite and character. *Contemporary Psychoanalysis, 2*:87, 1966.

Hendin, H.: *Suicide in Scandinavia.* New York, Grune and Stratton, 1966.

Hollingshead, A. and Redlich, F.: *Social Class and Mental Illness.* New York, Wiley, 1958.

Lesse, S.: The psychotherapist and apparent remissions in depressed suicidal patients. *American Journal of Psychotherapy, 19*:436, 1965.

Meerloo, A. J.: *Suicide and Mass Suicide.* New York, London, Grune and Stratton, 1962.

New York Times, April 26, 1969, p. 39.

One every twenty minutes. *Medical World News,* April 7, 1967, p. 73.

Chapter 6

PHARMACOTHERAPY

GEORGE NICKLIN

*Primum non nocere**

A conservative approach to the use of medications is most beneficial in preventing the many complications which such usage brings about. However, there are times when the use of medication can both enhance and accelerate a patient's recovery. Accordingly, the therapist should be ready to recommend medication when it is appropriate.

Since 1950 when Charpentier (1952) synthesized chlorpromazine, and Deniker and Delay (1952) introduced it as a tranquilizing agent in 1952, there has been a revolution in the pharmacotherapy of mental disorders. Kline (1954), working at Rockland State Hospital in New York State, and other researchers in the state hospital system, popularized the use of such agents for the severely ill mental patient. The end result of this revolution has been a marked decrease in the number of admissions to state hospitals as well as an increase in the number of patients available for psychotherapeutic techniques. Correspondingly, the governmental health care systems have had to build fewer facilities for the chronic mentally ill patient. There has also been an acceleration of the community mental health program permitting patients to be cared for locally.

The ready availability of many chemical substances has greatly complicated the modern psychotherapeutic scene. The thereputic sword has cut in both directions. While there has been a tremendous improvement in the drugs available to patients, there has been a concomitant rise in the abuse of such drugs. This has become flagrant in the United States population during the last third of the past decade (1966-1970) especially among college-age

*"The first premise is to do no harm."

118

and high school students. Many factors have contributed to this epidemic of drug abuse. One of the most prominent of these is availability secondary to the evolution of chemical therapy. Many physicians have been unaware of the complications of the new drugs, and it is not until they have been on the market for a period of time, that all the complications eventually emerge. Therapists in general should be alert to new drugs being used with their patients in the event that complications occur. Concerning this, I have a special three-year market test. This means that I do not prescribe any new pharmacotherapeutic agent until it has been on the open drug market for at least three years. As is well known, many of the new drugs do not pass this test and have to be withdrawn for reasons of vascular complications, blood dyscrasias, and the complications of drug addiction. An example of such an evolution during World War II was the synthetic analgesic meperidine hydrochloride (Demerol®), which is now regulated as a narcotic. Some of these complications can naturally be controlled by stricter regulation.

Despite the recent epidemic of drug abuse, it must be realized that the discharge rate from American mental hospitals has climbed steadily in the past fifty years, until at last more patients are being discharged annually than are being admitted. This has meant a revolution in mental health care. Many patients are now treated in their community where they can work and live productively. New mental health planning calls for the hospitalization of patients in their local community at small centers and their rapid reambulation into home and work experience. These new drugs have meaningfully shortened the duration of mental illness in a field where for many years such steps were unavailable. In the future, new methods of therapy must be found to accelerate mental health recovery in those so afflicted. These chemical therapeutic agents have opened a door to this new milieu and are a great aid to the psychotherapist.

CLASSIFICATION

Much has been written about the dilemma of classification. Recently, conferences have been called to clarify the dilemma which the evolution of the new drugs has brought about. As in all such evolutionary phenomena, the initial classification was one outlined by the chemists and physiologists who first discovered and utilized the drugs. As the psychotropic agents have multiplied, they have created a confusion as to how these drugs should be classified. Accordingly, the World Health Organization (Rep. Ser. No. 371) at a recent conference set up a classification which is outlined in Table 6-I following. This new classification, which was introduced in 1967, is an attempt to combine several previous classifications. Categorizations go from the antipsychotic agents known as neuroleptics through the anxiolytic sedatives, to antidepressants, and into the psychostimulants. In addition, there is a fifth category of psychodysleptics, which are those agents recently undergoing extreme abuse in American society for their hallucinogenic powers. They have also opened possibilities for the study of hallucinatory phenomena and aided psychiatric research.

Neuroleptics (Antipsychotic Agents)

The pharmacotherapeutic laboratories have been so successful in producing numerous phenothiazine compounds that it is virtually impossible to present the total group. Accordingly, only a limited number of the more commonly used compounds will be discussed. The picture is also complicated by the fact that each chemical agent is marketed under several different trade names. For example, the popular agent chlorpromazine is marketed under the trade names of Thorazine®, Largactil®, Megaphen®, and Aminazin®. Now let us first consider chlorpromazine hydrochloride. This agent is the most widely used of the neuroleptics at this time. Since 1952, it has been utilized with acutely agitated patients. It has been found to produce very satisfactory results. This agent remains bound in the body tissues for periods of 6 to 12 months after administration has ceased. It is well absorbed on oral administration and can also be given intramuscularly.

This drug has been very effective in the aggressive, destructive patient. It is usually initiated in therapy in the hospital setting or in the physician's office. The agitated patient is especially likely to benefit from it. The hallucinating schizophrenic will note a remission frequently in such ideas during the first

TABLE 6–I

CLASSIFICATION OF PSYCHOTROPIC DRUGS

Category	Representative Members
Neuroleptics	Phenothiazines Butyrophenones Thioxanthenes Reserpine derivatives, benzoquinolizines
Anxiolytic sedatives	Meprobamate and derivatives Diazepoxides Barbiturates
Antidepressants	Monoamine oxidase (MAO) inhibitors Imipramine and other tricyclic compounds
Psychostimulants	Amphetamine, methylphenidate, pipradrol Caffeine
Psychodysleptics (hallucinogens)	Lysergic acid diethylamide (LSD) Mescaline Psilocybin Dimethyltryptophan (DMT) Cannabis (marijuana, hashish, etc.)

week or two of therapy and indeed often in the first 24 hours. As in most psychotic conditions, the longer the patient has been ill, the less likely he is to improve with drug therapy. Despite this, many chronically ill psychotic patients have been rehabilitated. The agitation of depressed patients may be relieved or masked by chlorpromazine. However, it is no longer the therapy of choice in depressions. While chlorpromazine is recommended in acute alcoholic states, its demand on the liver for detoxification is such that it should be used conservatively. It is also useful in other delirious conditions. Also, it still may be helpful in aiding addicts who go through withdrawal symptoms, especially to the morphine derivatives.

Many patients complain of faintness on initial administration, since there is a concomitant fall in blood pressure related to individual variation and dosage. Initially, there may be an increased need for sleep which disappears after a few days. Many patients liken the effect of this drug to "having a blanket thrown around them." This drug also increases the effect of narcotic agents and barbiturates. There may be a transient leucopenia as well as some lowering of basic metabolic rate and temperature, pulse and respiration. The drug can be administered in tablets, which have an effect up to 6 hours, or in long-acting (12-hour) capsules.

Dosage levels vary with the needs of the patient, and they must be regulated individually. If a patient is on a sustained dosage level of this agent, he should have blood counts every 90 days to assess any leucopenia which may occur. While the usual patient is sustained on dosages of 600 to 800 mg per day if he is chronically disturbed, levels up to 2000 to 4000 mg in 24 hours have been given. The large dosage levels are accompanied with confusion and unsteady gait associated with extrapyramidal symptoms.

Two benzene rings joined by a sulphur and nitrogen atom represent the source of most of the phenothiazines as well as other tricyclic neuroleptics. By substituting at the R1 and R2 areas in the chemical formula, the numerous phenothiazine and tricyclic derivatives have been developed. The widely used chlorpromazine derivative comes from the substitution of a dimethylaminopropyl side chain at R1. This is also true for triflupromazine and promazine. Substitution of other chemical chains in this area leads to thioridazine and mepazine, if piperidine side chains are used, or with piperazines to development of perphenazine, prochlorperazine and trifluoperazine.

Complications

The complications seen with chlorpromazine range from minor skin reactions to fatal blood dyscrasias. Patients' lethargy may reach such a state that fecal impaction has been reported. Pains in the legs or abdomen may be secondary to hypotension previously mentioned. Patients with cardiovascular disease or atherosclerosis should receive the drug with caution. Abnormal skin pigmentation has been reported. Also, photosensitivity from mild to extreme has been noted with some patients. However, skin complications have been noted in only about 5 percent of those receiving the drug.

Liver complications are seen in 4 percent and are of a varying degree. Jaundice may appear from the second to the eighth week after the drug is initiated. This is due to an obstructive phenomena in the intralobular canaliculi. The jaundice may also be accompained with a pruritis. Naturally, if this complication of liver involvement appears, the drug should be discontinued. A high-carbohydrate, high-protein, and low-fat diet is recommended with vitamins. A liver study program is advisable.

Approximately one patient in 333 develops agranulocytosis. This usually appears within six weeks of the initiation of the drug. It is more common in women, especially in those over forty. Presenting symptoms of agranulocytosis are sore throat, mouth lesions, or a rise in temperature unaccountably. Despite immediate therapy including penicillin and broad-spectrum antibiotics, the prognosis is often poor. Transfusion and corticotropin (ACTH) may be used.

Earlier mention was made of the dyskinesia (difficulty in performing voluntary muscular movements) which appears with the use of chlorpromazine. This also involves akathisia (difficulty in sitting, posture) and dystonia. Parkinson-like symptoms may be treated with benztropine-methane-sulfonate (Cogentin®). On occasion, suicide has been attempted with chlorpromazine. However, only one death has been reported. When complications occur, withdrawal of the drug is recommended. However, its long-term use in schizophrenic reactions appears to have been quite beneficial when the dosage is adjusted to the individual. Discontinuance after such long-term usage should be done with caution.

Promazine

Promazine is a popular drug outside of psychiatry. It is useful in obstetrics and has been used in eclampsia and other postpartum conditions. It has also been used in psychiatry in alcoholism but is subject to criticism for its effect on the liver, since alcoholics usually have an already endangered liver. Some therapists have used it for treating withdrawal symptoms from opiate addiction.

Insofar as psychiatric practice tends to be specialized, the neuroleptic agents are used most often by those therapists treating psychotics. They are less likely to be utilized by therapists who see neurotics or character disorders in their practice. Complications for promazine are similar to those seen with chlorpromazine. Its manufacturers claim it has less hypotensive effect than chlorpromazine and is therefore useful in treating senile and arteriosclerotic brain disease. Dosage is adjusted to the individual needs of the patient. This preparation can be administered orally or intramuscularly. It has been given in amounts up to 1000 mg daily.

With the exception of a missing chlorine atom, this drug is identical to chlorpromazine. Chemically, it is ten (3-(dimethyl amino)propyl)-phenothiazine.

Triflupromazine

Good results have been reported with this drug with psychotics, especially paranoids, but some research workers have found conflicting evidence as its value. It appears to be no more effective than chlorpromazine in some studies done by Roebuck *et al.* (1959). Daily dosage ranges from 20 to 200 mg. However, as much as 6000 mg daily has been given to paranoid schizophrenic patients.

Chemically, this drug is ten (3-(dimethylamino)-propyl)-2-

(trifluromethyl)-phenothiazine. It is marketed under the trade names of Vesprin®, Vespral®, and Psyquil®.

While there are many other phenothiazine-promazine derivatives, the previously mentioned are the more commonly used.

Thioridazine

Because of reduced side effects and toxic manifestations, this drug has achieved wide usage. It is extremely useful in the treatment of psychosis, as well as psychophysiologic reactions, e.g. tension headaches, insomina, and fatigue. Schizophrenics who did not respond to other therapy have responded to the administration of thioridazine. Also, it does not have such side effects as drowsiness. This gives it an advantage over other phenothiazines. This drug also has some antidepressive effect. It is one of the few phenothiazines to have this trait. Usual daily dosages range from 20 to 800 mg. The lower dosages are associated with therapy for neurotics and the higher dosages with therapy for psychotics.

Comparatively speaking, complications with this drug are much rarer than those with the other phenothiazines. However, while less frequent, complications tend to follow the same patterns, though of a milder nature.

This drug is marketed as Mellaril®. Chemically, it is 2-methyl-mercapto-10(2-(N-methyl-2-piperidyl)-ethyl)-phenothiazine. This is a phenothiazine derivative with a piperdyl ring in a side chain. It is the most widely used of its group.

Piperazine Derivatives

While several popular drugs are included in this group, only three will be discussed here. These are the ones in more common usage in the United States.

Perphenazine

It has been used by large numbers of patients. Supposedly this drug is popular due to a fewer number of complications than chlorpromazine. This drug has not only been found useful in the treatment of schizophrenia, but also certain neurotic conditions including neurodermatoses and even in one patient with an acute epileptic psychosis. It has been used in combination with other organic therapies. It is believed to have fewer side effects than the more popular phenothiazines. Dosages range from 6 mg to as high as 64 mg daily. Higher dosages have been reported as high as 768 mg daily by Larson *et al.* (1959).

This drug is marketed under the trade names of Tralafon®, Fentazin®, and Decentan®. Chemically, it is 4-(3-(2-chlorophenothiazine-10-YL)propyl)1 piperazine-ethanol.

Fluphenazine

This drug is a powerful antipsychotic agent. It, too, has been used with neurotic patients in lower dosage levels. The neurotics with lower anxiety levels have been treated with as small a dosage as 0.5 mg daily, though dosage levels from 300 to 1000 mg have been reported, with minor extrapyramidal complications. Chemically this drug has a trifluoromethyl group substituted for the chlorine group in perphenazine. It is marketed under at least six trade names, of which two of the more popular are Prolixin® and Permitil®.

Trifluoperazine

This drug is found to be useful with apathetic, withdrawn schizophrenic patients. In clinical practice, it has become less popular in recent years. Some workers have reported it useful in the treatment of the hallucinations of delirium tremens. Dosage levels vary from 3 mg a day for neurotic patients to as high as sixty mgs. daily for psychotic patients. This drug is sometimes combined with chlorpromazine. Dosage level is usually gradually raised to meet individual patients' requirements. Chemically this drug is 10-(3-(4-methyl-1-piperazinyl)propyl)-2-(trifluoromethyl)-phenothiazine. This drug is marketed under the names of Stelazine® and Jatroneural®.

Prochlorperazine

Initially this drug was quite popular for its antiemetic effect. The drug has been reported to have an ability to raise the spirits of some patients. In clinical practice in recent years, this drug has become less popular. However, it is still prescribed for patients requiring antinauseant and tranquilizer control. It is also popular in the treatment of some gastrointestinal disorders. Dosage levels vary between 25 to 75 mg daily to as high a daily dose as 250 mg or above. This drug chemically is 2-chloro-10-(3-(4-methyl-1-piperazinyl)propyl)-phenothiazine. It is marketed under the trade names of Compazine®, Stemetil®, and Nipodal®. There are many other chemical derivatives in this currently studied group. However, they are not as popular in their usage and accordingly are not being discussed at this time.

Reserpine Derivatives

This drug is derived from the root of the plant *Rauwolfia serpentina*. It was popularized especially in the early 1950's for the treatment of schizophrenia. It is one of the pioneering drugs in this area, with chlorpromazine. Its use in recent years has diminished. It is likely to aggravate peptic ulcer due to an increase in gastric acidity and secretion. It also intensifies or induces depression at times to the depth of a psychotic depression. Kline (1954) was responsible for its introduction and popularization in the state hospital system in the United States. Lastly, there is a delay in the onset of the effect. The drug may be administered intramuscularly or by mouth. Maximum 24-hour does is 15 mg maintenance dose is usually 1 or 2 mg twice a day.

Anxiolytic Agents (Antineurotics)

These agents have become extremely popular since the introduction in 1946 of meprobamate. They are known colloquially as tranquilizers and have achieved extremely wide use for the treatment of moderate to severe anxiety states. The more recently introduced chlordiazepoxide and diazepam are now widely used in the United States. The latter has become especially popular, since it does not have sedative effect. Empirically the first two of these drugs, meprobamate and chlordiazepoxide, are sufficiently habituating to verge on the addictive in some patients.

Meprobamate

Berger and Ludwig (1952, 1964) introduced meprobamate in 1951. This drug is used in a variety of tension disorders. Its muscle-relaxant effects may correct muscle pain related to chronic contraction. In addition, it is used in virtually all of the anxiety states, including acute anxiety reactions, chronic anxiety reactions, phobias, neurodermatitis, premenstrual tension and also to correct sleeping disorders such as insomnia. Dosage of this drug is 400 mg three to four times daily. Double or triple this dosage level has been reported. Many toxic responses have been noted. These include acute nonthrombocytopenic purpura, skin reactions, and respiratory and vasomotor collapse in severe overdosage. In addition, addiction responses have been reported. Special care should be utilized if the drug is prescribed for drug addicts or alcoholics. On rare occasions, allergic reactions have been reported. These include erythema and urticaria of the skin, bronchial spasm and, rarely, loss of consciousness. Meprobamate chemically is known as 2-methyl-2-propyl-1,3-propanediol dicarbamate. This compound was derived from mephenesin, introduced in 1946.

Diazepam (Valium®)

This compound was introduced in the middle 1960's and has rapidly become one of the most popular tranquilizing agents. It is very popular in treatment of all the anxiety states including alcoholism, or central–nervous-system spasticity. Drowsiness is less common than with its closely related drug, chlordiazepoxide. It has also been noted to cause dysarthria, ataxia, headache, and motor hyperactivity. Addiction is a rare complication with this agent. Sudden discontinuance of the drug may cause some withdrawal symptoms, including convulsions in severe reactions. Dosage levels vary from 4 to 50 mg daily. Chemically this is 7-chloro-1,3-dihydro-1-methyl-5-phenyl-2H-1-4-benzodiazepin-2-one.

Chlordiazepoxide

This drug was introduced in 1960 and has been extensively studied. It is one of the most popular tranquilizing agents. However, it has recently been displaced to some extent by diazepam, which seems to have a slightly lower complication rate. It is marketed under the trade name of Librium®. It is used for the treatment of a wide range of psychiatric conditions involving mild to severe anxiety and including alcoholism. Dosage range may vary from 10 to 100 mg daily. This drug relieves anxiety, aggression, and agitation.

Its side effects are similar to those of diazepam. These include drowsiness, which is not uncommon, addiction, convulsions seven or eight days after withdrawal is initiated, as well as ataxia, dysarthria, headache, and hyperactivity. As much as 625 mg of the drug has been taken in a suicide attempt with no serious ill effects following gastric lavage. Chemically this drug is known as 7-chloro-2(methylamino)-5-phenyl-4-oxide.

The past two drugs described are benzodiazepine derivatives. Several other chemical variations of these drugs are available on the market but are not as popular as Librium and Valium.

Antidepressants

This group of therapeutic agents was introduced in the late 1950's, through work done by Kuhn (1957, 1958) in Switzerland. There are many tricyclic antidepressants. However, the two most popular therapeutic agents are imipramine and amitriptyline.

Imipramine

This agent is highly effective in psychotic depressive conditions. This is especially true of the manic-depressive reactions. It is not as effective with the agitated depressions. Clinical surveys have indicated that favorable results occur in 60 to 80 percent of all depressions so treated. In geriatric depressions, some researchers have found the drug not as effective. This confirms the impression that organic brain disease leading to depressive effect does not respond to this agent. This drug is also useful in the treatment of enuresis, due to its effect upon the muscles of the bladder.

Dosage levels vary from 75 to 250 mg or more daily. The dosage level should be increased slowly. Complications of this drug are relatively mild. It should not be administered in the presence of urinary retention or of glaucoma, and this is also true of analogs of this agent. Some patients have entered hypomanic states associated with imipramine. Mouth dryness, perspiration, dizziness or tremors may also occur. This drug is marketed under the trade name of Tofranil®. Chemically it is known as (5-(3-Dimethylamino-propyl)-10,11-dihydro-5H-dibenz(b,f) azepine).

Amitriptyline

This seems to have clinically fewer complications than the previously described imipramine. Accordingly, in recent years it has become more popular. It was introduced clinically three or four years after imipramine, about 1960. This drug also has a sedative effect that is useful in patients having sleeping problems with their depression.

Dosage levels vary from 50 to 300 mg daily. Maintenance therapy is usually 70 to 100 mg daily. The author has found clinically that this drug is the treatment of choice in severe neurotic or psychotic depressive reactions. When the patient is more accessible, pharmacotherapy should be utilized conjointly with psychotherapy. The drug has also been useful in patients with hopeless physical disease and in children with enuresis. Chemically this is 5-(3-dimethyl-aminopropylidene)-10,11-dihydro-5H-dibenzo(a,d)cyclopheptadiene. The trade name of this preparation is Elavil®.

Monoamine Oxidase Inhibitors

Imipramine and amitriptyline are the two most widely used tricyclic antidepressants. The monoamine oxidase inhibitors are an outgrowth of tuberculosis-therapy research based on niazid in 1952. These drugs change the liver enzyme chemistry of monoamine oxidase with a secondary effect on depression. There are at least ten drugs in use of whom seven are nonhydrazine derivatives, e.g., nialamide (Niamid®), isocarboxazide (Marplan®) and phenelzine (Nardil®) and three are hydrazine derivatives, e.g. tranylcypromine (Parnate®). Due to complications of high blood pressure and liver toxicity, these drugs are used with extreme caution. However, there may be some depressed patients who respond to them, and accordingly, the therapist will from time to time find them of benefit in his therapeutic armamentarium.

Nialamide

Some investigators such as Van Reeth (1959) found remissions with this therapy less satisfactory than those produced with ECT.

Patients with endogenous depression of the retarded type seem to respond best to this drug. There is conflicting data on neurotic depression response.

Dosage should be carefully regulated according to the manufacturer's instructions. Complications can be quite severe. Patients should be followed closely medically. Dosage starts with an initial dose of 100 mg daily, increasing to 300 mg or more over a two- to four-week period. Dosage is then reduced to 50 to 100 mg daily for maintenance level. Reduction can take place once improvement commences. Chemically this agent is called nialamide, 1-(2-(benzylcarbamyl)ethyl)-2-isonicotinoylhydrazine. It is marketed under the trade name of Niamid.

Isocarboxazide

It appearls that virtually all types of depressions respond to this drug. However, in addition to the aforementioned complications of monoamine oxidase inhibitors, some patients develop schizophrenic symptoms. Older patients do not seem to respond as well to this particular therapeutic drug. In some comparative studies, isocarboxazide was less preferable than imipramine or phenelzine.

Dose is 20 mg daily usually, increasing to 40 mg within two weeks, followed by reduction to maintenance dose. Maintenance dose is usually 10 mg daily. Up to 90 mg daily may be necessary to achieve benefit, and therapeutic response usually occurs within ten days. Chemically this drug is isocarboxazide, 1-benzyl-2-(5-methyl-3-isoxazolyl-carbonyl)-hydrazine. It is marketed under the trade name Marplan.

Phenelzine

This drug is highly effective in many varieties of depression, especially endogenous depression. Improvement can occur between the fifth day and the third week of therapy. Some investigators (Hutchinson and Smedberg) (1960) report that the inability to sleep and early waking are first symptoms to show improvement. This drug is well tolerated and has become one of the most popular antidepressants. Chemically this drug is known as B-phenylethylhydrazine. It is marketed under the trade name of Nardil.

Tranylcypromine

This drug causes a rapid remission in depressions. It is especially good in anxious and hostile depressions. However, its complications, especially hypertensive crisis, led to its withdrawal from the United States market and then its subsequent reintroduction. The latter was with the caution that it should be used primarily in a hospital setting.

Dosage is from 10 to 40 mg daily. It is expelled from the system in 48 to 72 hours after withdrawal. Chemically this drug is trans-2-phenyl-cylopropylamine. It is marketed under the trade name Parnate.

Because of the numerous side effects of the preceding four compounds, the author is extremely cautious in recommending them for the treatment of depression. However, patients who do not respond to other therapies should be considered eligible for these preparations. The most serious complications include acute liver necrosis with an incidence of about 1 in 4000. Partial hypotension may occur in elderly patients. In addition, hypertensive crisis may occur in some patients. It is a well-known fact that cheeses and wines should not be imbibed under any circumstances while using these medications.

Psychostimulants

Since the end of World War II, following a grave epidemic of amphetamine misusage, Japan has banned their manufacture. These drugs are widely used in the United States for the therapy of depression and also for appetite control with weight reduction. The drug has not been found useful in the treatment of schizophrenia. The drugs are popular to heighten concentration and increase ambition. It is of interest that Shepherd et al. (1968), in a controlled study of depressed patients, found no difference between amphetamines and placebos. Drug studies in American universities have revealed that these are among the most popular drugs used by students.

In addition to the earlier-mentioned danger of addiction, the complication of amphetamine psychosis has been widely reported. Connell's (1958) monograph on this subject points out that the syndrome is indistinguishable from paranoid schizophrenia. Empirical experience confirms this, noting the presence of delusions, ideas of reference, and hallucinations. Paranoid symptoms are often quite prominent and may be associated with acts of violence.

Three compounds are popular in this group: (a) dl-2 amino-1-phenylpropane sulfate, amphetamine (Benzedrine®); (b) Dextro-rotatory isomer of amphetamine sulfate, D-amphetamine (Dexedrine®); and (c) N-methylated amphetamine hydrochloride, meth-amphetamine (Desoxyn®, Methedrine®). These drugs are usually administered in dosages of 5 to 10 mg twice a day. They should not be given beyond 5 P.M. to avoid sleeplessness.

Methylphenydate

This substance has been popular for its antidepressant effects supposedly without effect on heart rate, blood pressure, or respiration. It has also been popular as an energizer and for weight control. Recent reports suggest that this preparation is useful in the treatment of hyperactive children. This may be especially true of those children with a minimal–brain-damage syndrome. The chemical formula for this substance is methyl-a-phenyl-2-piperidinacetate hydrochloride. The drug is usually administered at breakfast and lunch and consists of divided doses totalling 15 to 30 mg daily. This compound is marketed under the trade name of Ritalin®.

Caffeine

It is the most commonly available central nervous stimulant in the occidental culture, being present in both coffee and tea. One or two cups of coffee or tea contain 150 to 250 mg of caffeine.

Caffeine specifically affects the central nervous system and respiratory stimulation as well as increases skeletomuscle stimulation. It is often used in morphine and other drug overdosage since it specifically increases the sensitivity of the respiratory center and corrects depression of this center. In addition, the effects of caffeine in increasing central nervous system alertness and as a mild corrective for depression are well known. Children are especially sensitive to caffeine and for this reason should not be encouraged to engage in the ingestion of caffeine-containing drinks, such as coffee, tea, cola drinks, and also significant quantities of cocoa. It is contraindicated in patients with peptic ulcers, high blood pressure, cardiac conditions, and insomnia.

A syndrome of caffeine poisoning does appear in the culture characterized by restlessness, disturbed sleep, cardiac irregularities, and tachycardia. Some patients may develop diarrhea due to the essential ills of coffee. Psychic dependence is widespread in American society and is socially acceptable, though not desirable. Caffeine is 1,3,7-trimethylxanthine.

Psychodysleptics

Until 1968, experimentation in this drug group was extremely popular. These substances mimic psychopathology, such as schizophrenia. Recent abuse and problems arising with these compounds, and their violation of the principal enunciated at the beginning of this chapter, have increased caution in research. Some patients have developed nonreversible psychotic conditions. Compounds included in this group are lysergic acid diethylamide, psilocybin, and mescaline as well as marijuana.

Lysergic Acid Diethylamide (LSD-25)

This drug has become unpopular since 1968. The widespread occurrence of nonreversible psychosis, as well as sudden and unexpected flashbacks to the psychotic experience, have increased the cautiousness of most therapists in its use. In addition, its effect on the mutating rate of cells has raised questions as to its role in congenital abnormalities or other complications such as induced leukemia. It should only be used in a controlled situation present in a hospital.

Psilocybin

This is a hydroxytryptamine substance related to serotonin and derived from the mushroom *Psilocybe mexicana heim*. It requires one hundred times the dosage of LSD. The same cautions occur in the use of this drug. Whereas LSD's effects last eight to twelve hours, psilocybin lasts five hours. Patients utilizing both drugs are unable to distinguish the changes of LSD from those of psilocybin.

Mescaline (Peyote)

This substance has been widely used by Indian tribes in the United States, especially in the Southwest, to produce hallucinatory states. It has been investigated for use in abreaction of highly charged emotional states accompanied by repression. Research in this area is currently undertaken with great caution. The precipitation of latent depressions and suicidal tendencies, as well as nonreversal of psychotic states, have prompted caution.

Cannabis (Marijuana)

This substance has been described in the literature dating back to more than 4500 years ago. In the past seven years in the United States (1964-1971), there has been a tremendous popularization of this substance. I believe that this is directly related to social protest and feelings of despair against the American war involvement in southeast Asia. This social protest in the more sensitive portion of the population has produced an epidemic of drug usage involving hallucinogens, especially marijuana, on college campuses and in high schools in the United States. Nonreversible psychoses are reported in the literature with the use of marijuana. There is some question as to whether or not these occur in predisposed persons. Because of the current popularity of this substance, much research has recently been undertaken by federal and state agencies. The results of this are not as yet available.

Empirically, I have noted a popular use of this substance, especially in depressed patients. They report a relief of the symptoms of depression associated with increased appetite and weight gain. Subjects also report an increased awareness of paranoid sensation with some subjects developing paranoid ideation and delusional systems.

The medical preparations in this section should be approached with great caution, and results of recent and current research show no indication for any of these to be used on a therapeutic basis. They are most commonly now encountered as part of the epidemic of drug usage. Current developments in the therapeutic use of these drugs for treating psychogenic conditions are such that they should only be used in hospital settings under laboratory conditions for research purposes.

Tetrahydrocannabinol is now believed to be the active ingredient in cannabis.

Lithium

Cade (1949) in Australia reported the use of lithium salts with benefit for patients with psychotic excitement in 1949. He also reported positive response in manics. This has been validated by other research workers. There is a general consensus that the drug is of value in manic conditions. However, at least one fatality has been reported (status epilepticus developing on the eighth day of treatment). The drug is administered in 300 mg capsules, four to seven times weekly. It brings about excellent control of chronic and recurrent mania. The drug is toxic to the kidney and should be withdrawn if renal symptoms, vomiting, or diarrhea ensue. This is also true if undue tremor or ataxia develop. In 1970, this agent was introduced in the United States under the trade name Lithonate®. The manufacturer recommends up to 600 mg three times a day for acute manic states. Therapeutic blood levels can be maintained with 300 mg three times a day.

Barbiturates

These substances are the most commonly abused drugs in current usage in the United States. They also account for the largest percentage (25%) of suicides or accidental fatal poisonings in the United States. They are widely prescribed by physicians for insomnia and for undue tension associated with slight cardiac arrhythmia. Addiction is common and difficult to treat, due to the widespread availability of these substances. They are readily available on the illicit drug market. They are currently distributed by illicit narcotic distributors under the argot term, "downs." Empirically there seems to be a slight decrease in their usage in the New York City area.

DISCUSSION

The recent advent in the past twenty years of the antipsychotigens and tranquilizers has been so beneficial that it has enabled many patients to escape hospitalization for chronic mental illness. The development of these substances is a tribute to the pharmacotherapeutic researcher. This chapter has described current developments in the use of pharmacotherapeutic agents in the treatment of psychiatric disorders. Substances covered include the antipsychotigens such as chlorpromazine; tranquilizers such as meprobamate; antidepressants including tricyclic compounds and monoamine oxidase inhibitors; psychostimulants such as amphetamines; psychodysleptics—such as LSD-25, etc.; and other therapeutic agents such as lithium and barbiturates.

Caution is urged to the psychiatrist in his prescription of such preparations as well as encouragement to psychotherapists to recommend them when necessary and appropriate.

I note that in the metropolitan areas it is not uncommon to see patients suffering from irreversible chemical psychoses which require hospitalization. Also, addiction is quite common to these popular psychiatric treatment agents. In the background is the ever-present risk of severe drug abuse, including suicide. Accordingly, the author urges that prescription blanks carry necessary caution, and dosages should not be prescribed that permit lethal or addicting levels to be acquired by the patient. For more detailed evaluation of these therapeutic agents, the author recommends such books as that recently published by Kalinowsky and Hippius (1969). Whatever therapeutic course the psychotherapist embarks on, he should remember that drugs are a valuable adjunct to psychotherapy and should be ready to use them when appropriate but to be extremely cautious in recommending such usage, due to the many hazards which psychopharmacotherapy also involves.

REFERENCES

Berger, F. M.: The pharmacological properties of 2-methyl-2-n-propyl-1, 3-propaneidiol dicarbamate (Miltown), a new interneuronal blocking agent. *Journal of Pharmacology and Experimental Therapy, 104*:468, 1952.

Berger, F. M. and Ludwig, B. J.: Meprobamate and related compounds. In Gordon, M. (Ed.): *Psychopharmacological Agents,*

1:103, Medicinal Chemistry: A Series of Monographs, New York, Academic Press, 1964, vol. 4.

Cade, J. F. J.: Lithium salts in treatment of psychotic excitement. *Medical Journal of Australia, 2*:349, 1949.

Charpentier, P., Gailliott, P., Jacob, R., Guadechon, J., and Buisson, P.: Recherches sur les dimethylaminopropyl-n-phenothiazines substitutees. *Comptus Rendus, 235*-59, 1952.

Connell, P. H.: *Amphetamine Psychosis.* London, Chapman and Hall, 1958.

Delay, J. and Deniker, P.: Le traitement des derivee de l'hibernotherapie. Congres des medecins alienistes et neurologistes, Luxembourg, Juillet, 1952.

Hutchinson, J. T. and Smedberg, D.: Phenelzine (Nardil) in the treatment of endogenous depression, *Journal of Mental Science, 106*:704, 1960.

Kalinowsky, L. B. and Hippius, H.: *Pharmacological, Convulsive and Other Somatic Treatments in Psychiatry.* New York, Grune and Stratton, 1969.

Kline, N. S.: Use of *Rauwolfia serpentina benth.* in neuro-psychiatric conditions. *Annals of the New York Academy of Sciences, 59*:107, 1954.

Kuhn, R.: Uber die Behandlung depressiver Zustande mit einem Iminodibenzyl-derivat G.22355. *Schweizerische Medizinische Wochenschuft (Basel), 87*:1135, 1957.

Kuhn, R.: The treatment of depressive states with G.22355 (imipramine hydrochloride). *American Journal of Psychiatry, 115*:549, 1958.

Larson, A. N., Hamlon, J. S., and Sines, L. K.: A note on the clinical effects of perphenazine at very high dosages. *American Journal of Psychiatry, 116*:456, 1959.

Roebuck, B. E., Chambers, J. L., and Williams, E.: An evaluation of the therapeutic use of triflupromazine in mental disease. *Journal of Nervous and Mental Diseases, 129*s184, 1959.

Shepherd, M., Lader, M., and Rodnight, R.: *Clinical Psychopharmacology.* London, English Universities Press, 1968.

Van Reeth, P. C.: Nialamide in severe endogenous depression. *J. da Soc. das Ciencias Med de Lisboa,* supp., p. 210, November, 1959.

World Health Organization, Technical Report, Series No. 371.

Chapter 7

THE DECISION TO HOSPITALIZE

ABRAHAM LURIE

At one time or another, all practitioners in private practice are faced with the prospect of having to recommend hospitalization for someone they are treating. The decision to do so is difficult for the therapist, the patient, and the patient's family. The therapist can see this as a personal defeat. To the patient, it can be a signal that his therapist has found him to be too sick to be treated outside of an institution. For the family, it very often engenders guilt and feelings of failure. It can cause a family economic crisis, since the cost of hospitalization has reached an alarming high.

Philisophically, from a treatment point of view, hospitalization is often seen as a last resort. In private psychotherapeutic practice, hospitalization can be a very positive procedure. Even more significantly to the patient, if the therapist is aware of the route by which admission to the hospital can be made, the experience can be less traumatic for the patient, and the ability to accept hospitalization and be treated within the hospital can occur without trauma.

Before recommending hospitalization, a decision must be made regarding the need for this step. On the surface, this seems like a relatively simple evaluation. And yet this decision covers a process which includes many ambivalences of the therapist, the patient, and the family. A rule of thumb regarding the need for hospitalization is that patients who are dangerous to themselves or to others require a closed setting and should be hospitalized. But the determination as to what kind of behavior is dangerous is subjective and open to interpretation.

Some rare overt actions can easily be interpreted as dangerous; for example, significant suicidal threats or attempts. These require that the patient receive a period of intensive observation in a hospital setting. Acting out to the extent of endangering anyone's life requires continued and intensive supervision. An example of this is persistent thoughts of destroying people or destroying one's self. Anticipatory dangerous behavior is obviously a less-definitive criteria, but hospitalization is used to prevent overt action.

The decision to hospitalize a patient may be a specific to speeding up treatment. For example, a degree of depression which immobilizes an individual will be used by the therapist as an indication for hospitalization. The patient who cannot function and sinks deeper into the morass of indecision, depression, and literal pain will require a period of hospitalization so that the symptoms of the depression, if not the cause which is inducing this pain, can be alleviated. Hospitalization is used as a symptom alleviator. By relieving pain, it is possible for a patient to resume daily functioning which will enable him to become involved in therapy on an outpatient basis.

Sometimes the decision to hospitalize a patient is made not by the patient or his therapist but by the relatives. This is often true in the case of youngsters who are engaged in antisocial activities. The parents of such youngsters involved in judicial review or procedures feel that hospitalization will help judicial processes lean less heavily on youngsters if psychiatric treatment has been initiated. The motivation is greater on the part of the family than the youngster.

A family unit may make a determination that a member needs hospitalization to preserve the family. In this situation, the decision to hospitalize is hurried along by the insistence of the other family members so they can go about their business. Here the family will denegrate the patient and describe his activities in an exaggerated way which is based on the patient's behavior and is seen to be detrimental to the patient or others. Sometimes after a patient has been hospitalized, the family will, after a respite, retrospectively deny the degree of the behavior which has initially brought the patient to the hospital.

Having come to the conclusion to hospitalize the patient, it is necessary to implement this decision. Lack of knowledge about the hospital to use for this purpose and little information about the kinds of treatment programs available in the various hospitals brings indecision to the therapist and to the family. This is communicated to the patient. On top of this is the stigma which hospitalization brings to bear on the patient's perception of himself and the family's perception of themselves.

In discussing hospitalization, it is good practice for the therapist to know his resources thoroughly and to be familiar with aspects of admission procedures to the hospitals which he may use for this process.

From a practical point of view, it is well to know that many hospitals have psychiatric treatment facilities. General hospitals, the large voluntary teaching and training institutions, and city and county institutions usually include observation or treatment units. There are a few private or proprietary psychiatric institutions, but these are very expensive and are not large. The nonprofit institutions which offer psychiatric inpatient treatment expect the patient and/or the family to pay up to their financial limit. Rates for admission, therefore, may be high and can literally wipe out the savings of patients and families, even in general and voluntary hospitals. Fortunately, major medical insurance policies are providing some basic insurance which will help to defray expenses. In addition, in some states such as New York, it is possible for county, state, and voluntary psychiatric units to accept medically indigent patients, so that those who do not have funds can be treated in these institutions.

In spite of the tremendous growth of psychiatric inpatient units in general hospitals and county institutions, most patients who are hospitalized and require extended hospitalization find themselves in state institutions. In the last few years, the population in these hospitals has markedly decreased. Some institutions have dropped their census as much as 50 percent. The policies of many of the state institutions have also changed to accept voluntary patients. It is the voluntary commitment procedure which is now encouraged by state hospitals in the more progressive states. The decision, however, to accept the patient as a voluntary rests with many of the directors of the state hospitals.

The recent trend towards developing catchment areas encourages state, county, and psychiatric inpatient units to serve a geographic district. It is important for therapists to be aware of the geographic boundaries assigned to the hospitals they will be using for admissions. The therapist should become acquainted with the admissions officers and procedures. Admitting officers are generally receptive to giving information about their policies to those who request it. A card file with the hospital, the name of the admitting officer, and the telephone number is a very handy tool.

Many large institutions such as the state hospitals in New York State now have individuals designated as information officers whose job it is to provide specific information concerning admission procedures. They are particularly helpful in describing commitment procedures by which one can admit patients into a hospital as well as protecting the rights of the patient. This latter area is becoming increasingly important to diminish the stigma attached to hospitalization by insuring that patients who are admitted receive all the legal protection to which they are entitled. It is recommended that these officers who may have legal or social work background be contacted and become known to the therapist.

Personal contact with significant individuals involved in the admission process is very important. Commitment procedures vary from state to state, district to district, and hospital to hospital within the district. Many difficulties can be alleviated by personal knowledge of persons involved in the admission process. Hours of admission, the people involved, the process by which the admission takes place, and the office to go to are all small matters, but to the patient and the family who are entering the hospital, these become monumental. Each step arouses anxiety, and lack of knowledge of the details aggravates tension and produces more ambivalence regarding the decision to hospitalize. On the other hand, a clear explanation of the process, the names of people involved, and specific information on how to reach the offices all give a measure of authority of knowledge to the patient and the family and tends to allay anxieties.

Despite laws which spell out commitment procedures in considerable detail, the authorities involved in admission processes tend to interpret them somewhat differently. This is more complex when one considers that every state has a right to make, and has indeed made, decisions to change its commitment procedures. Instead of having the knowledge of each such procedure for each state, it is more practical to be sure that one is thoroughly acquainted with the different commitment procedures of the state institutions that one will need to use in hospitalizing patients. It is for this reason that personal relationships with admission people of all institutions are so important. The small differences and variations that take place in these procedures is useful information for the therapist which can be used to help patients and families accept hospitalization.

When emergencies arise and a decision to hospitalize the patient is made, then the first requirement is to move quickly. Alternatives available in cases of emergency hospitalization are not many. The first step is to move the patient to the appropriate hospital. Having selected the hospital to which the patient is to be admitted—following discussion with the patient and/or the family—it is best to call the hospital to be certain that a bed is available. This is a good practical procedure for hospitalizing patients in proprietary and voluntary psychiatric inpatient units and is now advantageous in using state institutions as well. If a bed and funds are available, then private ambulance services may be the most convenient and expeditious.

Many private ambulance services have their own rules regarding the number of attendants who must ride with the patients in the ambulance. Ordinarily the private ambulances are aware of the necessary manpower to transport patients and they are manned and well-equipped to handle almost any situation. A further advantage of the private ambulance service is their personnel's familiarity with various local hospitals in the community that accept psychiatric patients. They are familiar with admitting procedures and know to which service to bring the patient.

In an emergency situation in which there is some imminent danger to patients or others, it may be necessary to call the police. In large urban areas such as New York City and environs, police or city hospital ambulances with accompanying police in separate vehicles may come to handle most of the typical requests for this help.

Police and county ambulance services as well as private ambulance services are discreet in preparing patients for the trip and in transporting them to the appropriate place.

When police or county officials are called to provide transportation, the patients are admitted to a county hospital. In New York City, for example, if the police are called to provide ambulance service and they do respond, then the patient will be transported to the nearest county hospital. Today, in almost all large urban areas, county hospitals are equipped to deal with psychiatric emergencies, and when the police are notified and respond to such a call, they are effective, efficient, and tactful.

It is always advisable to notify parents, spouse, or adult children whenever decisions are made to hospitalize patients. Having someone in the family know what has been happening is therapeutically sound. But it is also a help to the therapist to involve the family at least at this point so that the therapist is not alone in making, planning, or implementing the decision for hospitalization. It is also important for the patient to have the family accompany or meet the patient at the admitting office. This gives the patient the feeling that he is not alone in this experience. If possible, and the family has the strength to make the decision for hospitalization and carry the plan through, it is best to have the family take on this responsibility. However, often in a crisis of this kind, families become disorganized and professional people involved in therapeutic situations should take the initiative in helping to make arrangements with the cooperation of the family and to motivate and help the family implement these decisions themselves.

After the patient is admitted to a psychiatric hospital, then laws governing the stays of these patients become effective. Unfortunately they vary from state to state and through practice, from county to county. Usually these regulations are a function of a State Department of Mental Hygiene or Mental Health. In New York state, these laws are explicitly detailed and have been amended and revised from time to time as a result of public hearings which are held throughout the state at intervals. Hearings are usually held after public or professional criticism which highlight inequities and injustices which creep into the state hospital system.

Experience indicates that constant attention must be paid to regulations pertaining to hospitalized psychiatric patients for a number of reasons. Primarily, these laws are necessary to protect liberties of patients so they receive the protection of the laws to which they are entitled. In the past, patients could be incarcerated in mental institutions by those who have been anxious to rid themselves of individuals. The strict enforcement of good laws pertaining to hospitalization, therefore, is a protection for the patients themselves. This procedure has been developed to protect the patient against involuntary hospitalization where the need is not justified.

A judicial procedure gives opportunity for the patient and his counsel as well as those interested in the patient to present their side. It also puts a burden of responsibility on professionals to prepare data which indicates that the patient, in fact, needs to be hospitalized for a longer period of time.

It is in this latter connection that legal procedures, such as certification and commitment have been developed. More recently, in some states such as New York following commitment of a patient, additional safeguards have been introduced to protect the patient's rights. At stated intervals, it is now necessary for patients who have been committed to be appraised again of the procedures which affect their stay and which advise them of their rights regarding the possibility of discharge from the institution in which they have been hospitalized.

In spite of these safeguards and the obvious concern on the part of many professionals, it is recognized that deficiencies and abuses creep into a system which limits the freedom of individuals. By the same token, public institutions are becoming increasingly wary of the kinds of patients that they admit and of the discharge procedures to follow when patients leave.

Therefore some relationship between the therapist and the person who is hospitalized can be a very important factor in helping the patient during his stay at the hospital. A visit to the institution or contact with the social worker in the institution or with patient's family brings to the family and to the patient the concrete feeling of the therapist's interest. This is crucial if the therapist is interested in continuing with the patient and with the families after the patient is discharged from the hospital. This also allows for the continuity of care following discharge.

Although the number of patients in psychiatric hospitals today is significantly less than they have been, the number of admissions has not decreased. At least as many, if not more people, are availing themselves of psychiatric hospitalization, but they are not remaining in the institutions as long as they have been. It is incumbent upon the private practitioner to become aware of the hospital as a resource to make certain that he is fully knowledgeable of hospital admission procedures in his community with which he will be working and that this knowledge can be transmitted in a therapeutic manner to the patient and the family.

Chapter 8

ETHICAL PROBLEMS AND SOME GUIDELINES

Thea C. Spyer

Significant contribution in systematic ethical thought has come from the philosophers. Struggle with concrete ethical problems remains with such groups as the helping professions who are often caught in the cross currents of conflicting or varying social, professional and personal opinion. In addition to the familiar ethical concern of guiding his professional behavior so as to assure maximum benefit to the patient, the mental health professional has two quite distinct ethical problems: (a) he must find a way to be true to both his avowed suspension of judgment in the therapy room and his concept of the "good" end product of his work and (b) he must be prepared to help in resolving the patient's own ethical struggles.

Although psychology is historically close to philosophy, it has produced few people sufficiently versed and seasoned in the two disciplines to promote a meaningful synthesis. The first part of this paper is an attempt to encourage an orderly approach to thinking about ethical problems—to hear, at least, that message of orderliness which is so highly developed among philosophers. The second part of the paper consists of some guidelines aimed specifically at private practice and designed to reduce the likelihood of getting into situations which may be fraught with ethical difficulties.

The dimensions of ethical thought are the same in private and agency clinical practice; it is the manifestations of ethical problems which differ in the two settings. The following examples serve to illustrate this point.

A psychologist working with patients in a low-fee clinic does not meet the problem of a patient who suddenly has real financial reverses in the middle of an intensive therapy and is unable to

146

pay future bills. However, he is confronted with the ethical issue under this problem when he is tempted by a better salary at a clinic which will not accept transfer of a patient who is in the middle of an intensive treatment with him. In either instance, the psychologist may struggle between the financial disadvantage of continued treatment and his explicit and implicit commitment to his patient.

Similarly, the hospital psychologist working on a salary with an assigned caseload does not have to worry about the problem of referring a patient to a more suitable colleague when he does not know where his next patient (meal) will come from. However, the hospital psychologist may meet the problem of being pressed to accept an administrative procedure which would force him to treat a patient who might receive more appropriate treatment from another staff member. Here again, in both settings, the psychologist must put his financial security on the line if he does not wish to violate his ideas on selective referral.

Despite the common ethical referents in the problems of psychologists in various forms of clinical work, and despite the fact that most clinical psychologists are decent human beings, it is difficult to gain consensus on any basic ethical points other than those dealing with blatant violation of professional responsibility and role. Clinical psychologists in private practice are particularly divergent in their views in that they are extremely individualistic. They work for themselves, generally by themselves; and through a very direct use of themselves, they work toward the goal of helping their patients gain freedom to dare to be and to fulfill themselves.

This paper focuses on the problems of dedicated clinicians who struggle to define their professional and ethical responsibility: the people who are interested in defining what is right, not those who struggle to skirt around generally accepted violations. Obvious violations would include willful misrepresentation of qualifications, use of the influence of professional role toward personal gain which is harmful to the patient, accepting fee kickbacks, spreading of slanderous misinformation about a colleague, or the breaking of confidentiality bonds for sensational effect. Psychologists involved in such acts are not addressed in this paper.

Once in debate, the people who are interested in what is right (not simply what is obviously wrong) generally find themselves unable to differentiate professional behavior which is governed by ethics from professional behavior governed by their particular theoretical and technical convictions. One man's technique built on defensible theory is another man's unethical behavior. For example, vehement humanists call psychoanalysts irresponsible in not recognizing that their technique only reinforces the very self-consciousness, shame, and inhibition it purports to relieve, while the counterattack rings with outrage over humanists' irresponsibility in flirting with acting out potential and personality disorganization. Rationalists accuse psychoanalysts of financial motives in adhering to their long-term techniques. Psychoanalysts accuse behaviorists of partial curing which has no enduring value and of neglecting the right of free will (Lomont, 1964). It is quite understandable that one who has totally subscribed to the validity of any of these approaches, for which he claims near universality, would find another's willful ignorance or knowledgeable resistance either stupid, unreasonable, or outright unethical. These quite gross accusations will continue among dedicated clinicians as long as there is no acceptable methodology for measuring personality change.

In the present paper, a clinician is considered ethically questionable when he willfully performs, or fails to take reasonable precaution against performing, an act which is likely to be detrimental to the most efficient, safe and thorough means of reaching the goals explicitly and implicitly set for the patient.

The following section carves out the basic dimensions of ethical debate.

BASIC DIMENSIONS OF ETHICAL DEBATE

The Unit of Judgment: Act or Outcome

A given action can be judged in terms of its worth as an act in itself or in terms of the worth of its probable consequences. These alternatives can be referred to as the deontologic and teleologic positions, respectively (McCord and Clemes, 1964). Both approaches are of course ultimately geared to successful outcome. The difference lies in the deontologist's conviction that a certain set of acts or role is most likely to bring about success and he sticks with the matter of defining and debating the ethics of acts, in and of themselves. The teleologist feels that the ethical focus is the effect of acts, that ethical value can only be judged by observing consequence.

For example, in an ethically nonsensitive area: both teleologist and deontologist might refuse to write a letter supporting a patient's application to some social institution, but for quite different reasons. The teleologist expects that his compliance would simply reinforce that patient's tendency to turn people into functions. The deontologist might refuse on the principle that a therapist's job is to analyze behavior and that the patient's job is to conduct his life using that analysis toward whatever end he wishes. By writing the letter he would weaken a patient's motive and facility to do his job.

In practice there are few pure form deontologists or teleologists, but strong tendencies are discernible in most experienced clinicians. Many clinicians would be surprised by their own position if they examined a number of their decisions in these terms. The most far-reaching implication in the choice of unit of judgment is whether one considers the psychologist responsible for certain acts toward the patient or responsible for the patient.

The Source of Judgment: Intrinsic or Extrinsic

Where does one look for moral standard? Those who have no faith in the natural goodness of man (Freud being an excellent example) advise looking toward standards which are logically derived, or at least defined in some terms other than what comes naturally. Counter to a very common misunderstanding of this position, looking towards factors extrinsic to the person does not imply that there is necessarily an opposition or mutual exclusion between what comes naturally and what is right. The probability of agreement in the untutored person is simply expected to be quite small.

In contrast, those who recognize a natural goodness in man

look to the individual for the source of moral judgment. If he is good, his moral responsibility is to behave in accordance with his natural feelings and tendencies. Right is what he thinks is right. Difference of opinion is of no moral concern, since all men share the natural goodness. Although many find the intrinsic position naive and dangerous, there is a very strong tendency for people to feel that the position is right and safe when its application is limited to their own actions. Those who supervise may recognize a form of this idea when they counsel trainees against actions which they themselves would take quite casually.

The Variability of Judgment: Absolute and Relative Standards

This is the most familiar point of ethical debate in clinical practice. Individually and as a group, psychologists have neither begun to reach an absolute standard which applies under all conditions, nor have they accepted the intrinsic position which would put an end to the ethics committees. The search for a relative position is really an attempt to make absolute statements of right under each of a number of defined conditions.

The development of a truly relative position requires very sophisticated thinking, since each problem situation represents a gestalt of interacting separate absolutes. Each of these absolute ethical standards has weight which varies with the nature of other absolutes it accompanies. It happens occasionally that a patient is in a position to be of help to the therapist. He may have "connections" or expertise which tempts the therapist. Limiting ourselves to the "act" as an unit of ethical judgment, the absolute tends to be a simple predetermined pro or con statement, such as the rule that personal interests of the therapist have no place in the office. The relative position can not necessarily be stated in lawful fashion since unforeseen variables may come into play. Continuing with the example, the relativist may not wish to accept services of any kind from the patient, however he is moved to change his view when he learns that the patient offers services as payment for treatment during a time of severe financial reverses. Assuming a few additional factors which he considers, a true relativist would have to create an absolute rule derived from the interaction of these factors, which rule would apply in every other essentially similar situation. This is, of course, an unlikely ideal, but it is presented to show that the idea that the relative position means simply "take every situation on its own merit" is quite misleading and unfortunately only too common.

A Few Individual Approaches to Solution

The following quote is from a very well-trained Sullivanian psychoanalyst. "One of my own personal rules of thumb for patients and myself has been 'Does it hurt anybody?' and then if it does not, 'Why not do it if you want to?' " Analyzing this man's position along with the dimensions discussed in this paper, it is clear that he is strongly teleologic in his focus on judging if the act could result in harm to others. He takes a relatively strong intrinsic position in trusting that his acts, once checked out for harmful consequences, are quite likely to be naturally good, no matter what they are, and he skirts the issue of absolute standards, since his criteria for identifying action of potential harm is unstated.

This stance may be contrasted with the very strong and clear ethical views of Thomas Szasz, who defines his responsibility professionally and ethically (which he considers identical) as analyzing the patient's communications, no less and certainly no more. ". . . Although the analyst tries to help the client, he does not 'take care of him.' The patient takes care of himself" (Szasz, 1965). This view represents a pure form example of an deontologic stand in defining the unit of judgment, combined with an extrinsically derived standard whose status is absolute for a person who identifies himself as an analyst, regardless of any other role identification attributable to him. The principle criticism of this view is the ritualistic potential in combining a rigid absolute standard of behavior with a total exclusion of concern about consequences as they appear on the spot.

With the current growth of the experientially oriented therapies, there are many practices which are justified by an ethic which closely resembles classical hedonism. "If during the session I feel fully involved and in it myself, I know it has to be an exciting experience for the patient, too. I can tell what's good by my own excitement." The criticism is that the zeal for creating excitement for the therapist represents an ontologic emphasis which is always vulnerable to losing sight of the avowed goal for the patient. Even if excitement in the therapist is a pure perfect index of excitement in the patient, there is still the problem of whether excitement in therapy sessions has a positive effect in the patient's life. It could have the opposite effect by satisfying the patient's excitement quota in a dead-end situation.

As is undoubtedly amply clear from the emphasis thus far, the opinion of the present writer is that an important safeguard against undue ethical stress or potential ethical abuse is an awareness of a systematic conceptual scheme for describing ethical and theoretical positions. The availability of such a scheme as a background for one's work facilitates the following:

1. Recognizing ethical problems.
2. Clarifying the issues in ethical conflict.
3. Making decisions.
4. Knowing what one's decisions were.
5. Relating follow-up observations back for possible modification of original position.
6. Providing a language for communication with colleagues.

Another major safeguard lies in the development of a set of fairly distinct guidelines which are designed to reduce the likelihood of getting into ethical problems. A sample of such guidelines is presented in the remainder of the paper.

The areas were selected on the basis of their frequently being at issue in everyday private practice. It is emphasized that the guidelines are not meant to stand as ethical principles but rather as ideas about professional conduct which may help the clinician avoid some ethical traps. The strong deontologic framework for the guidelines will be apparent. This is the only way in which some "practical" information can be given. A teleologically oriented ethics paper would begin with the basic rule that one may do anything that is likely to be to the patient's advantage and would elaborate into a treatise on various views of what constitutes advantage and which advantages are proper goals for psychotherapy (Lowe, 1969). Although generally applicable, the guidelines refer mainly to problems in private practice of individual psychotherapy. In each of the areas chosen for guideline, a reference to the APA official ethical standard most closely related is given in the footnote (American Psychologist, 1963).

GUIDELINES

Expectations and Demands of Patients

Patients who suffer from fairly severe ego lacks or who live without people to take on some of the essential interpersonal roles for them generally carry some expectation that their therapists will take on a good deal of their ego function or fill the emptiness of their world. These patients have very strong tendencies to "live" their transferences with little capacity to develop sufficient distance from the effect to permit analytic understanding. This type of patient, who is generally borderline psychotic or otherwise deeply disturbed characterologically, tries to place considerable responsibility for his everyday well-being and survival onto the therapist. The therapist's acceptance or rejection of this responsibility is the central issue here.

Guideline

A therapist should meet a patient's expectations and demands only when:
1. The action is consistent with his theory of practice.
2. He is prepared to deal with the consequences of the act of confirming the patient's expectations, such as greater dependencies, altered transference, and new demands.
3. His personal life situation can absorb this act and its probable consequences.
4. The patient has maximum possible knowledge as to the reason for the therapist's act, its limits, and conditions.
5. The therapist expects no return from the patient for having put himself out—not even an attitude of gratitude.

Example of Violation

This case illustrates an instance wherein virtually all of the conditions expressed above were ignored. The son of a narcissistic alcoholic mother is in treatment with his fifth therapist. Each of the four previous therapists had "disappointed" him within the period of a year, and in each instance he had left in an intense negative transferential rage. Early in treatment with the present therapist, he almost systematically tested out to see which of his many demands could be met. He wants to be seen six days a week; the therapist must be oblivious to all insults (not analyze, simply accept); the therapist must be available for phone conversations at all times and without indicating any annoyance if these calls continue over half an hour.

The therapist, a young psychiatrist newly out of residency, recognizes that the patient is without any internal resource to maintain himself on a level of tolerable anxiety, fears suicidal potential, and is very interested in establishing his practice. He makes the decision to accept the demands of the patient pretty much as stated. Initially the patient responds well, gets his first job, moves away from his parents' home and goes out with several girls. After some months during which the patient exercised all his "rights," he falls into a negative transferential rage centered around the feeling that the therapist is not really interested but rather tolerating him and collecting the fee. The therapist is also caught up in a rage since he expected some gratitude for having put himself out well beyond the call of duty. Also, in view of his just starting practice, he was not happy to lose this patient. The relationship was finally terminated, and the patient was referred to another therapist who was fully appraised of the patient's demands.

Confidentiality*

Guideline

In order to assist the patient in gaining maximum benefit from the freedom that he experiences in the atmosphere of confidentiality and suspension of judgment, the therapist should avoid actions which the patient could rightly take as evidence of disregard of the code of confidentiality.

---

*The parts of Principle VI of the APA Code which deal with confidentiality applicable to clinical practice state that confidentiality may be broken (a) with conditions of "clear and eminent danger to an individual or to society, and then only to appropriate professional workers or public authorities" and (b) for professional purposes and only with persons clearly concerned with the case.

Examples of Violation

1. In order to communicate a sense of "I'm on your side of the line," a therapist confided in his pubescent patient and told him some of the things his parents had said to the therapist in a session.

2. A fairly authoritarian analyst adopts an air of intrigue and collaboration in telling his patient that he is going to read him exactly every word that has been written about him in a report received from a diagnostic testing consultant. Although such a recital may be very appropriate in certain cases and situations, the message that came across here was that the patient was privileged to confidential information. (The APA Code Principle VI deals with this problem from another standpoint.)

3. At a dinner party, an analyst refers by name to a former patient who was a public personality and had died several years before. He alluded to several matters which he could only have known as her analyst. In so doing, the analyst shook the confidence in confidentiality of a man at that dinner party who was newly in analysis and who later asked me if confidentiality ends with one's life.

Countertransference*

Members of allied disciplines, the lay public, and nonclinical psychologists are often very "concerned" about the matter of objectivity in clinical practice, which is a polite way of pointing the finger at clinicians for the existence of countertransference.

> However much the analyst would want to be objective in face of his patient, his material, his mood, his whole personality, he cannot listen to him, perceive, nor understand him except with his own whole personality; that is to say, with his ego, his id, his super ego, and his internal objects. The constellation among these internal instances differs from analyst to analyst and from one era to another" (Racker, 1966).

*APA Code, Principle II c: The second half of this section reads that the psychologist "refrains from undertaking any activity in which his personal problems are likely to result in inferior professional services or harm to a client; or if he is already engaged in such an activity when he becomes aware of his personal problems, he seek competent professional assistance to determine whether he should continue or terminate his services to his client."

This listening through internal objects is a source of limitation which is here to stay. The therapist's responsibility is to know to distinguish those countertransferential reactions which are inevitable, which are structually given in the interaction of two particular human beings, from those which are imposed due to his pathology or preoccupation. As early as the 1930's, Racker, who was reared in classical analytic circles, already noted with great sophistication that the analyst of serious mind must be freed to use the structurally given countertransferential reaction to his patient's advantage. He implies that the very fear of the resonance of internal objects in the therapist can do more harm than an occasional counter-transferential abuse.

Guideline

A therapist is vulnerable to harmful and possibly unethical actions stemming from countertransferential anxiety when the activities of his patient have real potential to threaten his own personality integration or the stability of his adjustment. Although the therapist is sometimes deeply affected by a patient, he may not be dependent on that patient for a significant contribution to his own self concept or other ego function.

Examples of Violation

1. A therapist puts tremendous pressure on his patients to get better. Patients become conditioned to bring him elaborate reports of success with an occasional confession of failure thrown in parenthetically. The therapist who promotes such a reaction may suffer from a deep sense of impotence and ineffectiveness or any one of a number of dynamics which is experienced in an excessively strong need for proof of his being Good and Able. In effect, the patients are burdened with supporting his ideal self-concept.

2. A therapist is concerned that a nervous twitch in his eyelid may start if a patient discusses certain sexual fantasies. Whether this man's patients were indeed conditioned to avoid free presentation of sexual fantasy or whether they introjected the sense of the therapist's shame and guilt in relation to these fantasies

is not known. All that can be said is that the therapist's anxiety about his own exposure, through his being caught in voyeuristic excitement (the eyelid symptom), may inhibit progress or even reinforce symptoms.

3. A therapist maneuvers patients into a crystalized role of weakness such as sick one, child, inexperienced or naive person. Since patients in these roles usually exhibit strong positive transferences, the polarization of brilliant therapist and weak, incomplete patient can continue for a very long time. The therapist is clearly dependent upon his patient to provide the setting for the establishment or maintenance of his own stature. The assumption is that the sense of stature is not available to this therapist outside his office.

Fee Reduction of Patient Already in Treatment*

During the course of psychotherapy, a patient may suffer financial reverses or increased financial responsibility such that he can no longer pay his customary fee. In a case wherein the reduction of frequency of sessions would be clinically contraindicated, the ethical issue is, of course, the definition of responsibility to a patient who cannot continue to pay a fair and already established fee for treatment.

The therapist is responsible for the consequences of the relationship that he builds with his patient. His permitting himself to fall into a role which is relatively critical and at the same time not easily transferable to another therapist commits him to take some responsibility when the patient cannot continue to pay full fee. He may temporarily reduce the fee, forego the fee, or arrange for later partial or full payment. It is generally not advisable to see the patient without fee for a long time, since such an arrangement can create thorny countertransferential problems. The latter reference is made to the therapist's vulnerability to feelings

---

*APA Code, Principle XII a: "In establishing rates for professional services the psychologist considers carefully both the ability of the client to meet the financial burden and the charges made by other professional persons engaged in comparable work. He is willing to contribute a portion of his services to work for which he receives little or no financial return."

of impatience at times of resistance, especially the tendency to self-referential interpretations of resistance.

Guideline

A therapist in private practice should have a sufficiently large financial margin between projected income from fees and projected expenses so that he is free to occasionally reduce or forego a fee should he judge this clinically advisable.

Example

The patient is a man in his late twenties who has had severe emotional problems since childhood. He had made two suicidal gestures and was frightened by a recent deepening depression and sense of depersonalization. He lived at home with his mother who paid for psychotherapy. The patient responded remarkably well in treatment and was able to back up his increased feelings of independence and self-sufficiency by moving away from home into an apartment which he financed through his first job. Once financially independent, he ran into some unexpected expenses which made it impossible for him to continue to see the therapist upon whom he was still rather dependent in making the remainder of the transition to adult responsibility.

The therapist reduced the fee by one half for several months. It was explained to the patient that if he were unable to arrange his finances during this time, the therapist would make referral to a younger colleague or a clinic where the fee would be lower. A very specific date was set for the time when the fee would be returned to normal. In this case, the patient made tremendous effort and landed a job which covered the return to original fee at the set deadline.

Acceptance of Patients of Other Mental Health Professionals*

Unless a patient is legally directed, he has the right to leave one therapist and choose another. This does not imply that the

---

*APA Code, Principle II: "A psychologist does not normally offer professional services to a person receiving psychological assistance from another professional worker except by agreement with the other worker or after the termination of the client's relationship with the other professional worker."

chosen therapist should accept him. Although the decision is a clinical and not an ethical judgment, the whole matter of dealing with distraught, dissatisfied patients who are in treatment with a colleague is fraught with potential for unethical behavior on a countertransferential basis.

The aspect of the problem emphasized here is that the therapist should be free and able to accept or reject such patients and that he should not be subject to a strong bias which presses him to meet or reject the patient's manifest demands without some further investigation. Therapists who have a strong savior mentality are particularly prone to immediate acceptance. This policy is also seen among therapists who are isolated from their colleagues or who adhere to a given school and limit their professional contacts accordingly. These people are open to unethical acts in accepting patients who are in treatment with colleagues because they tend to catagorically downgrade work which differs from their own.

Guideline

The decision to accept a patient who wishes to leave treatment with a colleague is a clinical, not an ethical, judgment. Consultation with the previous therapist is strongly recommended in order to get more information from which to make this clinical judgment and in order to inform the previous therapist of the nature of the patient's dissatisfaction so that he also can make a clinical judgment and offer opinion. When the patient is accepted or rejected without an attempt at direct investigation of the previous treatment, it is likely that the judgment was made on unnecessarily incomplete data.

Example

A middle-aged woman consulted a psychologist whom she had heard at a panel discussion a year before. She was in treatment with a psychiatrist at the time and had continued to see him with good result. She called the psychologist at this time because of a recent dispute with her psychiatrist whom she accused of being "irresponsible" and "grandiose." The issue had been her belief that she had endocrine imbalance which was causing her mood swings. She claimed that the psychiatrist was unwilling to accept these findings of her internist and that he had gotten angry with her when she questioned his medical competence. She had terminated her treatment with him a week before.

The psychologist explained that he could not consider taking her on as a patient without speaking with the psychiatrist and the internist. The patient reluctantly gave permission, and the psychiatrist was contacted. The psychiatrist explained that the patient was hypochondriacal and had a long history of somatic delusion; he had spoken with the internist and had received reports which were all negative. Copies were sent to the psychologist. He explained that the current picture was the typical forerunner of an acute psychotic episode. Since a careful control of medication was required in this case, it was agreed that the patient would be referred to another psychiatrist if she were unwilling to return to the former one.

Treatment of Specific Symptoms*

It is often said that presenting problems of patients have moved from disabling symptoms to broad characterologic maladjustments over the years since Freud's repressed Victorian times. Whether or not this is so, a good number of patients still come complaining of definable symptoms for which they want relief as quickly as possible. A number of ethical issues arise when the psychologist consulted is committed to techniques designed to bring about personality change of some breadth. His tendency to demonstrate immediately to the patient that his symptom is like the above-water part of an iceberg and that the whole iceberg needs attention may be ethically challenged. The problem here is that the therapist must be free to consider several factors before he counsels the patient on the scope of treatment. He must consider: (a) the specific request of the patient, (b) the financial and other external strains of long-term treatment, (c) evidence in the professional field on the relative effectiveness of various

*The introductory section of Principle VIII of the APA Code: "The psychologist informs his prospective client of the important aspects of the potential relationship that might affect the client's decision to enter the relationship."

symptom-focused approaches in terms of immediate relief and sustaining benefit.

Guideline

The patient is to be thought of as coming for help from the field, not from the individual therapist, even though the referral may have been very specific. It is the therapist's responsibility to be well aware of developments in the field and to be prepared to present to the patient the techniques and demonstrated claims of other responsible methods of treatment.

Suicide Threat

In order to respond properly to suicide threats, the therapist must be able to make a fairly rapid determination about the meaning and seriousness of the threat. The differential diagnosis of the suicide idea is often extremely difficult to make; to wit, Sullivan's requiring the distinction between ". . . a pretty stable obsessional state" and "an indefinite obsessional schizoid reaction" (Sullivan, 1956). Once he knows the personality organization along these lines, he follows a corresponding differential technique of intervention for the suicidal patient. Other writers stress the importance of differentiating ego syntonic and ego alien suicidal ideation. Or, there is the matter of knowing whether the suicidal ideation simply serves as a safety valve, as in Nietzsche's "The thought of suicide has saved many lives."

Making these complex differentiations under time pressure requires that the therapist be as free from anxiety and other distracting emotions and considerations as is possible. This means that he must have available clear concepts of his responsibility to patients in general and to the suicidal patient in particular. Historically, such formulations follow the whole range, with again Szasz representing one pole in his statement that the analyst "cannot allow it (the suicide threat) to become a ground for modifying the contract. This understanding benefits both patient and therapist. For some people, self-destruction is more of a possibility than others. The analyst's task is to analyze this craving or fear as he would any other" (Szasz, 1965).

The nearly opposite view, wherein the therapist assumes some personal responsibility for keeping the patient alive, is well represented by Fromm-Reichman: "But no psychiatrist can carry the total burden of the responsibility for the self-induced death of his patients. This holds true especially with regard to the unpredictable suicidal impulses of some schizophrenics" (Fromm-Reichman, 1953). Her releasing us from "total burden" still leaves quite a residue!

The important point in view of ethical considerations is that both these analysts follow their statements with careful warning that the therapist not get embroiled in deep personal responsibility for life and death such that he is motivated by personal fear in his actions toward the suicidal patient. Frieda Fromm-Reichman speaks of a patient who said he "would have liked to kill himself if only he could be sure that it would matter to the doctor" (Fromm-Reichman, 1953).

Guideline

Although a therapist is free to formulate his own concept of responsibility to the suicidal patient, he should carefully reconsider formulations which would likely lead him to feeling personally threatened by a patient's suicide threat. This is likely to occur when a therapist views a patient's suicide as undeniable public evidence of a weakness in his own work or person. The most common errors made by threatened therapists are (a) inhibition about getting help from other professionals and (b) failure to act firmly in accordance with their own best clinical judgments.

Example

1. After a period of decrease in his effectiveness at work, a man of 42 confided to his boss that he was increasingly depressed and continually thinking of suicide. The boss referred him to his own former therapist whom he described as a savior, a man of exceptional talent who could no doubt help.

After an extended initial interview, the psychologist had no question that the patient was well beyond the suicidal ideation stage. The patient had already suicided psychologically, was becoming anorexic, and was waiting quite passively for a convenient time to perform the act. Suicide was extremely ego syntonic. At the close of the interview, the patient felt that he might try to work out his difficulties with this therapist; it certainly could not hurt. The psychologist did not take the patient but instead referred him immediately to a hospital-connected psychiatrist whose work he knew and whom he trusted. He felt that the psychiatrist would be a far more appropriate person to handle the immediate problems of the anorexia, possibly hospitalize the patient quickly and give ECT or drugs as indicated. The judgment was that drastic intervention was required.

2. A schizophrenic woman of 30 calmly stated during an interview that she sees no point in continuing life. After a carefully prepared and aggressive statement of her view, the room falls silent and she becomes very agitated because the therapist does not argue with her or even analyze her statement.

Although the suicide was described in detail in terms of its motivation and actual mechanics, the psychologist judged that the patient's hunger for a counterargument was a strong positive prognostic sign. The patient was not sent for any emergency psychiatric intervention. The patient did extremely well in therapy. Suicidal ideation was soon put aside when direct means of affecting significant persons in her world were developed.

Judgments Outside Psychotherapists' Own Discipline*

Patients in psychotherapy generally take services from a number of other professionals. On occasion they will talk to the therapist about suspicions of negligence or incompetence of such persons. Although the psychotherapist would have no professional knowledge from which to make judgments about such suspicions, there is an ethical issue as to whether he should concern himself

*APA Code, Principle II b: "The psychologist who engages in practice assists his client in obtaining professional help for all important aspects of his problem that fall outside the boundaries of his own competence." This principle requires, for example, that provisions be made for the diagnosis and treatment of relevant medical problems and for referral to or consultation with other specialists. Principle VII i: "In the use of accepted drugs for psychotherapeutic purposes, special care needs to be exercised by the psychologist to assure himself that the collaborating physician provides suitable safeguards for the client."

with the matter when his knowledge of the patient does not clearly contraindicate the possible validity of the suspicion.

Guideline

When there is credibility to a patient's suspicion of incompetence and negligence in the service he receives from a professional of another discipline, the therapist should help the patient to act on his suspicions. He might best begin by using the treatment tools on which he relies customarily. For example, the analyst may interpret around the fear of confronting authority, and the behaviorist may help prepare the patient for the confrontation through some specially adapted assertion training. When such customary tools are ineffective and there is insufficient time for modification and new attempts, the therapist may avail himself of the freedom assumed by any concerned person and suggest that the patient get an independent opinion from a reliable member of the discipline involved. (If the situation permits, it is advisable that the therapist contact the professional in question to inform him of the advice he plans to give or has given the patient.)

Example

A middle-aged man with serious physical disability of several years' duration is referred to a psychologist by a neighbor who is in treatment with the psychologist. History reveals two psychiatric hospitalizations, a suicide attempt in his thirties and a generally marginal adjustment. The present picture is mounting depression and feelings of depersonalization, alternating with periods of high anxiety and explosive behavior. Physical pain is described as torturous. After the first few months of therapy, the patient became more directly expressive and complained of his physician's lack of attention, overly optimistic prognostications which only added to disappointment, no descernible improvement, and particularly the physician's lack of attention to complaints of pain in body systems previously not affected. Considering the patient's mounting depression and increase in suicidal fantasy, the psychologist helped the patient to act on his desire for another medical opinion and contacted the physician to inform him of this action. In this particular case, the specialist consulted was able to help isolate a factor which was causing spread and general exacerbation of symptoms.

Some readers will find these guidelines far too restrictive to permit what they would call effective practice while others will find them too loose to be of real use. I can only hope that these readers will take the guidelines as a spring board for their own formulations. The fundamental ethical responsibility of all clinicians is to set out their ideas first for their own scrutiny and then for interaction with others.

It is probably naive to set a goal of real ethical uniformity in the field. In addition to all the professional divergence, there is research evidence that there are demonstrable personality variables which operate systematically in the choice of ethical stance in normal adults (McCord and Clemes, 1964).

At this time of exploration and revolution in the field, it is critical that the more traditional ethics which are reflected in this paper, not be tossed aside without something to replace them or at least that old ethical debates are replaced by new ones.

REFERENCES

American Psychologist, *Ethical Standards of Psychologists, 18*:56-60, 1963.

Lomont, James F.: *The Ethics of Behavior Therapy,* Psychological Reports, *14* (2):519-531, 1964.

Lowe, C. Marshall: *Value-Orientations in Counseling and Psychotherapy,* Chandler Publications, 1969.

McCord, Joan and Clemes, Stanley: *Conscience Orientation and Dimensions of Personality,* Behavioral Science, *9* (1):18-29, 1964.

Racker, Heinrich: *Ethics and Psychoanalysis and the Psychoanalysis of Ethics,* International Journal of Psychoanalysis, *47* (1):63-80, 1966.

Fromm-Reichman, Frieda: *Principles of Intensive Psychotherapy,* London, George Allen and Unwin, Ltd., 1953.

Sullivan, Harry Stack: *Clinical Studies in Psychiatry.* New York, W. W. Norton and Company, 1956.

Szasz, Thomas S.: *The Ethics of Psychoanalysis.* New York, Dell Publishing Company, Inc., 1965.

Chapter 9

PSYCHODIAGNOSTIC PRACTICE

Florence Halpern

The first thing that must be said in discussing a psychodiagnostic practice is that it should never be exclusively that. To be an effective diagnostician whose reports have value for the patient and the therapist, the diagnostician must also have firsthand experience with the treatment process. Only when he has such experience can he really know what kinds of information a therapist finds truly useful and what actually will add to his understanding of his patient, as well as the ways in which he can best explore with the patient the problems which caused him to seek therapy and then develop in the patient the strengths he needs. While it may be a matter of circumstances or temperament that causes a psychologist to turn primarily to diagnosis rather than therapy, in the final analysis, these two activities are closely related aspects of an integrated process—two sides of the same coin—and should not be arbitrarily separated.

A young psychologist starting out in private practice is actually very likely to accept whatever referrals come his way, be they diagnosis or therapy. As his practice grows, he may focus more and more on one or the other aspect of this interrelated process, but hopefully it will never be solely one or the other. However, as his practice expands, the psychologist is very likely to be seen by his profession and by referring agencies and individuals as primarily either a diagnostician or a therapist.

STARTING A PRIVATE DIAGNOSTIC PRACTICE

The diagnostician generally begins his private practice as a part-time operation, while working full or part time at a hospital, clinic, social agency, school, etc. His referrals are therefore likely to come from his co-workers, from the psychiatrists, psychologists,

166

social workers, pediatricians, speech therapists, etc. who, in addition to their hospital and clinic affiliations, are engaged in private therapeutic practice. In addition, once it becomes known that he is in private practice, the diagnostician may get referrals from former teachers, fellow students, and others who knew him and worked with him in the "early days." For instance, a student may have so impressed his diagnostic supervisor that he is happy to refer his therapy patients to him. The same thing may happen as a consequence of the contacts the diagnostician made during his internship.

From such beginnings, other sources of referral develop. A patient changes his therapist, and the new therapist requests a copy of the diagnostic report. Finding it helpful, he begins to refer some of his own patients to the diagnostician. Similarly, one therapist may tell another about "this psychologist" whom he has found very helpful, "who really seems to know what it's all about."

In addition to the referrals that come from friends and colleagues, the psychologist seeks referrals by sending out announcements to individuals whom he thinks might find his services helpful. Such an announcement would indicate the psychologist's right to practice; namely, that he is certified in the state in which he works, what his specialties are, where his office is located and the hours he can be reached. Most psychologists indicate that patients are seen by appointment only. If the psychodiagnostician has an ABEPP diploma, this may be indicated on the announcement. However, membership or fellowship in the American Psychological Association is not to be used as an indication of competence.

In addition to sending out announcements, it is sometimes helpful to write a letter or possibly even visit some of the large social agencies in the immediate area, explaining the type of service offered, the fees involved, etc. In this way, the diagnostician may become part of a panel of diagnostic consultants to whom the agency turns when testing is required.

As a practice grows, referrals are likely to come from patients as well as professionals. A mother whose child had a pleasant testing experience and who benefited from the test findings may tell another mother whose child has problems just how constructive the testing was in her case. Similarly, an adult who wants to know if he "really needs therapy" may be encouraged by a friend who has been tested to seek out diagnostic services for this purpose.

While the young diagnostician naturally welcomes all referrals, he should certainly not accept those which he is not equipped to handle. To do so would be a grave mistake professionally, as well as ethically unacceptable. For example, some students receive little or no training with children, and subsequent experiences during internship and other affiliations have focused around adults rather than children. For such a psychologist to attempt to interpret the test productions of children or work with infants would be quite disastrous.

THE OFFICE

Opening an office can, of course, be a somewhat risky financial venture. Rather than do this at the outset of private practice, many psychologists have found it more expedient to rent an office on an hourly or daily basis. In large cities, such rentals are generally available. As a practice flourishes, sharing an office with a colleague or having an office of one's own becomes the next appropriate step.

Using a portion of one's house or apartment as an office has advantages and disadvantages. The advantages are financial (some of the rental and upkeep of the home can be deducted as a business expense) while the expenditure of time and energy in going from home to office and back again avoided. However, if the home is used, the physical layout becomes most important. Patients must be able to come and go without encountering members of the family; and the family should not be required to curtail its activities to accommodate patients. Furthermore, the location of the home and its accessibility to transportation and parking facilities are important.

The office should not be excessively large or small, and while it should be tastefully furnished, it should not offer distractions. Test materials should be so placed that the psychologist has access to whatever he needs at any moment without having to leave his seat at the desk. Certainly moving about the room with any great frequency is not desirable. Attention should, of course, be paid to adequate lighting.

MAKING APPOINTMENTS

In most cases, the patient is told by his therapist to make an appointment with the diagnostician. The therapist generally provides the patient with the diagnostician's name, phone number, and address. However, in some instances, the therapist may arrange the appointment, and in the case of a referral from a social agency it is almost always the social worker who arranges the time for the client she wants tested.

Some therapists call before giving the patient the diagnostician's name, asking if the latter has time and is interested in testing his patient. In such instances, the therapist is also likely to give some details about the case, his reasons for referral, and the specific questions he would like to have answered. In other instances, especially when the therapist and the diagnostician have worked together for some time, the patient is likely to call and state that he has been told by his doctor to make an appointment to "take some tests." Occasionally the therapist whom the patient names as the referral source is a stranger to the diagnostician, someone he does not know at all. It is not advisable to communicate this to the patient but simply to make the appointment and then contact the therapist in order to learn from him what he expects from the diagnostician, what his experience with diagnostic testing has been, etc.

In arranging his appointments, the diagnostician should allow sufficient time to complete a test series. He should not make appointments so close to one another that he feels rushed because while he is testing one patient, another is waiting outside. For the relatively experienced diagnostician, two hours is usually sufficient time for a test battery, but naturally this varies from individual to individual. One is never sure about the patient until one starts working with him and learns how productive or unproductive, how fast or how slow, how compulsive and detailed he may be in his responses. If testing goes on much over two hours, the patient is likely to be fatigued or there will be another patient waiting. Under such circumstances, a second session can be arranged, even though most patients seem to prefer completing the testing in one session, and this can usually be done. However, there are advantages in setting up a second visit, especially with small children. It is not unusual to find that the child's (and even the adult's) mood and attitudes change from one visit to the next. Even his appearance may alter, being quite "sloppy" on one occasion and very neat the next.

FEES

When the therapist arranges the appointment for his patient, he will probably inquire about the fee unless he has worked with the diagnostician previously and therefore knows what his charges are. There may be occasions when the therapist indicates that his patient is not in a position to pay the usual fee (currently from 100 to 150 dollars), explaining that he is seeing the individual at a reduced fee and requesting the diagnostician to show the patient some consideration. On the other hand, there are times when the therapist makes a point of telling the diagnostician that a particular patient can well afford top fees or that the patient will have no respect for the psychological report unless he pays heavily for it.

If the therapist has not gone into the monetary aspects of the matter with the patient, the patient himself is likely to ask about this when he calls for an appointment. However, some patients do not raise the question, and it is then advisable for the diagnostician to tell the patient what the fee will be. Some patients know what the testing is likely to cost them, having had previous experience along such lines or having heard about testing costs from relatives or friends. Others are quite shocked at what they consider "exorbitant charges." They see the testing as the equivalent of a therapy session and cannot understand why they are expected to pay more than they would for a therapy hour. Not only should it be pointed out that testing takes more than an hour, but that the diagnostician spends several subsequent hours scoring, interpreting, and communicating his findings.

An experienced and skilled diagnostician can generally work faster than a neophyte and so finishes in a comparatively shorter time than the beginner. A patient may then complain that his friend or relative had three hours of testing, and he does not understand why he should pay the same amount for an hour and a half or two hours of testing. It is not always easy to get the patient to appreciate that he has received the same tests as his friend, very possibly more skillfully administered and interpreted, and probably with less strain for him. However, the effort has to be made. The picture of the beginning typist or piano player, compared with the virtuoso, sometimes helps clarify the issue.

INITIAL CONTACTS WITH THE PATIENT

Some patients call and make their appointment in business-like fashion without many questions, discussions, or arguments. Others seem unable to accept any time offered them, and one cannot help but feel that there is some element of resistance in such cases. Among the questions asked are, of course, the matter of fee, how long the session will take, what kind of tests are used, what happens to the results, and so on.

In response to the question about time, the answer should be to the effect that the testing generally takes somewhere in the neighborhood of two hours but that every individual is different and an exact statement of time cannot be made. How one answers the questions about the kinds of tests to be administered depends to a degree on the amount of sophistication the patient possesses in this connection. Hence, it is advisable to ask him if he is familiar with tests and gear the explanation accordingly. In most instances, saying that they help the therapist understand him more fully and that they are generally called "personality" tests seems to satisfy the questioner. In rare instances, there is a concern about the inclusion of some kind of physical test. For instance, a mother called to make an appointment for her child, saying that the therapist wanted him to have a "raw shock." She then immediately asked, "Will it hurt him very much?"

If the patient does not ask appropriate questions when he phones for his appointment, they should be raised, at least briefly, before actual testing begins. With knowledgable patients, aside from the discussion of fee if this has not been settled, all that is required is a brief sentence or two such as, "You know that I'm going to give you some tests that your therapist wants you to have. They will help him understand you better and so they'll be of help to you." With less sophisticated and more anxious patients, more time and effort may be needed to reassure them.

Some patients use such opening statements to begin a long, overly detailed discussion of their difficulties and the episodes in their lives that they feel are responsible for these difficulties. Thus, a patient may go on and on about her insomnia, with accompanying descriptions of the traumas she experienced when her mother died and her husband had to go out of town, etc. In certain instances, it becomes necessary to interrupt such a recital, stating that you have the picture and that it is now necessary to start the tests.

The majority of patients fall between the extremes of sophistication on the one hand and excessive anxiety and/or circumstantiality on the other hand. For most patients, then, relatively little time needs to be spent developing a relationship or establishing "rapport." While the relationship should be one which makes the patient feel as comfortable as possible and leaves him with the impression that the experience was a positive or even an enjoyable one, the contact is generally a one-time affair and questions of transference or countertransference do not enter into the picture to any extent, though they cannot always be totally avoided.

Patients frequently ask if they will be informed about the test results, if they will be given a copy of the report, or at least allowed to read it. The customary response to such requests is that the diagnostician does not give reports to anyone but the referring professional. What happens after that is up to the therapist or case worker. If the therapist wishes to give the patient a copy of the report or read portions of it to him (and a number do this) that is his decision to make. Some therapists state that with certain patients, the reports have a catalytic effect, speeding up communication and associations.

Even when the patient accepts the idea that he cannot have the written report, he is likely at the end of the testing to ask for some impressions. Explaining that it takes a number of hours to analyze the results generally resolves that issue. Sometimes the patient will call a few days or a week later to ask for the results. Once again he has to be told that the therapist has the report and will probably discuss it with him when he feels the time is appropriate.

There are a number of reasons why it is inadvisable for the diagnostician to discuss the test results with the patient. One of the chief ones is simply a question of semantics. He may talk about the same problems that the therapist does, but because he uses different words, the patient may get a very different concept of what his problems and possible solution for his problems are. In addition, the diagnostician in interpreting may bring into focus areas that the therapist prefers to leave dormant for a time.

Because he so much wants to have the report or because in certain instances he is actually considering a change of therapist, the patient may insist that he have the report to give his new doctor. He is then assured that the report will be sent to any therapist he designates.

Some patients are very concerned about the confidentiality of the report. School children and even high school and college students sometimes ask if the results are going to their school or their parents. Occasionally an adult will even ask if the report will be shown his wife or his boss should these individuals request this. It is most important to reassure the patient on this point, advising him that the report will go only to the referring therapist unless he, the patient, asks that it be sent elsewhere. It is advisable to get such requests or releases in writing.

In the case of the patient who has referred himself rather than come at the suggestion of his therapist, teacher, guidance counselor, etc., the story is, of course, a very different one. The diagnostician then has the responsibility of telling the patient what the test findings indicate. This is not done in technical language but in a way that is understandable and meaningful to the patient and above all else, helpful to him in planning subsequent steps. Such an interview or interviews with the patient do not take place at the conclusion of the testing, although the patient often expects this to occur. Such questions as, "Well, doc, what do you think? Am I a candidate for the bughouse?" or less dramatically but more pathetically, "Do you think anyone can help me?" convey the patient's deep concern about himself. Yet it would be a mistake to respond to such pleadings without carefully evaluating the test findings. The patient must therefore be told that it takes a little time to analyze his productions and an appointment should be set up for sometime in the near future at which time the diagnostician will be in far better position to answer his questions and make constructive suggestions than he is at the conclusion of the testing session.

In discussing his test results with him, it is well to begin with the problem the patient offers as his reason for seeking help, since this is an issue of which he is aware and about which he can talk. The underlying causes for this problem, its etiology and its impact on significant aspects of the patient's life need not be entered into at this point, even if the tests provide information about these matters. At this juncture, emphasis should be on the possibilities for change in the patient, his environment, or both, and suggestions should be made as to how such changes could be brought about.

In the greatest number of cases, the recommendation is likely to be "therapy." However, this is not a simple formula or a pat answer. The diagnostician must determine what kind of therapy would be best for the patient—whether analysis, psychoanalytically oriented therapy, supportive therapy, group therapy, family therapy, behavior therapy, sensitivity training, etc., would be most efficacious. He must also be ready to make appropriate recommendations, taking into account what the patient can afford, where he lives, whether he is likely to respond better to a man or a woman therapist, and so on. There are, of course, instances when therapy is not indicated, and other solutions to the patient's difficulties must be sought and implemented.

TESTS

Which tests the diagnostician will administer depends in part on the reason for the referral and the questions to be answered. In almost all instances, the concern is with dynamics and diagnosis, and so with few exceptions, the Rorschach and a second projective test (Thematic Apperception, Make-A-Picture-Story Test, etc.) are given. Most diagnosticians also rely heavily on figure drawings, and these have become part of the customary battery for most psychologists. For all children, and for adults when there is any question of thought disorder, impaired functioning, or limited intelligence, a formal intelligence test is certainly indicated. Even when such questions do not arise, it is helpful to administer certain selected subtests of the Wechsler Adult Intelligence Scale in order to ascertain the way in which the patient conceptualizes.

Where specific questions have been asked or where the patient's mode of responding raises questions in the diagnostician's mind, additional tests should, of course, be used. In cases where the issue of neurological impairment arises, the Bender Gestalt test and other tests geared to detect organicity should be given. Proverbs and fables are generally quite helpful in establishing the diagnosis of schizophrenia.

While the interview cannot be considered a formal diagnostic tool, it certainly plays a part in helping the diagnostician formulate a global picture of the patient. However, judgement must be exercised in using the interview. When a patient is referred by a therapist and has been seeing the therapist for some time, the chances are that he has had an extensive and intensive interview and might well resent going through the same biographical and emotion-laden material again. However, if such is not the case, if the therapist has not engaged the patient in an interview, or if the patient has come to the diagnostician of his own accord rather than being referred by someone else, then an interview is certainly required. Skill in interviewing is certainly as important as skill in giving and interpreting tests.

What the diagnostician knows about the patient is likely to vary greatly from case to case, depending on who makes the referral. As has already been indicated, some therapists always call in reference to the patient, providing the diagnostician with relevant information and the reasons for wanting diagnostic testing. Others communicate nothing about the patient, and some even insist that no questions be asked the patient, so that the test findings are, in a sense, uncontaminated by what the diagnostician knows about the patient's history.

In general, a certain amount of biographical data seems pertinent, along with the patient's reasons for seeking help. In some cases, the interview which permits the patient to talk about himself serves to relieve his tension and acts as a kind of ice breaker, leading into formal testing. In other instances, the patient is so anxious about the testing that the sooner testing gets started, the better. Once they realize what the tests are like, they generally can relax a bit. In such cases, any interviewing that needs to be done is best left until the conclusion of the actual testing.

SPECIAL PROBLEMS

Occasionally during the course of testing, a patient may ask the diagnostician what he thinks of the therapist he is currently seeing. Such a question should never be answered directly. Instead, the response should be something like, "If you have any questions or doubts about your therapist, why don't you discuss it with him. That's really the best way."

Sometimes a patient may phone anywhere from six months to ten years after the testing occurred. After reminding the diagnostician of the previous contact, the patient may go on to ask advice about a specific matter, anything from should he get married, should he change his job, to a request for recommendations for a therapist. If the patient is in therapy, he should be urged to raise the question with the therapist. If he is no longer seeing a therapist—and such is usually the case—the earlier material should be reviewed by the diagnostician and an appointment made with the patient to discuss his current problem. The diagnostician is then in a relatively good position to make a constructive recommendation or referral.

CHILDREN

Children naturally do not ask for therapy or for testing. These things are arranged for them by their parents, and what the child is told about the testing experience varies greatly from case to case. When asked why they think they are being tested, the majority of children insist that they do not know. If pushed to guess, they are likely to say something about "finding out how smart I am." When asked what his mother told him before bringing him to the diagnostician's office, the response generally takes one of two forms. Either the mother explained about a lady who "plays games," or told the child nothing beyond the fact that he was going to see someone who would ask him questions. It is the rare child who can formulate a statement about his problems or relate the testing to them. Occasionally, a child indicates that "The doctor I go to wanted me to do this," but he generally cannot or will not say why he goes to the doctor.

Sometimes in phoning for an appointment, a mother will ask, "What should I tell him about where he's going and what he's going to do?" Not knowing the child, this is not an easy question to answer. It is a good idea to ask if the child knows he has problems. For example, a bed wetter may want very much to overcome his difficulty so that he can go to camp; or a child who has trouble with other children yearns to make friends. In such cases, the child can be told that he is going to see someone who tries to help children with their problems. When the child is not aware that he has a problem or refuses to admit to one, the testing can be explained as a kind of "check-up." Parents should be warned not to give the child the idea that all he will do is "play games," since this is likely to interfere with a sustained effort at meeting assignments as well as he might.

Although the child cannot or will not communicate his difficulties when asked why he goes to a therapist or why he is being tested, he generally responds informatively to the diagnostician's efforts to state his problems for him. For instance, if asked whether or not he fights with his siblings, a child may agree quite happily that he "sure does," or may insist that "They always start with me." Similarly, it is possible to get answers to questions about the adequacy of school work, relations with neighborhood children, etc. Only on rare occasions has a child stated, "I asked to go to a head doctor." Such children are generally extremely anxious and depressed and also intelligent and sophisticated enough to realize that their distress can be alleviated with appropriate help.

In addition to whatever "interviewing" or conversation one has with the child, an interview with the parents is certainly indicated. It is best if this interview does not take place at the time of the testing, thus leaving the child sitting in the waiting area, well aware that he is the subject of discussion. If the interview has to take place at the time of testing, it is better to hold it at the end of session rather than keep the child anxiously waiting, unsure of what is going to happen to him.

The interview with the parent, whether it occurs at some time before or after the child is sesen by the diagnostician, is very likely to be seized on by the mother or father as an opportunity to elicit answers to the problems that are disturbing them. It requires considerable understanding and strength to resist such pleas for help before one is ready or able to do so effectively. If the interview occurs sometime before the actual testing session the situation is not so difficult since the diagnostician does not yet know the child. However, this does not necessarily stop an anxious or guilt-ridden parent. When the interview takes place after the testing, the parent is very likely to be most insistent on knowing what the diagnostician has discovered, what he thinks the problem really is, and if it can be overcome. Again, as in the case of the adult, it is best to refer the parent to the therapist who is treating the child, rather than offering his own interpretations. Most parents agree to this, albeit somewhat reluctantly, but others continue to press for a firsthand interpretation.

Not infrequently, it is the parent who needs and wants help, but because he cannot or will not recognize his need, he uses the child as the entering wedge to therapy. Sometimes a parent can be readily brought to a realization of her need by asking a simple question. For instance, a mother who spent more than ten minutes explaining how upset she gets when her six-year-old does not keep his room as neat as she would like him to, stopped short when asked, "Why is this so important to you?" or "Why does this mean so much to you?." At this point she asked, "Do you think I need therapy?" to which the diagnostician responded with "Let's talk about it." The upshot of the matter was that the mother, not the child, was seen in treatment.

Sometimes on the basis of the test findings, the possibility of neurological impairment comes into consideration. Suggesting that the child have a neurological examination is extremely disturbing to some parents. They can tolerate the idea of emotional problems and/or learning difficulties, but somehow the idea of even minimal brain damage proves very frightening.

Because of the anxiety it mobilizes as well as the additional expenses it entails, the question should be raised about the need for or value of a neurological examination. Even if brain damage is established, what can be done about it? Yet, in the case of a child, awareness of the existence of such damage may alter educational recommendations and procedures and may enable the parents to be more realistic about their goals for the child. Moreover, one cannot be sure that the damage is not the result of an ongoing process which requires medical attention.

In the case of a parent who has come to the diagnostician at the suggestion of a friend or relative, rather than at the recommendation of a therapist, "interpretation" of the test findings by the diagnostician is essential. Such interpretation should involve a careful exploration with the parent of what he sees as the child's difficulties and his general picture of the child. Such interviews usually provide the diagnostician with a valid concept of the parent's feelings and attitudes toward the child, thus rounding out the picture obtained from the tests. In discussing the test results with the parent, formal diagnosis is certainly not necessary; neither are the details about the underlying dynamics. What is required is a relatively simple explanation of what the child is experiencing and how these experiences and feelings tie in with the behaviors that are troubling the parents. In many instances, the parent is not only seeking understanding and advice but also reassurance and alleviation of guilt feelings.

No matter what one says to parents, there is a strong tendency on their part to see the situation in very fragmented and concrete terms. For example, after spending considerable time explaining to a parent that what the child does is essentially a bid for attention, a mother is likely to respond with, "But Doctor, what do I do when he hits his sister?"

Whether a child was sent for testing by a therapist or at the suggestion of a friend, it often happens that the parent asks that a report be sent to a pediatrician, a teacher, a guidance counselor, the family doctor, etc. The report to the pediatrician should not employ the same language used in the report to the therapist, if as is usually the case, the language tends to be somewhat technical. The same applies to the family doctor. As far as sending a report to a school is concerned, it is a good idea to ask the mother why she wants this, whether the school has actually requested the report. Even when a child has come for testing because of school problems, what is communicated to the school has to be carefully considered. The school does not need and cannot use past history, etiological factors, or dynamics with any great skill. Instead, in a school report, emphasis should be on the constructive ways that the school can help the child learn and adjust. Diagnostic labels should again be avoided.

Sometimes the diagnostician is familiar with the school and its educational philosophy. When he has such knowledge, when he has worked with the school personnel in the past, he is better able to gauge what the school can be told. He is then also in a favorable position to help the parents determine whether or not the school is the right one for the child. If the diagnostician does not have such information, he should try to get it by contacting the school or talking with parents he knows who have children in the school. Anyone who plans to work with children, even if children do not constitute his entire practice, should be well informed about the schools in his area, both public and private.

REPORTING TEST RESULTS

Test findings are usually transmitted to the referring agent in writing. However, written reports are sometimes preceded by a telephone communication if the therapist expresses urgency in a particular case or because the therapist may wish to communicate something that for one reason or another should not go into a written report.

Traditionally written reports begin with a description of the patient's behavior, how he experienced the examiner and the testing situation. The extent of the patient's anxiety in relation to the experience and his way of coping with that anxiety are especially important. For instance, there are patients who try to deny their discomfort by recourse to persistent and inappropriate laughter. There are others who treat the situation in a belittling, even contemptuous fashion, asking such things as, "Does this stuff really prove anything?" or, "Wouldn't what I said be different on a different day when I wasn't so tired?," etc. Such patients want desperately to minimize the significance of anything that the tests may say about them. Some patients do everything possible in order to delay the actual introduction of the tests, much like people who put off going to the dentist. Such people are likely to spend an inordinate amount of time answering the few questions they are asked at the outset of the session, that is, their age, marital status, number of children, type of work and educational level. It is amazing the ingenuity some patients develop in talking about such commonplace matters, all in an effort to avoid coming to grips with basic issues. In such cases, every last detail about every member of the family will be recounted, as will the difficulties that brought the patient to therapy. If such a recital is interrupted by the diagnostician, as it must inevitably be, the patient still has some tactics in reserve such as asking for a glass of water or needing to use the bathroom, etc. Such behavior obviously carries a significant message both for the diagnostician and the therapist since it can be assumed that the same kind of avoidant tactics will be used in treatment, at least initially, when any truly significant issues are approached.

In contrast to the patient who resorts to denial or delaying tactics, there is the patient who exaggerates his feelings of discomfort, hoping thereby to elicit sympathy and support from the examiner. Then there are the patients who try to reassure themselves and build up self-confidence by straining in every possible way to demonstrate how knowledgeable, able, and creative they are. All these behaviors give considerable insight into the patient's modes of adjustment, his way of meeting stress. Also significant are the modifications in behavior that are likely to occur during the course of the testing. Initial anxiety should and frequently does abate, and with this goes a lessening of defensive reactions. If the patient's adjustment remains a highly defensive one, he is probably a very rigid individual, and unless there are other factors at work on the day of the testing or in the relationship with the diagnostician, the prognosis for treatment seems somewhat guarded.

On the basis of his observations of the patient's general behavior, his interview material and his test findings, the diagnostician formulates a picture of the patient as a functioning individual, with problems to be solved and strengths and weaknesses which facilitate or hinder such resolution. He can generally determine whether the problem is a long-standing one or a reaction to some recent trauma; and he can assess the way the patient is presently coping and the effectiveness of such coping techniques.

In seeking to convey this picture to the therapist, it is good practice to begin the paragraph following the description of behavior with a broad, encompassing statement about the individual in question. Such a paragraph might begin with an introductory sentence somewhat like the following one, "This is an individual who, despite many assets, is persistently plagued by long-standing feelings of inadequacy. In reaction to such feelings, he vacillates between exaggerated self-assertion on the one hand and withdrawal from such self-assertion to attitudes of self-derogation on the other hand." The report then goes on to describe how this problem and this particular way of coping with it affects the patient's life in many areas—social, emotional, sexual, and possibly intellectual and vocational.

Sometimes the final sentence in such an opening paragraph may give a formal diagnosis, or sometimes this is left until later, when substantiating evidence for a diagnostic label has been offered. The way this matter is handled depends in part on the preferences of the diagnostician, but more so on the importance of the diagnosis in a particular case. For example, if a patient is psychotic, it is usually important to indicate this early in the report. The psychotic struggles with the same problems that the normal and the neurotic individual does; that is, he has to find himself, develop a role for himself, relate to others, come to terms with his impulses, etc. However, he is doing this within the framework of an impairment that makes the solution of his difficulties a very different matter from what it might be with a normal individual or a character disorder. Hence, elaborating on the psychotic's struggle without indicating how disturbed he is can be misleading to the therapist. Similarly, when the diagnostician finds indication of neurological impairment, it seems inappropriate to give a two- or three-page report on the patient's psychodynamics, and only at the conclusion of the report note that there is very probably organic damage present.

Once the overall picture has been outlined, it should be filled in with relevant details. Specific areas of the personality should be taken up, one at a time, and the effects of the patient's difficulties on his emotional development, his social adjustment, and his sexual life be evaluated and woven into the total picture. The weaknesses that are likely to impede adjustment, such as difficulties in impulse control, excessive recourse to displacement, exaggerated dependency needs, and so on, should be pointed up; and even more important strength's and assets should be emphasized. Some discussion of the patient's way of perceiving himself and experiencing himself and how this affects his perceptions of others is also indicated.

It is not always possible to find confirmatory evidence for all the things one thinks and feels about a patient. Some facts stand out clearly; others are only hinted at or suggested; some can only be inferred. Such inferences can and should be communicated to the therapist but always clearly labelled for what they are—educated guesses—not validated findings.

His understanding of the patient and how he operates is, in most instances, so complete that the diagnostician should be able to make predictions about the course and outcome of therapy. Also, as was noted above, he should be able to indicate the type of therapy that is most likely to achieve results.

Prediction is, of course, always dependent upon external circumstances which in most instances cannot be controlled. Consequently, although the diagnostician may feel that the patient is a serious suicidal risk, he cannot tell exactly when the self-destructive attempt is likely to be made. However, even the possibility of suicide should be reported immediately to the therapist, even if the full report is delayed.

Predicting a possible psychotic break is another event which the diagnostician cannot pinpoint in time. However, he can generally state what is most likely to bring about such a crisis. He also should be in a position to indicate to the therapist that the patient who is making such a tenuous adjustment is not able to tolerate or benefit from anything but supportive therapy, at least at this time; or on the contrary that despite his brittle adjustment he could respond to therapy constructively.

It should be apparent from all that has been said about report writing up to this point that the focus is exclusively on the patient, while the tests are simply the tools that help us understand the patient. Yet unfortunately, partly because of the history of testing and partly because of formal academic training, the beginning diagnostician frequently feels compelled to "justify" or validate tests and/or his use of them, rather than talking about a living, feeling human being.

Similarly, because intelligence testing came first in the development of applied psychology and also because intelligence tests are often taught before projective or personality tests are brought into the picture, the novice is likely to begin his report to the therapist with several lengthy paragraphs describing the details of the patient's intellectual functioning. As has already been noted, if there is a question of retardation, disturbed thinking, or neurological damage, then the intellectual functioning should be explored. However, in many cases, the patient's educational and work history bear witness to his mental ability, and at best a few subtests might be administered to see just how he thinks and organizes his ideas. In any event, in most cases, unless he has stipulated otherwise, the therapist is not overly concerned with the patient's mental endowment, and a discussion of the patient's performance on the intelligence test is certainly not the place to begin the communication to the therapist. Any special aspects of his mental functioning, particularly such matters as the patient's tendency to be overly concrete, to become bogged down in nonessential details, etc. should be incorporated in the report, not at the very outset, thus giving them undue importance, but where they fit in appropriately. Even in the case of children where an intelligence test is practically always given, the report rarely begins with a discussion of intellectual level unless this is the major question, the reason for referral. Instead, after personality organization and emotional difficulties have been explored, the reasons for any limitations or deviations in intellectual functioning are likely to become readily apparent.

Reports naturally vary in length, depending in part on the productivity of the patient and in part on the skill of the diagnostician to extract from the test material all the relevant issues.

However, length is not an indication of effectiveness. Short but pointed, well-organized reports are likely to prove as helpful as lengthy ones, and their brevity is welcomed by a busy therapist. It behooves the diagnostician to select from the tests and other material the significant factors and relate them to one another so that the end picture is not only valid but an integrated and living picture of the patient. To achieve this, it is not necessary to convey to the therapist every last little peripheral detail that the diagnostician dredges up from his material. Only when such minutiae have meaning in the total constellation should they be included in the communication to the therapist; and if they have relevance, then they are no longer insignificant.

A frequent complaint from therapists is that diagnosticians take too long to send out reports. Actually, the therapist would like to have the report the very day that the patient is seen, especially when there has been any delay in scheduling his testing appointment. For most diagnosticians such speed is virtually impossible, although they can generally give the therapist the highlights of their findings on the phone. This is certainly indicated if there is any danger of a suicidal attempt or likelihood of a psychotic blow-up.

As a rule, a therapist should not have to wait more than three or four days for a report. For the diagnostician, some sort of secretarial service is essential. Many use a dictating machine and then arrange to have the dictation transcribed, either by a full- or part-time secretary, depending upon the extent of his needs. Others dictate directly to a secretary. Whatever the arrangements, every effort must be made to get reports out promptly.

RECORDS

The test materials and a copy of the report that is sent to the therapist should be kept for a number of years. Most diagnosticians regard seven years as the desirable length of time. Certainly it should not be less than five. There are a number of reasons for holding onto the material this long. Perhaps the most important one is the use to which such material is put when retesting is required. Comparing the raw data obtained from the patient before and after therapy is just one example of the need for keeping test materials. In general, such comparisons provide indications of the extent, nature, and areas of change, of growth, or of regression that are invaluable in any study of a given individual.

Sending the raw data to another diagnostician or therapist when such a request is made becomes a debatable matter. For the very busy diagnostician who sees many patients every day and who takes down patient responses in his own private shorthand, responding to such requests can become inordinately time consuming. Some diagnosticians therefore make it a rule to send only the numerical findings, that is, the scores on the various subtests of the intelligence scale and the psychogram of the Rorschach.

After seven years from the date of testing, the raw data can be destroyed if storing it creates a problem. The report, however, is generally kept for ten years, and then that too is disposed of. At that time, a small card with the name of the patient, the referring therapist, the date of testing, the tests given and the diagnosis are all that is necessary.

CONCLUSIONS

For those who enjoy an intellectually demanding task and who like fitting together the pieces of a puzzle, diagnostic testing can be an exciting and rewarding experience. The problem is to tease out from a mass of material the basic issues and ascertain their impact on the total personality. Once the essential thread or threads are identified, unraveling the tangles becomes relatively easy. Then the individual threads must be rewoven to develop the picture that lies behind the picture so to speak, the latent forces that nevertheless explain the manifest functioning, spelling out what the patient really thinks and feels, explaining why he is the way he is.

Aside from its great value to the patient and the therapist, diagnostic testing also provides an excellent way of learning about people and personality functioning. Tests provide a kind of road map of the individual's inner life. Such a map enables one to search out different areas of experience, to explore the relationships between one area and another, laying bare the whole psychic life of the individual.

The major frustration that the diagnostician experiences is the lack of follow-up. He rarely gets any feedback from the therapist or the patient (although this is not always so), never learns if his analysis of the patient has been helpful and what the end result of the whole experience, testing, and treatment, has been. If he is very deeply concerned, he can, of course, get in touch with the therapist who referred the patient, but this cannot be done in every instance, mainly for reasons of time. Sometimes a collaborative relationship can be established with a therapist, and in such cases, because of mutual interest, each case that the diagnostician and the therapist have seen is gone over carefully, and the diagnostic material tied in with what is taking place in therapy. When such a relationship can be established, it is highly rewarding to everyone involved.

With the years, diagnostic testing has apparently become less appealing to the young psychologist, and hearsay has it that it is less in demand than it used to be. Yet the psychologists in any community who are known as diagnosticians are so busy that they are turning away referrals, and because of the apparent demand, there is almost no one to send them to, at least no one who can see them in the near future. If, then, the demands of psychodiagnosis, the need for careful analysis and synthesis of patient productions, and the transmission of one's interpretations of such material to a colleague has any appeal, being primarily, though not exclusively, a psychodiagnostician can be intellectually and financially a very satisfying and rewarding career.

Chapter 10

PSYCHOTHERAPEUTIC AND PSYCHODIAGNOSTIC ASPECTS OF PHYSICAL DISABILITY

IRVING SHELSKY

During the past quarter century, professional and lay attitudes towards individuals with disabilities have changed dramatically. The tendency towards unreal sterotypes is slowly being replaced with an awareness that the handicapped are people, just like the rest of us, with potential for growth and self-actualization. The phenomenon of the "closet child" or the blind beggar with cane and tin cup may still exist, but by and large they are today the exception rather than the rule.

World War II and the defeat of an ideology which preached the supremacy of one race over another and found justification for the murder of tens of thousands of physically and mentally "impaired" persons stirred both the conscience and the consciousness of mankind. This new awareness, coupled with the return to civilian life of large numbers of wounded servicemen, gave impetus to a previously limited field of medical and psychological study under the collective designation of rehabilitation. Psychology's contribution to this field has been and continues to be of major importance. As members of rehabilitation teams, psychologists have contributed to the ongoing treatment of the disabled. After the surgeons, physiotherapists, and other experts have stamped "case closed" on a patient's file, there still remains the task of helping him return to society and a meaningful life. This task would be significantly more difficult to accomplish were it not for the psychodiagnostic, psychotherapeutic, and research skills of psychology. These disciplines have been employed on the individual, family, group, and community levels to assist the handicapped assume their rightful role in society.

This paper will concern itself specifically with the psychotherapeutic and psychodiagnostic approaches to individuals with auditory and cardiovascular disability. It is hoped that within the framework of these two disabilities—one sensory, the other physical and life-threatening—the reader will be able to generalize his approach to other types of disability. Psychosomatic conditions, as defined by Dunbar (1954), Weiss, and English (1943) and specifically explored in journals devoted to psychosomatic illness are not here included.

At the outset, it is necessary to state that this author has a rather strong philosophical bias towards a body of knowledge called somatopsychology. As defined by Barker *et al.* (1953), somatopsychology deals with ". . . variations in physique that effect the psychological situation of a person by influencing the effectiveness of his body as a tool for action or by serving as a stimulus to himself or others." In other words, somatopsychology addresses itself to the interaction between the individual and his environment as well as to his feelings about himself and his disability. While this author's orientation is psychoanalytic, this paper by no means stresses the value of one orientation over another. Quite the contrary is true. Inherent in all that is to follow is the basic belief that any orientation (Freudian, behavioral, Gestalt, etc.) is valid provided the practitioner feels comfortable with it and can utilize it to help his patient grow.

GENERAL APPROACH TO PSYCHOLOGICAL ASPECTS OF PHYSICAL DISABILITY

Hamilton (1950) and Wright (1960) define physical disability as a condition or impairment of an individual as diagnosed by a physician (medical condition). Handicap is the effect the disability has on his functioning in society, interpersonally, intrapersonally, vocationally and avocationally. A physical disability need not necessarily be a handicap if it does not interfere with general functioning or if it is not experienced as an interpersonal or intrapersonal threat. On the other hand, an insult to the body (mastectomy, facial disfigurement, etc.) may be seen by some as a disability purely on the basis of the social and/or psychological meaning it conveys.

Persons with disabilities, who seek or are referred for psychological assistance, confront the psychologist with a constellation of problems. Societal attitudes about disability may be shared by the therapist as well as by the patient. Because even the psychotherapist is not immune to underlying prejudices and beliefs for which there is little basis in fact, he should be on guard against allowing them to intrude upon his relationship with his patient.

Prior to embarking upon our discussion of the two disabilities mentioned above, it is necessary to consider some myths which might well be shared by professionals and the general public alike.

Myth No. 1: Certain Physical Disabilities are Associated with Particular Personality Constellations

A survey of the literature (Barker *et al.*, 1953; Wright, 1960; Shontz, 1970) reveals that researchers have consistently concluded that there is no evidence to support the hypothesis that a specific physical disability results in particular personality types. This author's experience, likewise, tends to indicate that the onset of disability does not produce consistent personality changes per se. With additional stress, however, underlying dynamics become exacerbated and more apparent. It is therefore fairly evident that the therapeutic approach employed in treatment would depend on the training and orientation of the therapist and not on any dynamic factors implicit in the disability itself.

Above all else, in order to understand the effect that a disability has on a specific individual, we must first study the personal meaning it holds for him. Such avenues of inquiry can uncover not only the threatening aspects of a particular disability but certain features which, in fact, lend support to the underlying dynamics of the individual, i.e. secondary gains. Psychotherapists and diagnosticians (Fishman, 1962; Whitehouse, 1962; Raskin, 1962; Levine, 1953, 1962; Garrett, 1962; Berger, 1953; Harrower, 1953) caution against treating individuals with specific disabilities on the basis of preconceived notions (people with hearing loss tend to be paranoid). Treatment must always be oriented towards the specific meaning the situation and the disability have for the individual patient. Psychological impact can never be assumed to be constant from one disabled person to another.

Myth No. 2: The More Severe the Disability, the Greater the Consequent Psychological Disturbance and the Greater the Adjustment Problem.

With respect to the above statement, we must once again remind the reader that it is not the disability, per se, which produces a particular response but rather the personal dynamics of the individual. Each person will interpret and utilize a disability in accordance with his own personality structure and will integrate it on the basis of his own dynamics. A specific disability can have profound regressive effects on one individual, positive effects on another, and no marked effect on still another.

To reiterate, available evidence indicates that there is no consistently accepted and/or generalized insult to the personality as a consequence of a specific disability. Shontz (1970) states: "Radical changes in body structure have little or no prolonged effect on personality." Researchers investigating the effects of such gross alterations of body as hemicorporectomy (Freiden, 1969), bilateral hip disarticulation (Hirchenfang *et al.*, 1966), ileostomy and colostomy (Dlin *et al.*, 1969) and the introduction of cardiac pacemakers (Gladston and Gamble, 1969) all report little or no evidence of permanent personality change as a result of these interventions. While temporary disorganization may take place, there is a reestablishing and reorientation of the personality once the stress is overcome and the disability integrated.

Myth No. 3: Depression Is Indicative of An Inablilty to Cope With and Integrate Disability

A third aspect of disability which requires discussion involves the two-sided coin of acceptance and/or denial. Inasmuch as acceptance and denial are themselves coping mechanisms, all too often the latter is interpreted as an indication that a patient has, in fact, suceeded in integrating his disability. Depression, on the other hand, is seen as a negative feeling and an inability to cope. In reality, the reverse may be closer to the truth.

It is depression which, more than any other factor, may be an indication that the patient is in the process of integrating and accepting his disability, and it is depression which usually provides the impetus through which the disabled individual and the therapist are brought together. Only rarely will a person who utilizes denial as a defense be seen in therapy and then usually only if some specific crisis arises. It is essential to stress, as in all areas, that the above discussion is not offered as an absolute "truism" to be applied in all cases.

If, however, there is one rule that a therapist can follow in dealing with individuals who have disabilities, it is that he evaluate each one on the basis of his particular life space, life style, personality structure, etc. and that he, the therapist, not allow himself to generalize from one person to another. It is valuable to train oneself to think of persons who have disabilities as just that rather than as "disabled persons." Such a distinction eliminates the tendency to make the disability the chief identifying factor rather than just one aspect of a total human being.

AUDITORY DISABILITY

Auditory disability represents a sensory loss that can have profound effects on the growth and development of an individual. Psychotherapists specifically and psychologists generally are hypersensitive to the impact of interpersonal communication on personality development and growth. Auditory disability early in life impairs language development, and the child is robbed of one of the most important avenues for the development of his emotional, social, and intellectual capacities. When a hearing loss occurs later in life, familiar modes of communication built up during a lifetime are disrupted and a period of reorientation and new learning must take place before the individual can adjust to his disability and continue to grow.

Any discussion of auditory disability requires at least a working knowledge of some of the technical terminology associated with varying degrees and types of hearing loss. The following classifications are here reproduced directly from Levine (1962).

Classification of the Hearing-Impaired Population

1. *The Hypacusic or Hard of Hearing.* This category includes those whose hearing loss is not or has not been severe enough to prevent the natural learning of language and speech either

with or without a hearing aid. To distinguish persons with usable hearing from those whose hearing is no longer functional, the term "deafened" is conveniently applied to the latter.

2. *The Anacusic or Deaf.* This category includes those with irreversible deafness since birth or childhood, severe enough in the speech range to prevent the natural learning of language and speech even with the help of a hearing aid.

3. *The Dysacusic.* This category includes those with disorders in the synthesis and/or interpretation of acoustic stimuli (including spoken language) that are not due to loss in auditory acuity but may exist in the presence of unimpaired (as well as impaired) hearing ability. Persons with such conditions as auditory agnosia or word deafness fall into this category.

4. *The Psychodysacusic.* This category includes those with disorders of hearing or of response to acoustic stimuli (including spoken language) that are due to the action of the psychic mechanisms. Persons with such conditions as functional, psychogenic, or hysteric deafness fall into this category.

Levine (1962) cautions her readers against making the assumption that any of the preceding categories are mutually exclusive. Degree, amount, and type of hearing loss can be evaluated by trained otologists, audiologists, and other specialists. Techniques for doing so have been dramatically improved in recent years with the most startling advances being in the area of early childhood diagnosis.

Before psychotherapy can begin, there are a number of reality-based factors which must be taken into consideration. Among these are the patient's ability to use a telephone, whether the hearing loss effects him more in large groups than in small ones, whether the loss was sudden, progressive, profound, minimal, congenital, etc. In other words, when in the individual's life the hearing loss occurred, how it occurred, and how severe it is or is likely to become.

As Levine (1962) so aptly states:

When an individual's auditory relationship with his environment is abruptly destroyed, the impact is one of psychology's most traumatic events. When the muting process takes place in increasing increments, it can lead to chronic emotional instability; and when a child is born into a soundless environment, he encounters one of the greatest development obstacles known to man.

Because auditory disability by its very nature produces communication difficulties, the earliest rehabilitative efforts should be directed towards the development of compensatory skills. The congenitally deaf and the very young child are able to learn language more easily than the older child or adult. Lipreading, hearing aids, speech therapy, speech training, auditory training, and sign language are all valuable adjuncts to improved communication. Written language, gestures, and touch are other available means of communication especially useful in one-to-one relationships.

Because persons with hearing disabilities have many complex problems, it is not unusual for psychologists to function as members of a team consisting of all or any of the following: physician, audiologist, otologist, special educator, social worker, speech therapist, counselor, family members, and of course the patient himself.

Establishing Rapport

The task of establishing rapport with a patient, be he handicapped or not, is largely a matter of the skill of the individual therapist. However, when dealing with hearing-impaired persons, the task can be made significantly easier if the therapist tries to employ the following guidelines as suggested by Levine (1962). When interviewing lipreaders,

1. Make certain mouth and face are visible at all times.
2. Speak clearly and naturally, no mouthing, shouting, or slowing down. Use nontechnical language and noninvolved sentences.
3. Watch for signs of lipreading fatigue; drop in lipreading ability (restlessness and irritability, exhausted appearance).
4. Have pad and pencil ready to write key words or expressions.

When interviewing nonlipreaders,

1. With poor or nonlipreaders with good speech and language proficiency, pad and pencil will have to be used

for questions and comments. Patient, of course, communicates with speech or, if deaf, through manual communication if the interviewee prefers and the interviewer is able.

2. With nonlipreaders with incomprehensible or no speech and with verbal language deficiency, unless the interviewer is familiar with sign language, an interpreter will be needed. It is preferable that the interpreter not be emotionally involved with the patient and that if possible he be a person who works with the deaf.

Under optimum conditions, a person who will be working with the deaf should himself master manual communication.

Psychological and Psychodiagnostic Testing

Psychological evaluation of individuals with hearing impairment generally calls for the same type of information as is required with nondisabled persons (case history, interview, psychological testing, psychodiagnostic testing, etc.) When working with children, the utilization of multiple resources (teachers, physicians, family members, etc.) for the gathering of information produces a clearer picture of the child and the world in which he lives than would reliance on a single source, i.e. his parents.

With respect to the hearing-impaired youngster, he is, more often than not, referred for psychological assistance for one or more of the following reasons:

1. Behavior disturbances such as withdrawal and other acting-out behavior.
2. Evaluation of appropriate learning and educational programs.
3. Evaluation of intellectual status and potential; academic ability and achievement; social adjustment.
4. Rejection of a specific rehabilitative program (hearing aid, speech therapy, etc.) and/or the total program.
5. Interpersonal difficulties with peers, parents, siblings, etc.
6. Evaluation of specific strengths and weaknesses as related to communication and learning.

At the adult level and with adolescents, the presenting problems generally fall within the following categories:

1. Emotional disturbances such as depression, denial, over-

whelming anxiety, and acting-out behavior. Not infrequently, referrals call for differential diagnosis involving hysteria and the question of possible malingering.

2. Exaggerated effect of the disability on the life of the individual, be it in school, at work, or in his interpersonal relationships.

3. Rejection of rehabilitation aids and programs.

The Case History

In the taking of a case history, certain avenues of inquiry are mandatory. When dealing with a hearing-impaired person, or any person with a disability, at least a working knowledge of the medical aspects is essential. With auditory disability, data as to the type, amount, cause, age of onset, and whether or not there are other hearing-impaired persons in the family needs to be obtained. Other pertinent information would include such things as the patient's major mode of communication; the social, educational, occupational and domestic changes resultant from the disability; how the onset of disability altered the patient's behavior; and a history of all diagnostic, rehabilitative, and educational measures undertaken since the onset of the disability.

Psychological Testing

As stated above, the first order of priority is the collection of a complete history including all aspects of the patient's life. Furthermore, before the psychologist can select an appropriate test battery, he should have a good idea of his patient's attitudes about his disability and how he thinks it will effect his test performance.

Once again, it is important to stress that certain basic rules apply to all persons, handicapped and nonhandicapped alike. Whenever psychological tests are used, the person who is being tested should be fully aware of exactly what is expected of him. Such a task, needless to say, becomes especially difficult when the subject has a hearing impairment. Tests standardized on the basis of norm groups with normal hearing have to be modified to meet the needs of the hearing-impaired. Instruction manuals cannot be used dogmatically, and with certain instruments, sub-tests which measure ability to communicate have to be deleted. The goal should always be to measure that which the test is designed to measure and not the patient's ability to communicate.

Likewise, interpretation of test results must allow for the area of disability. In the case of the hearing-impaired, relying too heavily on the verbal areas will result in grossly underestimating your patient's potential in other areas.

Let us take, as an example, the Wechsler Intelligence Scale for Children and the Wechsler-Adult Intelligence Scale. When both scales (verbal and performance) are administered to a hearing-impaired person, the results may indicate overall functioning within the dull normal, or retarded range. All too often, no attempt is made to allow for the fact that the area of disability—in this case hearing loss—is given as much weight as are the perform-ance areas. When this happens youngsters and adults are classified as retarded when, in fact, they are not. When such an error is made with a child, he is often placed in a special class for the retarded rather than in a class for the hearing impaired where he could learn skills that would help him to achieve his potential.

If, however, instruments are broken down into subtests of strength and weakness, the result is a clearer picture of not only intellectual functioning but of potential ability and personality factors as well.

To still further enhance diagnostic understanding, the aid of other significant persons (teachers, peers, parents, spouse, em-ployer, etc.) can be sought. With the hearing-impaired, evalua-tion and possible modification of the milieu in which he functions can be of major importance in decreasing his frustrations and thus paving the way for growth and self-actualization.

Selection of the specific test or tests to be used will depend on a wide range of factors including what it is you wish to meas-ure; the patient's experiential background (deprived, enriched); amount of residual hearing, if any; and patient's ability to com-municate, respond, and follow directions.

As indicated above, with the hearing-impaired, performance rather than verbal tests give a more adequate picture of an individ-ual's potential. The following is a listing of test instruments from which, depending upon the needs of the specific patient, a complete battery can be assembled:

1. Performance Scale of the Wechsler Pre-School and Primary School Scale of Intelligence.
2. Gesell Developmental Schedules.
3. Bayley Scale of Infant Development.
4. Merrill Palmer Scale.
5. Grace Arthur Performance Scale.
6. The Hiskey-Nebraska Test of Learning Aptitude.
7. The Pictorial Test of Intelligence.
8. Performance Scale of the Wechsler Intelligence Scale for Children (WISC).
9. Chicago Non-Verbal.
10. Wechsler Adult Intelligence Scale.
11. Army Beta, Revised.
12. Arthur Point Scale.

Personality and projective measures can be selected from among the following:

1. Thematic Apperception Test.
2. Sentence Completion.
3. Figure Drawing.
4. House-Tree-Person.
5. Rorschach.
6. M.M.P.I.
7. Make a Picture-Story Test.

Certain clinical measures are valuable in evaluating the possible presence or absence of multiple disabilities (cerebral dysfunction, auditory perceptual dysfunction, academic retardation, etc.) The following list offers the psychologist a wide range of choices:

1. Illinois Test of Psycholinguistic Ability.
2. Bender-Gestalt.
3. Benton Visual Retention Test.
4. Flowers-Costello Test of Central Auditory Abilities.
5. Wide Range Achievement Test.
6. The Vineland Social Maturity Scale.
7. The Pre-School Attainment Record.

Other tests of intelligence, interest, aptitude, achievement, and personality can be utilized as needed and where appropriate. Some measures have been standardized on the hearing-impaired while some have norms for both impaired and nonimpaired.

The reader is referred to Buros Mental Measurement Year Books for a complete listing of all available tests.

Factors to be Considered in Therapy with the Hearing-Impaired

As mentioned briefly above, it is of major importance that the therapist be in touch with his own feelings about deafness and the deaf and that he feel comfortable when relating to persons with hearing impairments. Since most forms of psychotherapy employ verbal techniques, hearing-impaired persons face formidable obstacles when they become involved in conventional psychotherapeutic relationships. As for the therapist, he, too, has to overcome the reluctance he must surely experience when he is limited in the use of his favorite technique, verbal communication. Consequently, it is vital that during early contact between patient and therapist, a viable, mutually acceptable means of communication be decided upon. Possible choices include lipreading, note writing, gestures, and with children, play therapy. Still other techniques born of the inventiveness of both patient and therapist can be developed as well.

Relatedness will evolve as the relationship improves, and honesty and openness will begin to develop as growth occurs.

CARDIOVASCULAR DISABILITY

Cardiac disability, coronary heart disease, and hypertensive heart disease differ markedly from sensory and other types of physical disability in that it is not overtly apparent to others but, unlike blindness, deafness, crippling, etc., represents a serious threat to life itself.

Heart attack (myocardial infarction, coronary thrombosis, coronary occlusion) is the number one killer in the United States. It is, however, estimated that four out of five who suffer heart attacks do survive (Marvin, 1957). Having thus survived and come through the initial medical life-preserving phase, the patient may then be confronted with the realities of having to restrict a wide range of his activities as well as having to change his life style and many of his behavior patterns. Pain (angina pectoris) is a common consequence of coronary disability and occurs in different individuals with differing degrees of intensity and frequency. The reader is referred to Whitehouse (1962) for an in-depth discussion of the medical and psychological implications of cardiovascular disease.

Diagnostic Evaluation

Persons with cardiovascular disability require the professional services of a team rather than the attention of sundry professionals each working in his own area of expertise. Through his association with the Nassau County Cardiac Work Evaluation Unit, this author has functioned as the clinical psychologist on just such a team. The total team consisted of a cardiologist, internist, social worker, vocational psychologist and clinical psychologist. The role of the latter dealt largely with the psychodiagnostic evaluation of patients referred to the unit after having recovered from heart attacks.

The major tool employed in psychodiagnostic evaluation was the open-ended interview, so structured as to elicit from the patient his feelings about his disability, the meaning it holds for him and the manner in which it has changed his life. A form, reprinted below, was evolved, largely through trial and error, and proved a most valuable aid in the overall evaluation of the unit's patient population.

The clinical interview utilizes a life history approach focusing on previous, as well as present, adaptive patterns. The overall goal of the total evaluation is to isolate the obstacles which the patient is experiencing, to find his strengths and weaknesses and to determine what, if any, help he needs. His degree of readiness to accept therapy or other types of assistance is also studied.

While the phychotherapist in private practice cannot realistically hope to function within the framework of a team, he can, with his patient's awareness, call upon and consult with his physician.

NASSAU COUNTY CARDIAC WORK EVALUATION UNIT

Work Evaluation Unit   Psychological Evaluation   WEU No._____

NAME _____ DATE _____

ADDRESS _____ AGE____ OCCUPATION _____

1. GENERAL IMPRESSION OF ATTITUDE
   ____ Frank   ____ Evasive   ____ Conscientious
   ____ Spontaneous   ____ Guarded   ____ Withdrawn
   ____ Friendly   ____ Aggressive-
                            Passive

2. AFFECT
   ____ Normal   ____ Anxious   ____ Constricted
   ____ Depressed   ____ Flat   ____ Irritable
   ____ Hypomanic

3. INTELLIGENCE
   ____ Defective   ____ Average   ____ Superior
   ____ Below Average ____ High Average

4. ANXIETIES
   Causes   Pre: _____   Post: _____
   Resolution   _____   _____

5. NATURE OF FEARS
                   Pre: _____   Post: _____

6. ANGERS
   Causes   Pre: _____   Post: _____
   Resolution   _____   _____

7. HANDLING OF HOSTILITY
   Poor control   Pre: _____   Post: _____
   Moderate control   _____   _____
   Severe control   _____   _____

8. PLEASURES
   Sources   Pre: _____   Post: _____
   Effects   _____   _____

9. BASIC DEFENSES
   _____ Sublimation   _____ Rationalization
   _____ Avoidance   _____ Suppression
   _____ Denial   _____ Regression
   _____ Reaction formation   _____ Isolation
   _____ Compensation   _____ Projection
   _____ Somatization   _____ Introjection
   _____ Intellectualization

10. CHARACTER STRUCTURE AND/OR DIAGNOSTIC
    IMPRESSION
    _____ Character type _____ Psychoneurosis _____ Psychosis

11. STRESSES ASSOCIATED WITH THE PRECIPITATION
    OF ILLNESS
    Physical _____
    Emotional _____

12. REACTION TO ILLNESS
    Reasonably apprehensive _____
    Overly apprehensive _____
    Denial: Direct _____ Indirect _____

13. EMOTIONAL ACCEPTANCE OF DISABILITY
    Able to accept limitations realistically _____
    Difficulty accepting limitations _____
    Unable to accept limitations realistically _____

14. ATTITUDE TOWARD:
    Work   Pre: _____   Post: _____
    Family   _____   _____
    Security   _____   _____

15. MOTIVATION FOR EMPLOYMENT
    Overly motivated   Pre: _____   Post: _____
    Motivated   _____   _____
    Lacks motivation   _____   _____

16. PSYCHOLOGICAL READINESS FOR EMPLOYMENT
    _____ Ready   _____ Partially ready   _____ Not ready

17. NEEDS (MASLOW)   *Pre:*   *Post:*
    1 ... Physiological   _____   _____
    2 ... Safety   _____   _____
    3 ... Belongingness & love   _____   _____
    4 ... Importance, respect,
          self-esteem, independence _____   _____
    5 ... Information   _____   _____
    6 ... Understanding   _____   _____
    7 ... Beauty   _____   _____
    8 ... Self-Actualization   _____   _____

18. CHANGE IN HABITS AND ACTIVITIES AS RESULT OF
    CARDIAC DISEASE
    Diet   Y __ N __ _____ _____ __ M.D. __ self
    Smoke   Y __ N __ _____ _____ __ M.D. __ self
    Alocohol   Y __ N __ _____ _____ __ M.D. __ self

Hobbies &
   sports   Y __ N __ _____ _____ __ M.D. __ self
Work around
   house   Y __ N __ _____ _____ __ M.D. __ self
Sex   Y __ N __ _____ _____ __ M.D. __ self

19. REMARKS:

SIGNED: _____

Psychological Testing

Inasmuch as persons with cardiovascular disability do not usually have sensory, conceptual, or intellectual disabilities, the psychologist is free to use his preferred battery for personality assessment. There are, however, many somatic symptoms associated with cardiac disability. These do need to be evaluated on an individual basis within the overall structure of the patient's personality and as they relate to the test used. For example, the M.M.P.I. Hysteria, Depression, and Hypochondriasis Scales have many cardiac symptoms listed. A specific instrument, the Cardiac Adjustment Scale, has been developed by Rumbaugh (1964) and is designed to measure the potential for successful rehabilitation with cardiac patients.

Factors to Be Considered in Psychotherapy

With the onset of heart disease, there arises the need for radical changes in life style. The threat to life quite frequently evokes a marked increase in anxiety. After the acute phase of the illness has passed, the patient is in the unique position of having to evaluate not only his future, but his past as well. If it is at this point when his anxiety is high that he seeks psychotherapeutic assistance, then he would be very amenable to change. Under such conditions, a person's entire value system is threatened and his activity is frequently so curtailed that he can no longer employ previously learned defenses. Moreover, when an individual has cardiovascular disease, anxiety itself is seen as life-threatening and is usually the major factor which brings patient and psychotherapist together. Consequently, in the therapeutic relationship, the initial goal is to decrease anxiety by helping the patient become aware that he alone has the power to control his life in a constructive rather than a self-destructive manner.

For those individuals whose sense of personal worth depends largely on their ability to work, excell in sports, etc., and who are unable to accept limitations and dependence on others, the threat is formidable. Such persons can be helped to modify their strivings through insight into the bases of their drives.

Not infrequently, a cardiac patient is referred for psychotherapy because others believe that he is endangering his life thriugh the denial of his disability. Such a patient however, will rarely follow through with the referral.

As mentioned previously, anxiety is the most frequent cause for seeking psychotherapeutic assistance. Second in prominence are those patients who are depressed. In my experience, the depression must be dealt with before any progress towards meaningful growth and self-actualization can be made.

Pain (angina pectoris) sometimes becomes an important factor to be explored in therapy. What meaning does pain hold for the individual patient? Is its onset precipitated by emotional factors, physical factors, or both? How, other than through medication, can the patient learn to cope with it? Does pain provide the patient with conscious and/or unconscious secondary gains?

The acceptance or rejection of medication and medical advice is yet another indication of the meaning which the disability holds for the patient. It is, of course, important that the patient be able to communicate meaningfully with his physician, but more important are his prior attitudes towards authority which more than likely will be reflected in his behavior vis-a-vis his physician, hospital nurses, etc. Likewise, family relationships, peer group relationships, on-the-job relatedness, etc., are all fruitful avenues of investigation and are amenable to change, where appropriate, by virtue of the effects of the disability.

Family or group therapy are at times valuable aides in the overall psychotherapeutic experience. A recent study by Ruskin *et al.* (1970) supports the notion that patients cannot be dealt with in a vacuum. The study finds that the emotional strength of the spouse and the positive relationship between patient and spouse, correlates highly with successful rehabilitation.

As indicated earlier, the therapist must always be aware of his own feelings with respect to the meaning that a specific disability holds for him. Cardiovascular disease is an especially emotionally laden disability with all kinds of implications for the psychotherapist. The consequences of the life-threatening aspects of myocardial infarction and its sequelae can increase the therapists' anxiety and play a destructive role in therapy. He needs to explore the personal meaning cardiac disability holds for him and what role, if any, it has played in his life (parents, friends). The therapist must be on guard against these countertransference problems should they arise.

Summary

The preceding discussion of the psychotherapeutic and psychodiagnostic aspects of physical disability might, in a condensed form, come down to the following basic assumptions.

There are no specific personalities that are universally related to or associated with specific physical disabilities. In other words, there is no such thing as a cardiac personality, deaf personality, tubercular personality, etc.

The personality of the individual and the psychopathology or disturbance which we observe after the onset of a physical disability are not related to the disability per se but to the premorbid personality structure and/or the personal meaning that a particular disability has for a specific person.

Diagnosticians and therapists have to be aware of their own feelings about a specific disability. They have to do away with any preconceived notions they might have about certain universal effects of specific disabilities and approach each person as an individual. Having done so, patient and therapist can explore the effects of the disability in terms of the patient's day-to-day existence as well as its implications for the future growth of the individual.

The therapeutic approach utilized with handicapped as well as with nonhandicapped persons depends upon the therapist's own theoretical orientation and training and on the personality of the individual patient, not on the existence of characteristics universally associated with a specific disability.

REFERENCES

Barker, R. G., Wright, B. A., Meyerson, L., and Gonick, M. R.: Adjustment to physical handicap and illness: A survey of the social psychology of physique and disability. Social Science Research Council Bulletin 55, 1953.

Berger, S.: Paraplegia. In Garrett, J. F. (Ed.): *Psychological Aspects of Physical Disability.* Washington, D. C., Office of Vocational Rehabilitation, H.E.W., 1953, No. 210, pp. 46-59.

Dlin, B. M., Perlman, A., and Ringold, E.: Psychosexual response to ileostomy and colostomy. *American Journal of Psychiatry, 126*: 374-378, 1969.

Dunbar, F.: *Emotions and Bodily Changes.* New York, Columbia University Press, 1954.

Fishman, S.: Amputation. In Garrett, J. F. and Levine, E. S. (Eds.): *Practices with the Physically Disabled.* New York, Columbia University Press, 1962, pp. 1-50.

Freiden, F. H., Gertler, M., Tosberg, W., and Rusk, H. A.: Rehabilitation after hemicorporectomy, *Archives of Physical Medicine and Rehabilitation, 50*:259-263, 1969.

Garrett, J. F. and Levine, E. S. (Eds.): *Psychological Practices with the Physically Disabled.* New York, Columbia University Press, 1962, p. 1.

Gelfand, D.: *Factors Relating to Unsuccessful Vocational Adjustment of Cardiac Patients.* Pennsylvania Office of Vocational Rehabilitation, 1960.

Gladston, R. and Gamble, W. J.: On borrowed time: observations of children with implanted cardiac pacemakers and their families. *American Journal of Psychiatry, 126*:104-108, 1969.

Hamilton, K. W.: Counseling the handicapped. In *The Rehabilitation Process,* New York, Ronald, 1950.

Harrower, M. R.: Psychological factors in multiple sclerosis. In Garrett, J. F. (Ed.): *Psychological Aspects of Physical Disability.* Washington, D. C., Office of Vocational Rehabilitation, Department of Health, Education and Welfare, No. 210, pp. 68-79, 1953.

Hirschenfang, S., Cosla, H. W., and Benton, J. G.: Anxiety in a patient with bilateral hip disarticulation: preliminary report. *Perceptual and Motor Skills, 23*:41-42, 1966.

Levine, E. S.: The deaf. In Garrett, J. F. (Ed.): *Psychological Aspects of Physical Disability.* Washington, D. C., Office of Vocational

Rehabilitation, Department of Health, Education and Welfare, No. 210, pp. 125-146, 1953.

Levine, E. S.: Auditory disability. In Garrett, J. F. and Levine, E. S. (Eds.): *Psychological Practices With the Physically Disabled.* New York, Columbia University Press, 1962, pp. 279-340.

Marvin, H. M.: *You and Your Heart.* New York, New American Library, 1957.

Maslow, A. H.: *Motivation and Personality.* New York, Harper, 1954.

McDaniel, J. W.: *Physical Disability and Human Behavior.* Elmsford, New York, Pergamon Press, 1969.

Meyerson, L.: Somatopsychology of physical disability. In Cruckshank, W. M. (Ed.): *Psychology of Exceptional Children and Youth.* Englewood Cliffs, Prentice-Hall, 1971, pp. 1-74.

Raskin, N. J.: Visual disability. In Garrett, J. F. and Levine, E. S. (Eds.): *Psychological Practices With the Physically Disabled.* New York, Columbia University Press, 1962, pp. 341-375.

Rumbaugh, D. M.: *The Cardiac Adjustment Scale.* San Diego, California, Educational and Industrial Testing Service, 1964.

Ruskin, H. D., Stein, L., Shelsky, I. M., and Bailey, M. A.: MMPI: Comparison between patients with coronary heart disease and their spouses together with other demographic data: a preliminary report. Scandinavian Journal of Medicine, pp. 99-104, 1970.

Shontz, F. C.: *Physical disability and personality: theory and recent research.* Psychological Aspects of Disability, *17*:51-69, 1970.

Weiss, E. and English, O. S.: *Psychosomatic Medicine.* Philadelphia, Pennsylvania, Saunders, 1943.

Whitehouse, F. A.: Cardiovascular disability. In Garrett, J. F. and Levine, E. S. (Eds.): *Psychological Practices With the Physically Disabled.* New York, Columbia University Press, 1962, pp. 85-124.

Wright, B. A.: *Physical Disability—A Psychological Approach.* New York, Harper and Row, 1960.

Chapter 11

RESEARCH AND PRIVATE PRACTICE

GEORGE STRICKER

For many years, the model of training for the clinical psychologist has been that of a scientist-professional. Most university doctoral programs adhere to this model and devote varying amounts of space in their curriculum to courses which promote scientific values and professional training. If there is an overbalance between the two, it would clearly favor the scientist, as many universities seem to feel that it is the job of an educational institution to promote cognitive learning, and professional training can await postdoctoral institutes and experiences. Despite the profession's subscription to the model of the scientist-professional and the university training programs' emphasis on the development of scientists, most clinical psychologists choose one or the other components of the dichotomy, rather than actualizing an integration of the two aspects of training. Some clinical psychologists become pure scientists, devote their lives to research, and find employment in universities or in research positions within clinical installations. A great many other clinical psychologists choose a professional career, finding their employment in clinical positions within these same installations or in private practice. It is the unusual psychologist who can remain actively involved in research and also productively involved in clinical work. The divorce between science and professionalism is often so complete that the practitioner turns his back on the findings of research, thereby depriving himself of a means of evaluating his own functioning and also of enriching his current practice. Many professionals will defend their lack of attention to the scientific journals with the comment that there is little in contemporary research that is relevant to the everyday problems of clinical practice, so that the time that would be taken from their other professional or personal activities cannot be justified. To some extent it is true that much research is nonclinical, and a great deal of clinical research is superficial and of little practical value to the profession. At least some of the responsibility for this failure must be placed at the feet of the professional who ignores his training and does not produce the kind of research that he and his fellow practitioners would find meaningful. Even beyond this, many professionals who are approached with the opportunity of participating in well-designed and potentially meaningful research refuse this opportunity, thereby assuring that most research will be done using inadequately trained therapists, so that generalization becomes difficult. Any professional therapist who seriously considers himself an applied scientist, in the sense that his practice involves the application of general principles of behavior derived from personality theory, has the responsibility of cooperating with serious researchers in producing a meaningful body of literature. If he fails to do this, he cannot attribute sole blame to the researcher for failing to produce relevant and meaningful findings.

Although the contribution of research findings to applied clinical practice has been severely limited, there is a significant place for research in the life of the practitioner. My own practice is divided between research consultation and traditional clinical practice. I find that the ability to use my research background, training, and interests in a private-practice setting is personally enriching and provides me with a number of experiences that would not have been available had I ignored this portion of my background. There are two major focuses of this research practice —dissertation supervision and program evaluation—and I would like to discuss each one in turn.

DISSERTATION SUPERVISION

The private practice of dissertation supervision requires a large metropolitan area with a great many universities present. For this reason, it is unlikely that dissertation supervision could be a significant portion of the practice of a professional outside of perhaps a half dozen major metropolitan communities. One reason for this limitation is that most of the people who have sufficient skill to engage in this practice have a paid university affiliation. It has always been my feeling that students within one's own university are not appropriate candidates for this practice. If I am paid a salary to deliver services within a university community, I cannot in good conscience charge students of that university for that service. I have heard others say that their time is limited and that justifies charging students from other departments within their university. My feeling is that if my time is really too limited to see a person, then it will not suddenly be freed if he can produce a fee. Either I have the time to see him or I do not, and if I do have the time, it is part of my obligation to the university to see the student without charge. For this reason I will only see students from other universities in my research practice.

Since every university should provide thesis supervision to its students, the question may be asked as to why any student would wish to pay a fee for what he can receive as part of his tuition payment within his home university. For some students, the reason they come to see me is that they find communication within their own committee very difficult. In some cases, the reason for the difficulty in communication is the inability of the advisor to have enough time for the student, and in other cases it is his inability to provide sufficient structure or clarity of instructions. There are other students who could be very well served by members of their own committee, but they feel that they would prefer showing their ignorance to a stranger rather than to somebody in an evaluative role. From this, it is easy to see that a clinician with research skills is in a particularly good position to deliver meaningful consultation. Many of the problems that students seeking consultation present require particular skills in delivering the information rather than in developing knowledge. Some students require one consultation visit in which I can make a point of methodology clear, while others will require a number of sessions which often are concerned with how one relates to an advisor and makes best use of the facilities that he has available. In a few instances I have found that the problem is one of a significant learning block rather than any specific lack of knowledge, and students who came with the intention of getting research consultation soon realized that their real need was for psychotherapy.

Although my training was in psychology, my consultation is not restricted to projects within this area. I have found that I have been helpful to a wide variety of students from a number of social science areas. The major need that they share is in the general area of methodology, and psychology provides the opportunity to develop a methodology that is applicable to a great many problem areas.

The principal requirement of a private research supervisor is the ability to communicate with directness and clarity. The student does not wish an overly abstract presentation of a series of measurement issues, nor is he coming to be dazzled by your knowledge of the literature or of abstruse methodological problems. Rather, he is coming with a problem in need of a solution, and if the problem allows for a solution, it should be given readily. If the problem cannot be solved simply, then that should be explained to the student so that he is clear as to what his best choices are for future development of the problem area. While a knowledge of statistics is helpful, the highest premium is usually on clear, logical thinking and research methodology. Cookbook statistics usually suffice for the type of problems that are brought to me.

There is a very clear distinction between the way I would relate to one of my own doctoral advisees as compared to a student who has come to me for consultation. With one of my advisees I consider my role as that of a teacher, and part of teaching involves helping the student to develop a problem, to explore it in all of its implications, and to shoulder the major burden of responsibility. I help as much as I can but my ultimate goal is to have the student become a skilled researcher. When I am consulting I see my role as that of an expert, and I have no hesitancy in giving solutions directly rather than teaching the student the way to approach finding the solution. Since my goal for the two types of advisees differs, my approach to reaching that goal will differ accordingly. I can work much more rapidly with a consulting student, but I do not feel that they learn as much about research from me. Then again, they are not usually interested in learning very much about research in general but just want the answer to a problem.

Finding referrals for such a practice is very difficult. I feel most comfortable being passive about this aspect of my practice. A number of colleagues know that I am available for this type of consultation, and the largest source of referrals that I have are friends of people I have worked with in the past. I would not want to advertise this service widely because I do not want to recruit students away from their usual university channels. Theoretically, I would prefer a university system that would function well enough as to leave no room for a person with my particular skills. If a student can get this kind of advice from his own committee, and get it without cost, he is much better off. Furthermore, he will learn a great deal more if he will work with somebody who wants to develop his research education fully rather than as a source of answers. That is why I encourage students to use their own facilities more effectively. However, if a student has exhausted the usual channels of help within a university and does not feel any satisfaction, he will occasionally turn to a resource outside those channels. In such cases I am available to them.

The fee for this service is very easy for me to arrive at. Whatever rate I happen to be charging for my clinical work is also applied to research consultation. In my practice I am charging for my time, and I believe that my time is equally as valuable whether the help I am offering is in research, in diagnostics, or in therapy. Not only does this position make sense to the students who come for help but they often feel that it is something of a bargain, since their problems usually are solvable in a very limited number of sessions as compared to the usual time-extended therapy situation.

PROGRAM EVALUATION

The most exciting aspect of my research practice is in the area of program evaluation. I have been called upon to serve as project evaluator in a fascinating range of problem areas. As examples of the wide variety of problems to which a person with research skills can make a contribution, I have worked with a stop-smoking cruise, an evaluation of the need for a new children's newspaper as a supplement to primary school reading programs, a drug education program, an evaluation of the mental health of clergymen, a series of sensitivity training experiences, and an evaluation of an innovation in the teaching of reading. What is common to each of these areas is the need for skills in research methodology. The content is remarkably varied, but the solution to the problem of evaluation is not very different. These programs were exciting not only because of the variety of content, which gave me the opportunity to develop many new areas of interest and add to my education, but they also fed back into my clinical practice and my teaching. The attempt to solve a real field problem taught skills which were applicable in many other areas. Further, I am sufficiently concrete in my approach to problems and to what gives me satisfaction as to be particularly pleased by the opportunity to solve an immediate problem and to see the implications of that solution put into practice.

A program evaluator can find problems that arise from either end of the continuum of closeness to the administration of a project. One difficulty arises when the need for an evaluation is seen as symbolic rather than substantive. Because of the requirement for accountability, a number of project administrators will attempt to engage the services of a program evaluator without any desire for an evaluation. The evaluation is *pro forma* and nobody intends to pay a great deal of attention to the findings. Cooperation will be limited and the report will be filed quickly. When I have a feeling that an evaluation is being sought for that purpose, I will shy away from the task. It is singularly unrewarding to work at a project, no matter how interesting it might be, with the full knowledge that your work will not be given any serious attention.

The more usual relationship is one in which the administrator engages an evaluator and then relies heavily upon him to help shape the program from the very beginning. The evaluator then becomes a junior project director without portfolio, and becomes involved in many of the decisions that shape the functioning of the project. The danger to evaluation is that you will become too intimately involved with the program to render any objective judgments. On the other hand, there will be a great deal more in the way of satisfaction because the program really will be something of your own. When I sense that a program is developing in this direction, I often move towards it very eagerly, if it is an area in which I have some interest, because the sense of involvement is rewarding in its own right. Many objective indices will have to be included in the evaluation of such a program out of recognition of the dangers that can be introduced by excessive involvement. It is bad enough to have to say that somebody's brainchild is a failure, but it is even worse if it is your own brainchild. Nevertheless, the failure to adequately evaluate a program can lead to the perpetuation of error, and a decent evaluation can often spot mistakes at an early stage when they can still be corrected.

Although it would make a fascinating discussion, the purpose of this chapter is not to describe how to go about doing a program evaluation, any more than the other chapters will teach how to go about doing therapy. The major practical issues that the program evaluator must be concerned with relate to the relationships with the project director and other project personnel. Again, clinical skills are most helpful. It is important to recognize the vested interests and ego involvement, and it is both kind and effective not to step on toes unnecessarily. Further, the program evaluator will do a far better job if he can be sure of the cooperation of everyone involved, and that cooperation is far more readily forthcoming if the major personnel connected with a project have reason to trust your good intentions . Nobody is going to bend over backwards to aid in a hatchet job, and there is no particular satisfaction that can be derived from a whitewash. A thorough and objective evaluation is in the best interests of all the parties, but it should be delivered in a way that is intended to be helpful rather than destructive.

Referrals for program evaluation are not easy to come by, and each evaluation involves a great deal of intensive work over a long period of time. Most of the referrals have come to me through colleagues who are aware of the work that I do and feel that I might be in a position to contribute to a program. It is very difficult to state how one gets his first referral in this area, but if the initial job is done well, it seems that there is little difficulty in obtaining a great many other referrals.

Fees for a program evaluation are far more difficult to set, since the amount of time involvement is usually undetermined. In some cases, the fee is determined by the budget of a grant or an administrative unit. In many cases I will be asked to suggest a fee, and my suggestion often is arrived at through guess work. Again, I try to estimate the amount of time because that is the basic unit that I have to offer. In most cases I put in a great deal more time than I initially estimate, but the rewards of programs usually go far beyond the financial. It is the unusual program that I have evaluated where my fee is commensurate with the amount of time I put in, but fortunately it is also the unusual program where I feel that I have been underpaid when everything is considered.

In summary, the role of research in private practice can be manifold. Every private practitioner should be a research consumer. It seems to me to be irresponsible to ignore the contributions that science can make towards one's practice. A great many more practitioners can be research producers than is currently the case, particularly if one's involvement in research production is limited to cooperation with active research scientists. But the bulk of this chapter has described how research consultation can be a significant portion of one's private practice activity, and as such can be a very educational, fulfilling, and rewarding portion of one's practice.

Chapter 12

LAW AND PRIVATE PRACTICE

GEORGE L. JUROW and WILLIAM E. MARIANO

The literature concerning law and private practice is virtually nonexistent. This surprising fact may help account for the interest and apprehension with which many psychologists in private practice view the legal process. The legal consequences of private practice are indeed largely uncharted. For example, with one exception, no lawsuit alleging malpractice in psychotherapy—by either psychologists or psychiatrists—has ever reached an appellate court in this country. On the one hand, this statistic can be taken as pleasant evidence that psychotherapists rarely become involved with the law and need not fear legal consequences. On the other hand, the statistic reflects the alarming absence of legal guidelines in the performance of a task regarded as sufficiently hazardous by the over 3000 members of the American Psychological Association covered by malpractice insurance.

The basic issue the legal scholar faces is to what extent should the State intervene to reorder private relationships? The psychologist in private practice is likely to find the very posing of this question to be intrusive. The dyadic relationship of traditional psychotherapy is, after all, among the most private of relationships. Yet, the actions of the therapist have ramifications that carry far beyond the treatment room. To illustrate just a few: the psychologist may learn of his patient's intention to commit a crime and may be able to prevent the crime by intervening with the proper authorities; the psychologist may keep records, notes, or tape recordings which may be subpoenaed by a court; the psychologist is paid a fee for his services and may have a legitimate interest in taking legal action to collect an unpaid fee; more generally, the psychologist's actions may seriously affect the health, safety, and welfare of an individual, thereby also affecting his wife, children, or other relatives. The law, as the regulator of society's norms, has an arguable interest in the above and similar issues.

The purpose of this chapter is to survey three main areas involving law and private practice—privileged communication, the tort liability of the psychologist, and the psychologist as expert witness—with a view towards articulating the concerns of each profession. Although legal questions may arise in a myriad of other areas as well, the focus will be on a deeper study of the essential problem areas rather than a broader, but less intensive, survey of every issue. The emphasis is practical in its concern for assisting the psychologist faced with the task of considering the legal consequences of his conduct. The discussion, however, may well raise as many questions as it answers, both practical and theoretical, because of the nascent state of the law.

PRIVILEGED COMMUNICATION

In general, a witness summoned to testify at a trial must answer all questions asked of him. The object of compelling testimony is to ensure fair trials by encouraging maximum disclosure of evidence. However, in the form of "testimonial privileges," the law has carved out a major exception to the rule compelling witnesses to testify. A "testimonial privilege" is a right granted a witness to refuse to testify in court concerning communications passing between persons standing in a confidential relationship to each other. The privilege of nondisclosure is designed to protect confidential relationships which would otherwise be impaired through fear of future disclosure in court.

At common law, communications were privileged in only two confidential relationships: lawyer-client, and husband-wife. All states retain these common law privileges. In addition, some states have accorded privileged status to physicians, psychologists, priests, journalists, detectives, and certain others. At present, over half the states by statute privilege communications with physicians. Psychiatrists, as physicians, are implicitly included within these statutes but psychologists and social workers are not. Because of the special nature of the psychiatrist-patient relationship, several states have statutes specifically covering the relationship. Approximately half the states provide for certification or licensing of psychologist. Most, but not all, of the certification or licensing statutes grant privileged communication status to psychologists. The privilege section of New York's certification statute (N.Y. Educ. Law Sec. 7611) is illustrative:

> The confidential relations and communications between a psychologist registered under the provisions of this act and his client are placed on the same basis as those provided by law between attorney and client, and nothing in this article shall be construed to require any such privileged communications to be disclosed.

The late expert on evidence, Dean John Wigmore (1940), suggested four guidelines which should be considered before granting a privilege:

> "(1) Does the communication in the usual circumstances of the given professional relation originate in a confidence that it will not be disclosed? (2) Is the inviolability of that confidence essential to the achievement of the purpose of the relationship? (3) Is the relation one that should be fostered? and (4) Is the expected injury to the relation, through the fear of later disclosure, greater than the expected benefit to justice in obtaining the testimony?"

The granting of testimonial privileges has been much debated in the literature. Wigmore vigorously opposed the physician-patient privilege in terms of his four criteria because he believed communications only rarely were confidential, and that few people would be deterred from seeking medical help because of fear of disclosure. Wigmore's evaluation of the medical privilege did not include discussion of psychiatry or psychotherapy (his final treatise appeared in 1940). Most writers on the subject of privilege agree that Wigmore's tests are satisfied in the case of psychotherapy and that the privilege ought to be afforded psychiatrists, psychologists, social workers, and others practicing psychotherapy. The defining characteristic of psychotherapy is free disclosure of intimate and confidential material; confidence and trust in the therapist is vital to the treatment process; the treatment relation is of social benefit and should be fostered; and disclosure of information, even in isolated cases, would be disastrous to the relationship in terms of harm to past or present patients and in deterring future patients from seeking treatment.

The practice of conferring the privilege for psychologists in the context of certification or licensing statutes has been criticized on the ground that a blanket protection for all persons consulting "psychologists" certified or registered is too broad because it includes certain psychological work which should not be privileged. For example, industrial psychologists, polling specialists and social or experimental psychologists may not need protection. It would seem the better procedure to grant the privilege on a functional basis rather than in terms of professional title. An additional difficulty in linking certification and privilege is that these statutes do not protect persons consulting the uncertified or unlicensed psychologist, regardless of what duties he performs.

Before discussing how privileges operate, it is first necessary to clearly distinguish "privilege" from "confidentiality." Confidentiality relates to professional ethics. Member associations within many professions establish codes of conduct. These codes may require the professional to respect the confidentiality of communications in the course of his duties. These ethical standards may prohibit disclosure to any third party in a wide variety of situations (see section on Confidentiality in *Ethical Standards of Psychologist*, 1970). "Testimonial privilege," on the other hand, is a legally granted protection in a very specific instance, namely, when the psychologist is called to testify in court.

The law of privileged communications is a morass in terms of legal analysis for two reasons. First, as already indicated, each state sets its own rules on the subject. Some states accord the privilege to psychologists, while others do not; in some states, psychologists are privileged but psychiatrists are not; in some states, psychologists are privileged only if working under the authority of a psychiatrist, and so on. Second, to say that "communications between a psychologist and a person consulting the psychologist are privileged" tells you little about how the privilege operates in practice. In fact, the law of privilege is akin to plowing through a minefield. Although intended to protect the right of nondisclosure, the grant of privilege has been viewed with suspicion by courts and legislatures because it constitutes an exception to the general rule. Consequently, the law of privilege—in the form of statutes and often narrow judicial interpretations—is full of exceptions and restrictions. Far from granting absolute immunity from disclosure, the law of privilege often seems to take away as much protection as it first appears to grant.

In the following discussion on privilege, reference will, on occasion, be made to the Connecticut Model Statute. In 1961, Connecticut passed the first statute specifically covering the psychiatrist-patient privilege. The statute was prepared by a distinguished committee and received the endorsement of the Group for the Advancement of Psychiatry. The Connecticut statute has been the model for psychiatrist-patient privilege statutes recently enacted in several states. The statute covers clinical psychologists and social workers only if they work under the supervision of a psychiatrist. The drafters of the Connecticut statute were divided over whether to grant the privilege to psychologists working independently in private practice; the deciding factor in not granting the privilege was a fear of losing legislative support for the bill. In any case, the Connecticut statute promises to have considerable influence in the drafting of future legislation on privilege, including statutes granting psychologists an independent privilege.

When the privilege is granted in a particular state, the privilege belongs to the patient (or client), *not* the psychologist. Thus the patient has the option of waiving the privilege and requiring the psychologist to testify. Such a waiver may place the psychologist in conflict if adhering to his code of professional ethics prohibits disclosure. In addition, as Slovenko (1966) has pointed out, the patient waiving the privilege may not know what he is waiving. The psychologist may correctly consider it detrimental for the patient to see diagnostic test reports, diagnostic labels, or other material concerning treatment. Unless the court itself intervenes and creates a privilege in the instant case, which has occurred but rarely, the psychologist would face a contempt of court citation for failure to testify.

In most jurisdictions, as well as in the Connecticut statute, the privilege is waived if the patient brings a personal injury suit. The classic argument is that a plaintiff may not use the privilege as both "a sword and a shield." Thus, a defendant may ask the psychologist to testify in order to rebut the plaintiff's allegations concerning his mental condition. This waiver doctrine has been justly criticized (Slovenko, 1966) on the ground that alternatives exist to forcing a patient in therapy to choose between disclosing confidences and asserting a just claim. For example, court-appointed psychologists may be able to make as relevant an evaluation of the plaintiff as would the plaintiff's therapist, without disrupting the plaintiff's treatment.

In most jurisdictions, death terminates the privilege. If a will is contested, the mental capacity of the patient to execute the will is often an issue in litigation. Since the privilege is personal to the deceased, the psychologist or heirs may not assert the privilege. This rule places the psychologist in the difficult position of having to disclose confidences of the deceased as well as confidences of living persons associated with the deceased. Further, the psychologist may be forced to testify to whether or not his patient may have committed suicide, a circumstance which may prohibit payment of an insurance policy.

A defendant in a criminal case may be ordered by the court to submit to a mental examination. Federal law and the laws of most states provide that communications to a psychologist or psychiatrist in the course of such examination are not privileged insofar as they concern the defendant's mental condition. Thus, under this rule, there may be no testimony concerning admissions made about the crime. The Connecticut statute terminates the privilege when the patient needs hospitalization pursuant to state commitment statutes. But the termination is a limited one, restricting disclosure to communications relevant to the commitment proceeding.

Divorce cases can provide difficult situations in states without privilege protection. Since "fault" is still a legal issue in contested divorces, psychologists can be compelled to testify about confidences disclosed in therapy (particularly adultery or other sexual practices). The increasing use of conjoint therapy, or therapy where both spouses are seen separately by the same therapist, raise the question whether one spouse can compel the testimony of the therapist in the face of a privilege claim by the opposing spouse. There are no cases on this point, nor do the privilege statutes note the problem.

The growing use of group therapy provides a serious problem under the privilege statutes. Traditionally, no privilege attaches to otherwise confidential communications when the communication occurs in the presence of a third person. The theory is that confidentiality no longer exists. Some states have extended the traditional medical privilege to cover the physician's nurse or secretary, but others have not. In group therapy, the therapist might be prohibited from testifying, but other patients would not be. It appears necessary to modify most privilege statutes which consider only the narrow dyadic relationship. McCormick (1953) has articulated the better view concerning the medical privilege and third parties, a view which by analogy should govern the group therapy setting:

> . . . if the third person is present as a needed and customary participant in such consultation, the circle of confidence may be reasonably extended to include him . . . the nurse present as the doctor's assistant during the consultation or examination, or the technician who makes tests or X-ray photographs under the doctor's direction, who will be looked on as the doctor's agent in whose keeping the information will remain privileged. (McCormick, 1953)

Similarly, each participant in group therapy is an integral part of the treatment process and assists the therapist in treatment of other patients. At present, no state statute clearly grants privilege protection to a psychologist and the group he is treating, although the statutes in two states, California and Kansas, might be so construed. The Connecticut statute would cover group therapy, but only under the supervision of a psychiatrist.

Communication to a third party also presents a problem for psychologists working with children. Because parents, teachers, or others may be involved in the treatment process, the receipt of information to these third parties would invalidate any privilege in most jurisdictions. The Connecticut statute expresses the better view in allowing the patient to prevent disclosure of communications between members of the patient's family and the therapist. Should the privilege be held applicable in a case involving the treatment of a child, an unanswered question remains as to whether a child may waive the privilege. The law requires most waivers of rights by persons to be made "knowingly" and "intelligently." A minor may lack this necessary capacity to make an informed decision. In a child custody case, parents may want a waiver in order to compel testimony by the therapist, although such testimony may not ultimately be in the child's best interests. In such cases it should be the court's responsibility, aided by information from the therapist, to protect the interests of the child.

A very serious difficulty with the privilege rules concerns the so-called "future crime exception." The privilege is considered terminated for the physician-patient and attorney-client relations when the communications concern the commission of present crimes or the planning of future crimes. Patients in therapy may be involved in the commission or future commission of a variety of crimes including narcotics violations, homosexuality, abortion, violent assault, tax evasion, larceny, business fraud, or whatever. The disclosure of such information, if compelled later in court, would seriously disrupt the treatment process by deterring patients from seeking treatment and communicating freely. Further, most psychologists are aware that expressions of intent are different from acting out the intent. In fact, compelling disclosure may be of least service to society, since the therapist has the unique opportunity of preventing serious criminal behavior by continuing to work with the patient. Apart from disclosure in court, the law presently requires physicians to disclose to appropriate authorities a variety of situations that may come to their attention, including venereal and other communicable diseases; epilepsy (to Motor Vehicle Departments); gunshot wounds; and under so-called "battered child statutes," injuries to children that seem to have been inflicted by parents. Psychologists are not generally covered by these disclosure provisions. Certain situations, however, may present the psychotherapist with a need for immediate disclosure. The patient who is clearly and imminently dangerous to himself or others would be the primary example. In such instances, the psychologist can prevent serious harm to the patient or to others by acting under state statutes providing for short-term emergency hospital commitment.

Where the privilege exists, it would protect the confidentiality of notes, records, tape recordings, and the like. But it should be remembered by the psychologist that since the patient may waive the privilege, the content of such materials may be subject to disclosure in future litigation. Although the patient may desire a waiver for his own reasons, the psychologist who keeps records should weigh the consequences of disclosure to other members of the community. The problem is particularly acute with respect to patients who disclose information concerning adultery or other behavior which may be the subject of future divorce or child-custody litigation. In states where no privilege exists, the keeping of records in any form is particularly hazardous, since they may be subpoenaed . Attorneys are particularly interested in records because the therapist himself is likely to be a reluctant witness. Many psychologists make it a practice not to keep records of treatment sessions because of fear of subpoena.

TORT LIABILITY

A tort is a private injury resulting from a breach of duty created by law. Torts embrace a variety of conduct, including negligence, breach of privacy, assault, libel and slander, etc. Torts are distinct from wrongs involving breach of contract which arise from violations of obligations created by consent of the parties; and distinct from crimes, which involve wrongs arising from a violation of public duty. Certain torts, however, may also constitute crimes or breach of contract, so there is some overlap.

Malpractice

Liability for negligence (malpractice) is the tort of most significance to the psychologist in private practice. Professionals, including psychologists, physicians, attorneys, engineers, accountants and others, do not guarantee to accomplish a particular result or cure. But once he undertakes treatment of a patient, the psychologist, in the same way as the physician and surgeon, is obligated to conduct his examination and treatment in a skillful, competent and professional manner. The psychologist holds himself out as possessing the skill and knowledge commonly possessed by members in good standing of the psychology profession, and is consequently liable for harm or injury for failure to meet current professional standards.

With one exception, there are no appellate cases in this country involving a suit for malpractice of psychotherapy. There are a moderate number of malpractice cases involving psychiatrists, but these mainly involve the negligent administration of shock therapy where fractures can occur or the negligent administration of drugs. The psychologist in private practice is primarily concerned with malpractice involving psychotherapy.

In the absence of a substantial and settled body of case law, a general definition of malpractice in terms of failure to exercise the currently accepted standards of professional skill offers little guidance to the psychotherapist in private practice. However, two cases involving successful malpractice action brought against psychiatrists merit discussion.

Hammer v. Rosen was a malpractice action brought against John N. Rosen in 1955. Rosen is noted for his efforts in utilizing "direct psychoanalysis" with psychotics. The plaintiff was a diagnosed schizophrenic who had undergone over 150 electric-shock treatments with a previous therapist. Rosen treated the patient for seven years. Three of the plaintiff's witnesses testified that Rosen had physically beaten (slapped) the plaintiff on several occasions. The trial court dismissed the malpractice action without submitting it to a jury, but the New York Court of Appeals reversed (7 N.Y. 2d 376, 165 N.E. 2d 756, 1960), holding that the case should have gone to the jury. The Court of Appeals stated that the testimony of plaintiff's witnesses concerning the beatings "made out a prima facie case of malpractice which, if uncontradicted and unexplained and credited by the jury, would require a verdict for the plaintiff." Rosen argued that expert testimony was necessary to support plaintiff's charge of malpractice. The Court of Appeals dismissed this argument, remarking that "the very nature of the acts complained of bespeaks improper treatment and malpractice and that, if the defendant chooses to justify these acts as proper treatment, he is under the necessity of offering evidence to that effect."

Most medical malpractice cases have held that a jury may not find negligence in the absence of expert testimony to that effect. The failure of the New York Court of Appeals to require expert testimony has been interpreted by some commentators (e.g. Morse, 1967) as a decision hostile to the psychotherapy profession and out of tune with modern treatment concepts. This interpretation is arguable. The Court of Appeals noted in its opinion that Rosen's appellate brief itself characterized any type of treatment involving assaults upon a patient as "fantastic." In light of Rosen's own characterization, and his denial of having committed such acts, it was not unreasonable for the Court to hold that such unexplained assaultive conduct could constitute malpractice. The Court of Appeals' statement that the "very nature of the acts complained of bespeaks improper treatment and malpractice" is not necessarily a restrictive and limiting judicial view of psychotherapy. The opinion referred to the alleged acts as "beatings" and at no point was the conduct treated as less or placed in therapeutic context.

Landau v. Werner (105 Sol. J. 257, on appeal, 105 Sol. J. 1008, C.A. 1961) was the other successful suit for malpractice in psychotherapy. Although a British precedent, the case raises disturbing questions concerning judicial scrutiny of the psychotherapeutic process. The plaintiff was treated by a psychiatrist beginning in 1949. After 24 sessions, the plaintiff developed strong transferential sexual and emotional feelings for the therapist. The plaintiff discussed these feelings with the therapist who advised her that the feelings would decline and that she should continue treatment. The therapist feared that plaintiff would relapse to a previous anxiety state and so began to visit the plaintiff socially. The social visits included visits to restaurants, taxicab rides, and discussion of a holiday vacation. No allegation was made that the therapist made improper advances. The plaintiff thereafter relapsed, required electroshock treatments, and attempted suicide.

At the trial, several psychiatrists testified on behalf of the plaintiff that social visits under such transferential circumstances were improper. The defendant did not rebut this testimony with any expert witnesses of his own. The Court of Appeals held that a good cause of action for malpractice was made out by unrebutted proof of expert testimony condemning social visits to a patient transferentially aroused to the therapist, when the patient's condition declines thereafter. The decision in *Landau* implies that the therapist should have broken off the treatment relation rather than handle the transference through social visits. The Court decided that the therapist's judgment that the patient would deteriorate if not seen by the therapist (through social visits if the patient refused to continue therapy) was improper. The solution, as the Court saw it, was referral of the patient to her previous psychiatrist.

The Court's handling of the *Landau* case is questionable, although the plaintiff was burdened by the uniformity of the expert medical testimony condemning social visits. In medical malpractice cases, the courts have held it allowable to use innovative techniques in lieu of established procedures, although the guidelines are vague and controversial. If the burden is placed on the therapist departing from established standards to justify his treatment, at first blush an apparently reasonable proposition, the road may be closed for techniques departing from majority professional opinion. Since treatment techniques in psychotherapy have been characterized by considerable professional controversy, particularly in recent years as innovation has greatly increased, courts may be incorrect in assuming that a clear body of professional standards exists. Treatment techniques that would be abhorrent to the classical Freudian psychoanalyst may be accepted by a variety of other therapists whose techniques in turn might be condemned by still other therapists. The question is how courts should draw the line in order to protect patients from egregious treatment methods while respecting the variety of professional differences existing about therapy techniques. To solve the problem, as our adversary system does, by leaving it to the litigants to turn the trial into a "battle of expert witnesses" begs the question. It is precisely the innovator who is likely to lose the battle under these ground rules. More helpful would be increased judicial sophistication to look behind the "experts," who may be advocates of a narrow professional point of view, in order to place innovative methods in proper perspective.

Psychologists who lead encounter groups, sensitivity groups, marathon groups, and the like have few guidelines in assessing boundaries of legal liability. *Hammer* and *Landau* dealt with the dyadic therapeutic relation and were decided before the rapid proliferation of new group techniques. However, these cases are disquieting for therapists engaged in very innovative treatment techniques. The essence of the two cases is that a court will not uncritically assume that anything done by a therapist in the course of treatment may have a therapeutic purpose. The burden is thus placed on the therapist to justify radical techniques. *Hammer* involved acts that would constitute assault and battery unless otherwise justified as part of treatment. *Hammer* certainly would not rule out all touching of a patient by a therapist. The therapist who comforts a distraught patient in a reasonable manner, although he touches the patient, would not be engaging in assaultive conduct. But some practices employed in encounter and similar groups may run the risk of being labeled prima facie malpractice in the event of a lawsuit (for example, "games" whereby participants approach each other and express nonverbally how they feel may result in a fight, or where a person tries to fight his way in or out of a closed circle of people). The therapist might be responsible for assaults committed at his direction by other participants, although he did not personally participate.

Although there is no case law dealing specifically with these innovative groups, there are some points psychologists leading groups ought to consider. The psychologist leading an encounter or similar group may assume he has considerable leeway because of the absence of settled professional standards. Further, the unlicensed or uncertified psychologist, as well as a therapist without any formal academic training, might argue that he does not hold himself out as possessing special skill and knowledge in the same way as a physician, attorney, or certified psychologist. However, the very fact of "leading" a group where the ability to direct human behavior is assumed by the participants is an undertaking to use reasonable care in doing so. Even though group techniques may differ from leader to leader, there is a common element in most group work that raises the issue of potential malpractice. The common element is the danger of serious emotional injury to a participant. Although there is little data on the incidence of psychotic episodes or other breakdowns, the risk is there because of the very nature of the activity. The law on traditional medical malpractice has sometimes made the degree of care required depend upon the degree of danger should something go wrong, particularly when the elements of the procedure cannot be easily controlled. In *Landau v. Werner, supra,* the Court spoke as follows:

> A psychiatrist had explosive forces under his control and if they were released the consequences might be disastrous. He must exercise the very greatest care in dealing with the dark secrets of the human mind . . . if mistakes were made in psychotherapy, psychoanalysis, or other forms of psychological therapy which employed transference, the consequences might be disastrous and indeed irrevocable.

An analogy can be drawn, as Dawidoff (1966) has noted, to the tort doctrine of strict liability. There is a trend in the law to impose liability for injury without regard to fault, particularly when there is something inherently dangerous about the defendant's activity were something to go wrong. Although the strict liability doctrine is limited to certain specific situations, both *Landau* and *Hammer* suggest a hint of the doctrine. It seems unwise to impose strict liability for psychological treatment or to infer malpractice from the very fact of the injury (the so-called tort doctrine of *res ipsa loquitor,* literally, "The thing speaks for itself") and the courts have not done so as yet. But the psychologist must be prepared for judicial mistrust of therapy, particularly of novel types of treatment.

The most obvious way the psychologist involved in encounter and similar groups can guard against potential liability is to screen prospective group participants as carefully as possible. Group therapists of the more traditional analytic variety, who may see patients both in individual and group treatment, tend to do some screening. However, psychologists involved in the more transient encounter groups often do not. Screening is time-consuming and may be impossible under some circumstances. But the very fact of failure to screen may itself be taken as evidence of negligence. Failure to screen, in combination with the actual fact of an acute psychotic episode in the group, is a difficult case for the psychologist to defend in court.

Another way the psychologist might protect himself from potential liability is to obtain a written consent form whereby the patient releases the psychologist from liability for conduct which might constitute negligence. A written release may or may not be legally effective. The legal issue involved is the doctrine of "assumption of risk." In general, a plaintiff may consent to relieve the defendant of his duty of reasonable care and take his risk of the consequences. In fact, the consent to assume the risk need not be expressed in writing but may be implied from plaintiff's conduct in freely entering into a situation or relationship presenting obvious danger. The crucial element in assumption of risk is that the plaintiff (patient) must have *knowledge of the risk*. A plaintiff may not assume a risk of which he is ignorant; he must understand the nature of the danger. The psychologist may be reluctant to discuss risks with participants prior to the group experience for a variety of reasons. Primarily, he may not want to alarm the participant about a risk which has a low probability of occurrence. But failure to clearly spell out the potential dangers will invalidate the consent forms. The psychologist cannot assume that the participant is assuming the "obvious" dangers or risks implied in group experiences. The participant may be wholly ignorant of what the group techniques are, how they could affect him, and so on. The group participant who is injured is likely to be a person whose emotional problems render him incapable of clearly understanding what he is getting involved in. A court would be unlikely to find assumption of risk on the part of an emotionally disturbed person. It should also be noted that even if the consent form is valid, it would not relieve the psychologist of liability for "gross" negligence or intentional misconduct.

The principle of "knowledge of the risk" is part of the assumption of risk doctrine but it potentially may have an independent status. In the law of medical malpractice, the doctrine of "informed consent" has rapidly expanded. The informed consent doctrine prohibits surgery or other critical medical procedures without the prior consent of the patient. The informed consent requirement is independent of the equally important duty of reasonable care and skill in treatment. Similar to the assumption of risk situation, effective informed consent must be based on an understanding of the nature of the treatment and its risks. The consent problem is particularly acute in instances of innovative medical treatment where risks may be unknown. Here the plaintiff must disclose to the patient the possibility of unknown risks, since disclosure will affect the patient's decision to proceed with the proposed treatment.

The informed consent doctrine has not yet been applied to psychotherapy in any form. However, the encounter group movement may be a fertile field for extension of the doctrine. Prospective participants may not be aware of the variety of group techniques which may be employed, including caressing, nudity, genital contact, arm wrestling, and so on (see Goldman and Brody, 1970, for a description of the variety of group techniques employed). The naive participant who is injured may base his claim not on the psychologist's negligence but rather on his failure to inform the patient of what was going to happen. A court faced with an injured plaintiff who was the subject of unorthodox (to the court, perhaps, bizarre) behavioral techniques may well be tempted to apply some version of the informed consent doctrine. The best way the psychologist can protect himself is to inform participants of what techniques might be used and the possibility of risk (preferably in writing, signed by both psychologist and participant). Here again, unless the information given the participant is full and complete, it will be of no legal consequence. Further, since an emotionally disturbed participant may be held incapable of informed consent, the psychologist is ultimately thrown back on careful screening as his best precaution.

Right of Privacy

A defendant will incur liability for damages if he invades plaintiff's privacy. What constitutes legally protected privacy cannot be simply defined because of the variety of circumstances the cases cover. There have been several cases involving suits for breach of privacy against psychologists and psychiatrists, but none have been held liable. The potential for liability is present, of course, since the defining element of traditional psychotherapy is its confidential nature. The confidentiality section in the American Psychological Association code of ethics (1970) makes this professional responsibility plain. The following discussion will point out some obvious risks of incurring liability, although every eventuality cannot be covered.

Psychotherapists, like other professionals, are prone to discuss their work with colleagues, at home, or at social affairs. Cocktail party chatter is particularly hazardous if patients' names are used. Even if names are not used, the psychologist should be cautious because identity may be easily inferred from the facts of the case. Psychologists frequently present patients at case conferences, before one-way mirrors or before other groups. Presenting the patient or material about the patient without the patient's consent may violate privacy. A patient who consents to appear before a one-way mirror or on closed-circuit television must be precisely informed about who will be observing. Written consent forms, enumerating the observers, should be obtained from the patient. The psychologist should be cautious about presenting a patient who is sufficiently disturbed so as not to understand what is happening or who is watching. The psychologist who presents test or other written material about a patient is advised to delete the patient's name from the material. The psychologist who submits case material for publication is responsible for disguising the identity of the patient even though the case presentation may suffer. Where the patient may be identified from the material, prior consent to publication must be obtained. Written consent should always be obtained before information is released to others, whether professionals or nonprofessionals, or institutions such as hospitals, schools, and government agencies.

Suits to collect a fee may involve disclosure that the patient is in treatment, but this has not been held to constitute invasion of privacy. In several cases, a physician who turned his debt over to a collection agency was sued for invasion of privacy when the collection agency notified the patient's employer in order to help collect the debt. These claims for invasion of privacy were denied. However, a therapist might be responsible for invasion of privacy were the collection agency to act too broadly and unreasonably in disseminating information. It should be noted that a patient's testimonial privilege of preventing the psychologist from testifying in court does not apply in lawsuits between the parties. Thus, the psychologist may sue his patient for failure to pay his fee. It is not necessary that the psychologist, to establish his claim, testify about the content of sessions. The existence of the therapy relationship, the number of sessions and the fee are all that is necessary to allege in court. In this connection, his case is stronger when the psychologist keeps accurate books and sends out bills regularly.

THE PSYCHOLOGIST AS EXPERT WITNESS

Expert pesychological testimony is relevant to a variety of courtroom disputes. Of paramount importance is the insanity defense. Under the traditional "M'Naghten rule" in effect in most jurisdictions, a defendant may be acquitted of a crime on grounds of insanity if he can show he was laboring under such a defect of reason from disease of the mind as not to know the nature and quality of the act; or if he did know it, that he did not know he was doing what was wrong. Other rules exist in some jurisdictions, including the "Durham rule" which relieves criminal responsibility if the unlawful act was the product of mental disease or mental defect.

The psychologist, using diagnostic tests or interview methods, can testify about the nature of the defendant's mental state, his intellectual level, the possibility of brain damage, and so. The relevance of defendant's (or plaintiff's) mental state extends beyond insanity defense cases, including, as well, insurance claims, workman's compensation disability claims, will contests litigating the decedent's capacity to make a will, and child-custody cases.

The competency of the psychologist to testify as an expert witness has been upheld against challenge. In the leading case of *Jenkins v. United States*, 307 F. 2d 637 (D.C. Cir. 1962), the competency of psychologists was extensively reviewed. Jenkins was charged with assault with intent to rape, and pleaded insanity. The trial court excluded testimony offered by three defense psychologists. In overruling the verdict, the United States Court of Appeals for the District of Columbia stated that:

. . . the Ph.D. in Clinical Psychology involves some—and often much—training and experience in the diagnosis and treatment of mental disorders. Typically, candidates are trained, *inter alia,* in general psychology, theory of personality and psychodynamics, psychopathology, diagnostic methods, therapeutic techniques, selected aspects of physiology and anatomy, and clinical methods. A one-year internship in a mental hospital is required for the degree. After graduation some clinical psychologists administer and interpret diagnostic tests which elicit the patient's intellectual level, defenses, personality structure, attitudes, feelings, thought and perceptual processes. See 1 Rapaport, Diagnostic Testing 7-9 (1945). In many institutions and clinics their reports, which regularly include opinions concerning the presence or absence of mental disease or defect, are important aids to psychiatrists who customarily have the final responsibility for diagnosis. Some psychologists, moreover, regularly administer psychotherapy and related non-organic therapies in treatment of certain types of mental disorders. (307 F. 2d at 644-645).

In the *Jenkins* appeal, the American Psychological Association filed an amicus curiae brief supporting the competency of qualified psychologists to testify on the existence of mental disease or defect and to answer questions as to the causal relationship between such disease or defect and an alleged crime. The Court of Appeals opinion concurred with the view of the American Psychological Association, despite an amicus curiae brief filed in opposition by the American Psychiatric Association.

Serving as an expert witness is a challenging experience. The psychologist relying on diagnostic tests will face rigorous cross-examination concerning the reliability and validity of these tests. The successful expert witness avoids the arrogant assumption that the validity of his procedures should be self-evident to the court. Apart from a layman's inability to comprehend the usefulness of projective and other tests, there is considerable controversy in the literature concerning the validity and reliability of various tests. The successful witness is one who is familiar with the literature, who can acknowledge the presence of conflicting views (but place the data in proper perspective), and most importantly who can patiently clarify to the court or jury how he reached his conclusions using the methods he did.

Ability to testify as an expert witness is a very high art because most psychologists, like other professionals, are understandably defensive when their competency, and hence pride, is challenged. It is an unfortunate but real fact that distrust still exists among judges and jurors toward the mental health profession. This distrust is fueled by the controversy within the mental health profession itself concerning the scientific nature of mental illness. For example, Halleck (1967) and other authorities on forensic psychiatry and psychology have argued that consistent definitions of mental illness do not exist apart from vague and equivocal value judgments. The "medical model" or "disease" concept of mental illness is competing with the view that psychopathology is a function of social role adaptation, with different implications for criminal responsibility. The expert witness must have a respect and understanding for such opposing viewpoints while still being an effective advocate for his own position.

SUMMARY

Few psychologists have ever been sued concerning their professional activities. The likelihood of a given psychologist incurring monetary liability is slight. Nevertheless, the psychologist has a professional responsibility to be aware of the legal consequences of his professional practice. Even if he is not likely to be sued personally, his actions may have profound consequences for others. The psychologist who keeps records, case summaries, tape recordings, and the like must be cognizant of the risk of subpoena in his state, cognizant of who might be harmed by public disclosure of these materials, and cognizant of what alternatives he might take if he deems the risk too high.

The risk of personal liability, though still small, is increasing. Innovative treatment methods, particularly the growth of the sensitivity and encounter group movement, have raised issues of legal liability which will inevitably be tested in court. The growth of large-scale health insurance programs has encouraged litigation for personal injury. As any profession grows and achieves wide public acceptance, professional standards become fixed and accepted by the courts as relevant to holding liable those professionals violating such standards.

The private practitioner is most apt to assist the law in providing diagnostic opinions at insanity trials. Since the *Jenkins* decision, the psychologist's role in this large area has expanded. With the increasing expansion of the role of the private practitioner to include community involvement, bringing with it increasing contact with public agencies and community interest groups, the psychologist will inevitably become more active in the legal process.

Chapter 13

ACCOUNTING, TAX, RETIREMENT, AND ESTATE ASPECTS OF THE PSYCHOTHERAPIST'S PRACTICE

S. GEORGE GREENSPAN*

No one practicing a profession can avoid those affairs that relate to the financial aspects of his practice. They embrace a complicated network of economic relationships and activities in which each professional, as an economic person, is inextricably involved.

This chapter is concerned with some of these economic processes, how they affect you and place demands on you, and in what way you can resolve these demands and obligations. It is divided into four main sections with subtopics under each section. "Record Keeping and Accounting" is devoted to the recording of your monetary affairs. "Income Tax and Tax-Saving Methods" is an explanation of a number of tax ideas which, when properly applied, can reduce your annual tax bill. "Retirement Planning" concerns certain monetary strategies that will assist you in building up funds for future retirement. "Estate Planning" deals with methods that can be used to ensure that as much as possible of your worldly goods will be conserved in your estate when you pass away.

Considerable additional material concerning the economic affairs of your practice could have been included, while many topics included could have been expanded, but selection and treatment was limited by space considerations.

The subject matter is not intended to replace your accountant or lawyer whose professional skill and experience is indispensable in conducting the business aspects of your practice. It is hoped

---

*The author gratefully acknowledges the critical comments of Edward Brancati, Esq., consultant on pension and estate planning, for the sections on retirement and estate planning.

that the concepts, terms, and procedures discussed will enable you to better communicate with your professional advisors. You may consider jotting down some of the things that are particularly worthwhile to discuss with your professional advisors.

You should not approach the following sections with hesitation. It is neither abstruse nor incomprehensible. Much of it you have, in a general way, been exposed to in your daily activities.

The effort you make towards understanding and executing these practice concepts and methods will produce cash dividends and help assure a greater measure of material security for you and your family.

RECORD KEEPING AND ACCOUNTING
Purpose

The average psychotherapist usually operates his practice as an individual practitioner. He may have a full- or part-time secretary. If he has a secretary, her services may be shared with other therapists practicing in the same office. When a secretary is employed, the duties of keeping records usually becomes her responsibility. Business record keeping for a psychotherapist is a relatively simple procedure, since the time spent with the patient is usually charged at an hourly rate, payable monthly.

The following are several very good reasons that require the maintenance of accurate records:

1. They permit you to know whether your practice is providing an adequate income for your needs and goals, i.e. it discloses how your income and expenses are developing currently and how they compare with previous years.
2. They are the basis for information for patient invoicing, paying your bills, knowing who owes you for past services, and in general controlling the money end of your practice.
3. They enable your accountant to prepare a proper income tax return. The law requires every person gainfully engaged to maintain records to determine his correct tax liability.
4. They are needed to prepare employee tax information, like social security and withholding taxes.

Requirements

What to Keep

The income tax law requires that in regard to your expenses, the paid bills and cancelled checks which substantiate your book-keeping records be kept for possible audit. On the income side, you must be able to identify the source of your receipts as revealed by your bank deposits, your stock brokerage account, etc. Some of these receipts may be nontaxable like a repayment to you of a loan, a gift, or inheritance and unless properly explained or identified during a tax examination, needless embarrassment and difficulties will arise. Estimates and sketchy records approximating income and expenses are insufficient for legal compliance. They may cause you to lose proper expense deductions. Also, they may subject you to increased taxable income when, in fact, these receipts are not income subject to tax in the first place.

How Long to Keep Your Records

Income taxes may be assessed anytime within three years after the tax return is filed or six years if the taxpayer omits more than 25 percent of his gross receipts (fees, interest, gains on sales, etc.). It is prudent from a tax point of view to keep your records at least six years. In addition to the tax consideration, there are commercial law considerations. The laws of each state fix various time periods within which someone may sue you. In those states that have adopted the Uniform Commercial Code, and nearly all states have adopted the code, a suit for breach of contract, like a claim for payment, must be commenced within four years from the time of the original transaction. A suit commenced after four years can be defended by pleading the Statute of Limitation as a defense, thus barring recovery. During the four-year period, you will need to prove payment by a cancelled check, paid receipt, etc. After that time, the Statute acts as a good defense to the suit. A safe rule for all purposes is to keep your records for at least six years. All your records should be kept in a safe place protected from the dangers of fire or other casualty loss and secure from theft or vandalism.

Bookkeeping

Income Statement: Cash and Accrual Method

To properly record the various financial transactions of your practice, basic data and books of account are required. Most therapists record their basic data and books of account on a calendar year basis. They consider as income and expense for the year only what is received in payment from patients and what is disbursed in the way of expenses. This method of accounting is called the cash basis of accounting and is used by most therapists for tax purposes. Though simple, it is an inaccurate accounting method for determining what the true state of your business affairs may be, since it omits what you may still owe (your accounts payable) and what is owed to you (your accounts receivable). Unless you have been paid by all your patients in the year and in turn you have paid all your obligations for the year, which is unlikely, you must consider in your calculation your outstanding receivables and payables by using the accrual method of accounting for accurately determining your true net income for the year. It is not a difficult procedure. You first prepare your income statement on the cash method (cash receipts less cash payments for the year) and then you adjust the cash income statement by your outstanding accounts payable and receivable at the beginning and end of the year.

INCOME STATEMENT, YEAR 197X

	Cash Income Statement (Tax Method)	Adjustments	Accrual Income Statement
Receipts From Fees (Received)	$40,000		$40,000
Minus Due from patients at beginning of year		($5,000)	
Add Due from patients at end of year		7,000	2,000
Income totals	$40,000		$42,000
Business Expenses (Paid)	$15,000		$15,000
Minus Last years expenses paid this year		(7,000)	
Add This years expenses unpaid end of year		12,000	5,000
*Depreciation of car	1,000		1,000
Expense totals	$16,000		$21,000
Net income from practice	$24,000		$21,000
Drawings paid to you	20,000		20,000
Net income remaining in practice	4,000		1,000

*Major purchases like furniture, your business car, etc., are treated in a special way. The entire cost should not be considered a business expense in the year of purchase. They are capital assets to be depreciated (treated as an expense) over their useful life. A car with an estimate life of four years costing 6,500 dollars that can be traded in for 1,500 dollars is a depreciation expense of 1,000 dollars in each of the four years.

The Bookkeeping System

The totals that are used in the preparation of the income statement come from your basic data and books of account. If these records are up to date, you can prepare your income statement monthly or quarterly in order to know how you are financially progressing in your practice.

The minimum bookkeeping system for a therapist consists of basic data and books of account. The basic data to record payments is the bank checks you write, petty cash slips, and expense invoices (paid or unpaid). The basic data source for receipts is your appointment log or diary. Books of account record and classify the data sources chronologically. The account books consist of the cash receipts book, cash disbursement book,

TABLE 13-I

THE ORGANIZATION OF RECORD KEEPING AND ACCOUNTING

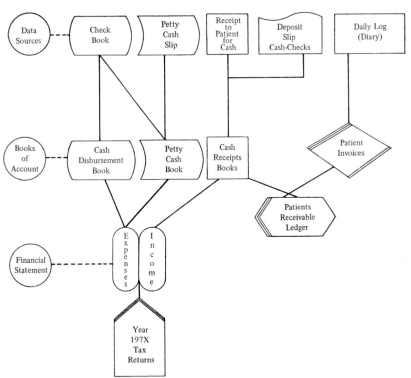

petty cash book, payroll book, and patients' ledger cards. All of these books of account and data source forms can be purchased in most stationery stores. A detailed explanation of the use of these data sources and books of account follow. By examining the specimen figures recording typical transactions, you will see how the business events flow from data sources to the books and then to the income statement. Table 13-I illustrates the organization of the record keeping and accounting process.

Data Sources

BANK CHECKBOOK, PETTY CASH SLIPS (CASH OUT). It is best to have two separate bank checking accounts—one for personal household purposes and one for your practice so you do not mix your business transactions with your personal affairs. It is practical to have both accounts in the same bank in order to facilitate transfers of funds from one account to the other. Pay your expenses upon the basis of bills rendered to you. Your expense invoices or bills should be filed alphabetically in two files, one for the paid bills and the other for unpaid bills. When you write a check to pay a business expense, clearly indicate on the stub part of your checkbook what it is for (see the Code of Business Expenses, Fig. 13-1). Then write on the bill a notation that it is paid plus the check number and date of payment. Your checkbook is designed to keep a current record of how much you have in the bank. The total of your deposit should be inserted in the appropriate place in the checkbook, and as checks are written, their amounts are subtracted from your deposit in order to arrive at the balance you have in the bank. Without this balance at your fingertips, you would not know if you had sufficient funds to pay your expenses. Although in most instances you will pay all expenses by check, periodically you will need to draw a check for cash in order to pay cash expenses. The payments made by use of the petty cash check are for minor expenses like supplies, carfare, postage, etc., and can be accounted for by a simple record book called a petty cash book. Where possible, obtain a receipt for petty cash outlays. If you cannot get a receipt, prepare one yourself on a simple sheet of paper, recording date, amount, to whom paid, and purpose. Most stationers sell petty cash pad

1. Automobile Expenses
    a. Gas and oil.
    b. Repairs and maintenance.
    c. Depreciation.
    d. Insurance.

2. Capital Expenditures
    a. Furniture.
    b. Car.
    c. Depreciation.

3. Professional Expenses
    a. Dues.
    b. Books and periodicals.
    c. Malpractice insurance.
    d. Client development (entertainment and promotion).
    e. Educational expenses.
    f. Travel and carfare.
    g. Convention costs.
    h. Gifts.
    i. Research expenses.
    j. Refund fees.
    k. Professional assistance, consultation.

4. Employee Expenses
    a. Salary.
    b. Social security expense.
    c. Unemployment insurance expense.
    d. Compensation insurance.
    e. Temporary—nonemployee help.
    f. Disability insurance.
    g. Employee welfare payments (life insurance, medical, etc.).

5. Administrative Expenses
    a. Rent.
    b. Light and heat.
    c. Stationery and supplies.
    d. Telephone and telegraph.
    e. Postage.
    f. Office maintenance and repairs.
    g. Accounting and legal.
    h. General expenses.
    i. Office expenses (noncapital items).
    j. Phone answering service.
    k. Property tax.
    l. Tips and gratuities.

Figure 13–1. Record-keeping and accounting code of business expenses. The code permits expansion for additional expenses by adding a letter under each classification.

books on which you can make a notation of your petty expenditures.

DAILY LOG OF COLLECTIONS AND CHARGES. Since the practice of psychotherapy is conducted on a time-spent basis, all of the therapist's working time must be accounted for in order not to overlook charging a patient. The daily log or diary records the

Record Keeping and Accounting
Cash Receipts
Month of September 197X

Date		Patient Receipt	Deposit	General Item	Column Amount
	Totals Forward-Previous Months	$14300 00	$15 7 25 00		$14 2 5 00
1	Mary Smith	50 00			
	Roger Jones	30 00			
	Abe Green	25 00			
	John Castor	25 00	1 30 00		
2	Dividend XYZ Stock			Dividend	4 5 00
	Rent - Subtenant			Rent	100 00
	Gloria Debs	30 00	1 75 00		
6	Tom Sloan	40 00			
	Virginia Dollack	25 00			
	Herman Snow	25 00	90 00		
	Total For Month				
	Cumulative Total				

Figure 13-2. Cash receipts book.

name of the patient in the appropriate hour when he is seen. To the right hand side of the appointment hour and the patient's name, the amount is entered representing the patient's charge for his visit. Very often this log doubles as an appointment book.

BOOKS OF ACCOUNT. When the patient remits his check to you for payment, the information as to patient name, date and amount is entered in the cash receipts book (Fig. 13-2). If cash is received in payment, the patient must be given a receipt. The carbon copy of the receipt remains in the receipt book and is used as a source from which cash entries are made to the cash receipts book. Deposits to the bank should be made as often as required. The individual items and total of the bank deposit slip must agree with the cash book deposit and cash column. Bank deposit slips are furnished by your bank for the purpose of making deposits of your patient's receipts.

The cash disbursement book (Fig. 13-3), which is a record of expense payments, is made up of multicolumn pages. There is a space provided to enter the name to whom the check was made out (payee), the date, and check number. In the columnar part, each column is headed by an expense description with a general column for less-frequent expenses. A new page is begun each month for both the receipt and disbursement pages. Cumulative total carry forward the totals of each month. In this way, you can quickly know the expenses you have paid and the receipts received for each month and for the cumulative period that has elapsed since the first of the year. By December 31 of each year, you will have a complete record from which to prepare your annual income statement and income tax returns. In practice, most books of account consist of loose-leaf sheets kept in a post binder and are easily removed at the end of the year for filing away. The post binder is retained and new sheets inserted for the next year to make up the pages for receipts and disbursements.

The petty cash book (Fig. 13-4) is similar to the cash disbursement book, in that it is multicolumnar for type of expenses. But instead of the recording data coming from the checkbook, the source for entry is the petty cash slips or receipts. A common method to control and account for petty cash checks is to use the "petty cash fund system." Let us suppose you have determined from experience that your cash-out-of-pocket requirements will amount to 50 dollars a week. A petty cash check is drawn from your checkbook for this amount and cashed in your bank. The 50 dollars is your kitty. When the cash in the kitty is diminished, you replenish the kitty or fund by drawing another check, not for 50 dollars but for the total amount of petty cash receipts you have expended in payments. Remove these receipts for filing and indicate on it the date and check number used to replenish. You replenish only in the amount you have expended or paid out since the last petty cash expense check. It will always be less than 50 dollars unless the kitty is completely exhausted. At all times, the total of the current receipts in the petty cash box plus

CASH DISBURSEMENTS

MONTH OF SEPTEMBER 197X

DATE	NAME	CHECK NUMBER	AMOUNT	WAGES	(TAX WITHHELD)	DISTRIBUTION OF EXPENSES PROFESSIONAL EXPENSES	AUTO EXPENSES	ADMINISTRATIVE EXPENSES	DRAWING	GENERAL ITEM	COLUMN AMOUNT
	TOTALS FORWARD		$1378520	$600 00	$(15000)	$873520	$152000	$308000			
1	ABC REALTY	107	30000					30000 Code 5A			
	ANNA FUND	108	8400	100 00	(520) (1080)						
	ACME STATIONERS	109	5220					5250 5C			
10	DINERS CLUB	110	8320			8320 Code 3D					
12	PETTY CASH	111	4300							PETTY CASH	$4300
	GEORGE FOREST	112	25000						$25000		
17	PETTY CASH	113	2200							PETTY CASH	2200
18	CONS EDISON	114	3750					3750 5B			
19	AETNA INSURANCE	115	120000					120000 3C			
19	AB AUTO REPAIRS	116	7820				7820 Code 1B				
	TOTAL FOR MONTH										
	CUMULATIVE TOTAL										

Figure 13-3. Cash disbursement book.

| Date | NAME | FUND BALANCE | CASH RECEIVED | CASH EXPENDED | DISTRIBUTION OF CASH EXPENSES | | | GENERAL COLUMN | |
					PROFESSIONAL EXPENSES	AUTO EXPENSES	ADMINISTRATIVE EXPENSES	ITEM	AMOUNT
	TOTALS FORWARD	$ 5000	$ 75000	$ 70000					
1	Replenished. Check 111	5000	4300	4300	Code 3F 1200 3H 1000		Code 5E 2100		
17	" Check 113	5000	2200	2200		Code 1A 700		4G	1500

Figure 13-4. Petty cash book.

the cash on hand will equal 50 dollars if accurately kept. If it does not add up to 50 dollars, you most likely have not made out a petty cash slip for an expenditure.

Each patient has a ledger card (Fig. 13-5) which can be kept in alphabetical order in a looseleaf book or in a card tray. Each sheet or card has on its top the name, telephone number, business and home address of the patient, the fee rate, and other billing remarks. The body of the card has three columns after the date space: debit (charge), credit (payment received), and balance. The debit comes from your copy of the patient's monthly invoice. The data source for the monthly invoice is the daily log (diary). Number the copies of your patient invoices consecutively

Date 197X	Description	Posting Ref. Invoice Page#	Charges	Credits	Balance
MAR 30		123	$200 00		$ 200 00
APR	Cash Receipts	4		$150 00	$ 50 00
APR 30		130	250 00		300 00
MAY	Cash Receipts	5		250 00	50 00
MAY 30		140	200 00		250 00
JUNE	Cash Receipts	6		250 00	-0-
JUNE30		152	150 00		150 00
SEPT 1	Cash Receipts	9		50 00	100 00
SEPT30		165	200 00		300 00

Patient - Mary Smith
210 Longworth Ave.
Kenilton, New York

Tel. 974 - 3821

Figure 13-5.   Patients' ledger card.

and keep the copies in a binder. The payment-received credit has its origin in the cash receipts book where patient payments received by you are recorded. The balance column represents what is due you. The balance is the difference between the total charges and total payments received. When the total charges and the total credits are the same, the patient's account is in balance, and he is completely paid up. An accurate patient's ledger system is indispensable for proper billing and collecting your fees, a matter treated in another chapter.

The payroll book is optional. Where you have no turnover in your office staff, the cash disbursement book which records your salary expenditures less employee tax deductions can be used for the preparation of the government payroll reports due quarterly and annually. Payroll reporting becomes difficult when there are a number of different employees during the year. To facilitate reporting in this kind of situation, a payroll book and individual employee ledger cards should be maintained. Whenever you employ someone in your practice for the first time, you are required to register as an employer. From then on, you must collect various payroll taxes during pay time from your employee to be periodically remitted to the federal, state and city governments. Some cities and states have no income tax and therefore no withholding from salary. Each state and city has different reporting requirements. When you register as an employer with a taxing authority, local or federal, you will receive an identification number, charts enabling you to determine how much to withhold and filing reports and instructions. Since in effect you are a trustee for the various government entities, strict compliance as to collection and remittance is imposed upon you, subject to various penalties for late filing or payment of the funds withheld from your employee's salary. Your employee is required to inform you about his tax status, whether he is married or single, his dependents, and to give you his social security number. This information enables you to make the proper tax deductions from his salary.

Computerized Systems

A number of banks and data processing companies offer a

service of preparing your books of account and financial reports from the data sources that you code in from a coding system supplied by them. Their fees are based upon a minimum charge plus a charge for each item transaction. On a yearly basis, this can amount to about $200. Computer applications in record keeping and financial reporting have worked out well where there are a great number of repeated transactions and the need for a large amount of analytical print outs. The record keeping and accounting of the therapist is simple in comparison, and financial reports can be easily prepared. It seems hardly worthwhile to incur this extra expense.

INCOME TAXES AND TAX-SAVING METHODS

The Importance of Income Taxes to You

As a therapist, you rely on your practice and whatever investment income you can accumulate for the funds to provide a proper standard of living for yourself and your family. From these funds you will be building the security needed when you will not be practicing any longer. The income you presently earn is subject to graduated rates of taxation, so the more you earn, the less remains with you. A precise knowledge of the constantly changing rules and regulations of the Income Tax Law is the concern of your accountant and lawyer. To keep up with these "ins and outs" and advise you accordingly is the duty of your professional specialist. However, he cannot be overseeing your daily business activities as they arise out of your professional practice, nor is it practical to communicate with him at each and every moment. You have a general obligation to be acquainted with the usual areas of tax significance as they affect your profession so that you can operate your practice with the greatest tax benefit to you. At the same time, you must be alert to the problem areas of taxable transactions that require prompt advice from your accountant or lawyer, and you must obtain this guidance before you may take some costly or improper action out of ignorance or imprudence. The following discussion deals only with the more important problem areas of taxes as they may affect a practicing therapist.

Business Deductions

As a therapist, you know that the cost of running your practice is a deductible expense in arriving at the net income. The expenses of rent, salary, supplies, telephone are the straightforward expenses that you can deduct if you know the rules, rules which you may now be overlooking. If you have not been deducting them, you have been losing a great deal of money because the government takes at least 50 percent of your income in taxes if you are a successful practitioner. Among a number of expenses that are in the area of possible "loss of opportunity," entertainment, travel, and education expenses are probably the most important. They are also the prime target of Internal Revenue scrutiny. If you understand the rules, you will have nothing to be concerned about when you are examined about these or other expenses. The tax department requires that you abide by these rules in your professional activities. Your accountant cannot live them for you. If you know about them and are able to prove that you incurred these expenses, you will have more after-tax dollars left for your financial needs.

Entertainment Expenses

It is best to illustrate the prickly nature of entertainment expenses by a number of examples concerning Dr. Forest's practice.

Dr. Forest's practice is about 50 percent referred to him by other professionals. The remainder comes from patient recommendations. He realizes that building his practice is an integral part of his professional responsibility. To create the professional goodwill needed for a successful practice, he has been doing the following.

1. He joined a country club where he entertains other professionals and residents of the community. His family also uses the country club extensively. During the year he gave a debutante party for the daughter of another doctor in order to create goodwill.

2. He entertains about once a month at his home, to which

social gatherings as many as 30 people from the community are invited.

3. When he is particularly obligated to someone, he invites that person and his wife out with him, asking his own wife to join. The two couples usually go to a night club or to the theatre.

4. Before attending the regular professional society meeting in town, he and a number of his colleagues have dinner out in an expensive, dignified restaurant and enjoy a quiet business dinner while discussing common problems of their practice. Frequently he picks up the tab for the group.

The events noted in these examples are typical activities of many therapists. Although they are all business-motivated, not all of them may be deducted from your income as a business entertainment expense.

1. The membership cost of country club dues can only be deducted as an expense if the facility is used more than 50 percent for business (direct business or indirect goodwill purpose) as measured by your daily use. If your family used the club 51 days out of 100 days that the club was used, there is no deduction for dues at all. Even if you pass the business-use test, only a percentage of the cost of your dues is deductible. This percentage is the fraction formed by total time used as it bears to the time spent to discuss business or have a quiet meal with business associates. Dr. Forest's club membership costs 2,000 dollars a year. He uses the club 75 days out of 100 days for business use. He has passed the 50 percent rule. Of the 75 days, only 50 days is the club used by him for directly related business or quiet business meals with professional associates. Therefore, only 50 percent of 2,000 dollars of his dues can be deducted, namely 1,000 dollars. You get no benefit for general goodwill entertainment. But the out-of-pocket costs, or so-called direct costs, for food, beverages, tips, etc., for goodwill purposes entertaining professionals, community residents, and your secretary are deductible if reasonable. A quiet business meal, even if no business is discussed, is a business expense. So is your wife's cost if she is present along with other wives. The debutante party is not deductible. Club recreation costs following or preceding a business meeting are also deductible by you as an expense.

2. Home entertainment is deductible only to the extent it is commercially and not socially motivated. You need not discuss business, but the person should be someone who can relate to your practice. Friendly social gatherings at home, although conducive to goodwill in general, are not direct enough to be considered a business expense.

3. "Out on the town" expenses are only allowed if you can show that you did discuss business at the event. This is impossible to do because a night club, theatre, etc., is the kind of surrounding not conducive to a business discussion. However, if your entertainment directly precedes or follows a substantial and bonafide professional discussion, you can get the deduction. This did not happen when Dr. Forest invited the person to whom he was obligated to be his guest at a night club or theatre.

4. However, his cost of paying for a dinner is deductible when, before attending a professional meeting, he associates with other professionals in a quiet atmosphere for business goodwill purposes.

If you cannot prove you paid the cost, you cannot deduct it. Estimates are not allowed. Any expense over 25 dollars must be backed up by a receipt and information usually in a diary form, giving information as to whom, where, when, why, and how much. A cancelled check by itself is no proof of that kind of deduction. Many taxpayers' to conform to the rules, write the information required on the back of the credit card club receipt.

Gifts are a form of goodwill practice building. But no matter how well documented, a gift is limited to 25 dollars per person.

Travel and Convention Expenses

UNITED STATES AND OVERSEAS TRAVEL. Psychotherapists, like all professionals, do a goodly portion of travel attending professional conventions. All of these travel expenses are deductible. This includes the cost of the trip and living expenses while attending the convention. Therapists are wont to visit foreign countries for the purpose of study and observation. These costs are also deductible. The problems arise where business and pleasure are combined and when your wife goes along and you wish to claim her as a business expense. The tax law distinguishes United States travel from foreign. United States travel is easier to deduct. For example, Dr. Forest attends a convention in Los Angeles, flying from New York. He spends three days at the convention and seven days sightseeing. The entire trip is deductible. Only the costs of sightseeing are nondeductible, being personal in nature. When domestic travel occurs, no separation between personal and businesss is required if the principal reason for the trip is business or employment.

Supposing the trip was abroad and Dr. Forest had gone to Rome for the convention, attending it for three days. The flight to Rome took one day. Then he did sightseeing in Paris and London for seven days on the trip back home. The return flight to New York was one day. He was out of the country twelve days. The cost of the meals and lodging for his stay in Rome is 100 per cent deductible. However only 3/12 or 25 per cent of his plane fare can be considered a business travel expense.

If, instead of sightseeing on the way back, his sightseeing was done beyond the point of his convention destination, like Athens, then no portion of the trip's expense beyond Rome is a business expense. Only 3/12 of 25 percent or the New York to Rome portion of the flight is deductible. However, there are three exceptions that permit the entire air cost to be deductible:

1. If you can establish that a personal vacation was not a major consideration of your trip, the sightseeing beyond the convention would be personal expense, but all of the plane fare would still be a business expense, similar to the United States travel, and no prorating is required. When time spent on pleasure travel is greater than convention or business time, you then have a problem proving a 100 per cent air fare deduction.

2. The entire air cost is deductible if you were outside of the United States a week or less (do not count day of departure as a part of the week).

3. The entire air cost is deductible if less than 25 per cent of the total time (count time coming and going) was on personal matters.

Adequate records similar to those necessary to prove business entertainment are required to be maintained.

A wife's travel expense when accompanying her husband are very difficult to deduct. You must first prove a bona-fide business purpose in taking her along. Among the tests to establish bona-fide are the wife's unique talents, how essential she is to her husband's business, and whether she is also in business with him. Her presence must be necessary, not just helpful.

LOCAL TRAVEL. The so-called commuting expenses, of whatever nature, in going from home to office or hospital and back again to your home are not a business expense. Only direct professional travel is deductible—going from office to office, home to patient, patient to patient, etc.

Automobile Operation

All expenses of operating the car (gas, oil, repairs,) insurance, depreciation, parking etc. for business use can be deducted as a business expense. But you must keep an accurate record of these expenses and the travel time that is part business and part non-business. If you have two cars, use the newer one as much as possible for business use. You will have less record keeping and a higher cost of depreciation in the newer car. The government permits a simple formula method of figuring auto costs: 12 cents for the first 15,000 business miles and 9 cents in excess of 15,000. This is in place of all expenses for the use of the auto, except parking and tolls. You can go from one method to another each year. However, if you use the 12 cents a mile you must own the car, use only one car and have claimed simple depreciation (straight-line) in deducting a portion of the original cost of the car when you did not use the formula method in prior years. The cost of a car is called a capital item. Its total cost cannot be considered an expense in one year. The same consideration is applied to other capital items you use in your practice, like office furnishings (usually 10-year life) equipment (usually 10 to 15 year life.) It may be considered an expense by treating a portion of its cost each year, called depreciation, over its useful life, usually four years. A car costing 6,000 dollars can only be treated as a business expense (depreciation) each year for 1,500 dollars, if we assume its useful life is four years. Even then, not all of the 6,000 dollars can be treated as an expense. In applying these rules, an allowance must be made for partial personal use and salvage value. Salvage value is the ultimate resale value of the car. If you sell a car at a profit and the depreciation taken for the car over the years is greater than the gain, you will be taxed on the gain for over-depreciating, in the year of sale. The following examples indicate how this is accounted for:

Depreciation

Cost of car	$6,000
less 10 percent personal use	600
Business basis	$5,400
Estimated salvage value at the end of four years	1,400
Base for depreciation	4,000
Yearly depreciation allowable	$1,000

Sale of Car at End of Four Years—Income in Year of Sale

	Total	Use for Business	Use for Pleasure
Cost	$6,000	$5,400	$ 600
Less: Depreciation taken	4,000	4,000	—
Total Undepreciated cost	2,000	1,400	
Selling Price	3,000	2,700	300
Gain or (Loss)	$1,000	$1,300	$ (300)

The entire 1,300 dollar gain is ordinary income because it is less than the depreciation taken. The 300 dollars loss in the pleasure column cannot be used as a business expense to reduce your 1,300 dollar gain arising from overdepreciating the car in the four years.

The Cost of Continuing Education

There is no end to new developments in science and therefore to the need for continuing education by therapists. This type of education has for its purpose the maintenance and improvements of your skills in practice.

Not only are the course fees deductible from your income, but any auxiliary costs like transportation, meals, and lodging while away from home are also a business expense. But your education cannot be deducted as a business expense if it is for the purpose of meeting the minimum educational requirements for establishment in a profession. These expenses are personal in nature. Thus a former lawyer, now a lecturer in psychology and hypnosis before adult audiences, was denied the right to deduct as a business expense the tuition paid to obtain a Ph.D. degree in clinical psychology. He was considered as going from one profession to another. In the well-known Greenberg Case (367 F

2d 663), however, a psychiatrist engaged in private practice of psychiatry was able to deduct all his costs of training to be an analyst at a psychonanalytic institute. His training did not qualify him for a new profession but enhanced his present profession. These training expenses could be deducted.

Research expenses are equivalent to educational expenses. The reasonable costs of problem researching, scientific investigation, and publishing in your technical area in order to enhance your professional status are business expenses. Expenses for travel related to your profession are also business expenses. A doctor and his wife were permitted to deduct 9,000 dollars of travel expenses incurred while studying the world-wide treatment of alcoholism. He specialized in treating alcoholics, and his wife ran a treatment clinic with him.

Prizes and Awards

Prizes and awards are not income if given in recognition of scientific, civic, educational, or charitable achievement. But the selection must be done without any action on your part, and no substantial future services must be rendered. Thus, the Nobel Prize award and teacher awards are not taxable.

Scholarships and Fellowships

To determine if the amounts of scholarships and fellowships are taxable, a distinction has to be made between degree and nondegree candidates.

If the scholarship is made to assist you in your studies as a non-degree candidate and is not to compensate you for employment (past, present, and future), or the study is not primarily for the benifit of the donor of the scholarship, then such funds are completely tax free to you.

Where a degree candidate receives payment for work of a kind required of all degree candidates, it is still tax free. But a nondegree recipient does not receive the award completely tax free. Nondegree candidates can only exclude the first 300 dollars per month they receive and then for a period not beyond 36 months. In addition, the donor of the grant must be a tax-exempt organization (school, international organization, etc.).

Some of the exempt awards that have been considered partial or completely tax free:

1. Grant research fellowship from National Institute of Health.
2. American Heart Research fellowship to pursue a heart-research career.
3. Grant of expenses by exempt organization to enable a teacher to do research.
4. National Science Foundation postdoctoral fellowship.

If your grant specifically designates what part of the grant shall cover auxiliary expenses (travel costs, research expenses, living costs for you and your family), this part is tax free and not subject to the 300 dollars a month limitation.

Deducting Home Office Expenses

Often a therapist will set aside a portion of his home for study, research, and seeing patients. If you can prove the regular business use or purpose of the office in your home and your business costs for the space used, you can get an office cost deduction. If this is your only office, there is no proof of need required. But if your principal office is away from home and your home office is of minor use, then you must prove you are required to use it. For example, it is a burden for a number of your patients to travel a considerable distance to see you at your principal office. Of course you must prove that it is furnished for professional office use. The method in arriving at a cost is usually based on a percentage of total home space to business space (room or area). The costs that can be allocated are rent, light, heat, telephone, depreciation (if you own the home), maintenance, gardening, domestic help, etc. Be sure to keep a record of the patients you see there. The cost for real estate taxes and mortgage interest if it is a home need not be considered, since these amounts are allowable anyway in itemizing your regular deductions in arriving at taxable income. They are in the same nonbusiness category as charity, medical, state and local taxes, casualty losses, etc. expenses.

Year-End Tax Planning

Individual tax returns are prepared and paid by most therapists on a calendar year basis determined by cash received and cash payments made. Because of this fact, a cash basis taxpayer is in a position to collect or delay receiving fees from patients. At the same time, he can prepay expenses that could be paid in the early part of the next year or wait till next year to pay many expenses he could pay this year. The effect of this is to lower or increase income in a particular year:

Increase Income	*Decrease Income*
1. Collect as many fees as you can this year.	Do not press to collect fees owing you this year.
2. Defer paying business expenses to early next year.	Pay all your bills this year.

When and how you will do this financial juggling will depend upon a number of situations:

Increase Income This Year	*Decrease Income This Year*
1. You expect a better year next year.	You have an excellent year this year.
2. Taxes will go up next year.	Taxes will be lower next year.
3. You have many personal tax deductions this year (charity, medical, investment losses, casualty losses, bad debts, higher realty taxes, interest payments, etc.)	You anticipate more personal tax deductions next year which you can apply against the higher income next year.

By timing the control of payments in and out, you are roughly averaging out your net taxable income. This is important to you. As explained previously, the same dollar of taxable income does not pay the same taxes; tax rates are applied variously upward to different levels of taxable income. Averaging out your income from one year to another keeps you out of the higher brackets (change of rate).

But you must keep away from a "constructive receipt" situation. Constructive receipt designates as taxable income any amount unqualifiedly subject to your request, whether or not it has been reduced to cash in your account. A good example of this is interest that has not been formally entered in your savings account passbook. It is yours. Merely a formality has delayed it being entered. The interest earned on your savings for a year is income. It has been constructively received. A note from a solvent patient is the same as cash and is considered income when received. The month of December is the time to take reckoning and plan your operations in this regard. You cannot plan anything when you do not have good up-to-the-minute records that can tell you what you have earned for the first eleven months of the year.

How the New Tax Acts of 1969 and 1970 Affect You

At the end of 1969 and 1970 a great number of changes were made in the tax provisions. Enlarged standard deductions, dependency exemptions and the concept of a maximum rate of tax for earned income directly concern the psychotherapeat.

STANDARD DEDUCTION—Tax Exemption. The standard deduction permitted a taxpayer to deduct 10 percent of his taxable income if his adjusted gross income was $10,000 or more. There was a maximum of $1,000. The standard deduction is in lieu of itemizing deductions, like contributions medical, local taxes, etc. Starting in 1971 the standard deduction, the maximum and dependency exemptions have been increased to give a greater allowance:

Year	1970	1971	1972	1973 and thereafter
Rate-Standard	10%	13%	15%	15%
Maximum	$1,000	$1,500	$2,000	$2,000
Exemption	$ 625	$ 675	$ 750	$ 750

MAXIMUM RATE ON (INCOME FROM) PROFESSIONAL EARNED INCOME. Presently a taxable income of 22,000 dollars and more results in a tax rate of 50 percent to 70 percent for an individual filing a tax return. On a joint return (husband and wife), the 50 percent to 70 percent rate is imposed when the taxable income is 44,000 dollars and more. Under the new law, the maximum marginal tax on earned income from a profession is 60 percent in 1971 and 50 percent in 1972.

TAX RELIEF FOR SINGLE PERSONS AND HEADS OF HOUSEHOLDS. The new rates, which are lower, begin in 1971.

In many other areas, however, the Tax Reform Act results in higher taxes by eliminating some tax loopholes and modifying certain tax advantages. Most of these changes do not pertain to the business activities of most therapists. A few of these changes which you may be affected by include:

1. Charitable contributions of property that has appreciated in value.
2. Curbs on the previous favorable treatment of capital gains.
3. Minimum tax of 10 percent on certain preference items such as capital gains, excess interest paid to carry an investment, etc.

The application of the higher tax on these items is quite complicated and you should consult with your tax advisor if you are affected by these kinds of transactions.

RETIREMENT PLANNING

The psychotherapist, like every working individual, is faced with the eventuality that in his later life he will retire by choice or necessity. To retire comfortably, funds must be set aside during one's productive years to realize this goal. Whether the funds set aside are put into a savings bank to earn interest or in security investments, insurance, or annuity plans for appreciation, the therapist is confronted with three problems: the risk of inflation, the safety of the investment, and our progressive tax structure.

Inflation

In the last 20 years, prices have increased 44.3 percent, with the largest increase in prices occurring in the last three years at a rate of 5 to 6 percent per annum. Inflation strikes hardest at those with relatively fixed income like retirees. Retirement plans which were based on salaries earned during periods of stable prices no longer provide sufficient retirement income to many presently retired persons. If we continue to assume an inflationary economy, any retirement plan must provide an investment program that can overcome the erosion of the dollar while your funds are accumulated for eventual use in retirement. The principal method heretofore used to overcome the erosion of inflation has been to invest part of the money of the retirement fund in stocks of publicly owned companies (equity securities). The theory has been that as prices rise, so will the value of equity securities. It is not clear whether this has solved the problem. During the current recession, inflation has continued while the values of many publicly held stocks have declined significantly.

Risk

It is a principle of investment that the greater the risk, the better the return on the investment ought to be. While savings banks and insurance companies provide a great deal of safety for funds invested with them, the earnings realized on these funds, guaranteed though they are, return about 3 to 5 percent. An adequate retirement plan must provide for a combination of guaranteed risk and higher yield if it is to meet its objective of balanced growth in an inflationary economy.

Progressive Taxation

Under the present income tax structure, the more one earns, the steeper is the tax rate applied to the increased income because the rate of taxation is graduated upwards. Fortunately, beginning in 1972, the maximum federal tax rate on earned income (income from salaries or profession) will be 50 percent instead of the present 70 percent. Even at this lower maximum rate, little may be left to be set aside towards retirement after you have paid for your required living expenses and income taxes. The tax laws recognize this difficulty and provide for tax-favored retirement plans. Money contributed to a qualified retirement plan is considered a business expense deductible from your gross income, like rent and salaries. Being an expense, the effect is to put aside money before taxes are deducted from this sum. The entire amount goes into your retirement fund and not the net amount after paying taxes which would occur if the plan were not tax qualified or approved. While these whole dollars are in the retirement account earning an investment return, the return itself is free from tax. Only upon retirement does this income growth become subject to tax. To illustrate the dramatic effect of a tax sheltered retirement plan, let us assume that you are in a 32 percent highest tax bracket. Your funds in the plan earn 8 percent per annum and you are also able to contribute 2,500 dollars a year to the plan. At the end of twenty years, you will have accumulated 123,550 dollars for retirement as contrasted with 65,850 dollars you would be able to accumulate under a non-tax-favored retirement plan.

Qualified Plans

There are three types of qualified plans available to the therapist. Only a qualified plan permits you to benefit from favored tax treatment for your contribution. These types are:

1. The *self-employed retirement plan* (also called, Keogh or H.R. 10 Plan) available when you practice in a nonincorporated form as an individual or partnership.

2. The *corporate pension plan* which is permitted when you incorporate your practice as a professional corporation.

3. *Tax preferred annuities* available to part- or full-time employees of nonprofit tax-exempt educational, charitable, and religious organizations (called Tax Law Section 501(c) (3) Organizations).

Each of these three types of plans has its special requirements. Because of the unique features of each plan and the importance of knowing what they are in order to make an intelligent selection appropriate to your needs, you should become familiar with their essentials.

SELF-EMPLOYED RETIREMENT PLAN (S.E.R.P.). Before the self-employed retirement plan (Table 13-II) was enacted into legislation, there was no way a self-employed psychotherapist could put aside money into a tax-preferred retirement plan. S.E.R.P. answers this need, but only in part, because it has a number of limitations and discriminatory features should you employ anyone in your practice. Objectionable features are several. It limits you to a maximum contribution of the lesser of 10% of net earned income or 2,500 dollars per annum that can be deducted as a business expense. It discriminates against you in that any employee you have who receives his money from the fund in a lump sum by severance or retirement will only pay a tax-favored capital gain tax on the income in excess of the employer's contribution. This income would arise from the appreciation of the investments in the fund. You as the employer will pay at ordinary income tax rates the money received, subject to a special five-year averaging procedure. Any money contributed by you to the plan for the benefit of your employee belongs completely to him when he leaves for

TABLE 13-II
THE SELF-EMPLOYED RETIREMENT PLAN (S.E.R.P.)

Effect as to:	Employer (Owner Employee)	Employee (Common Law Employee)
Eligibility	Self-employed individuals or partnerships. Must treat employees fairly (no discrimination), have terms in writing, and put contributions into an investment form trust.	All employees of self-employed person or with three or more years of service. Can include working wife in the plan.
Maximum contribution	10 per cent of net income but not exceeding $2,500 per annum.	10 per cent of salary, but not exceeding $2,500 per annum.
Tax deductibility	100 per cent but cannot exceed $2,500.	100 per cent but cannot exceed $2,500.
Income of trust (investment)	Tax-free accumulation while in trust.	Tax-free accumulation while in trust.

Forms of trust investment	Various—singly or in combination, to:

1. Bank trust fund—funds can be invested as you direct or at bank's discretion.
2. Insurance company to purchase non-transferable annuity contracts including variable annuity with incidental life insurance benefits, which are not deductible and cannot exceed 100 times planned monthly retirement income.
3. Mutual fund plans through a bank custodial account.
4. Purchase of United States retirement plan bonds.

Vesting (amount to your credit and available to you when you leave)	Unless permanently disabled, no withdrawals until 59½ years of age; must distribute all funds to your credit on reaching 70½ years of age. Premature distribution may result in a penalty.	Complete ownership to employee when contributed. Can receive proceeds on quitting or when disabled; need not wait to retirement age or 59½ to receive proceeds.
Distribution	1. Funds received are taxable at ordinary income rates but subject to a five-year averaging procedure if taken in one lump sum.	Only the employer contributions are taxed as ordinary income if taken in lump sum. The tax impact is lessened by a seven year averaging out procedure.
	2. If elect distribution as annuity, taxed on gain at ordinary income rates when received under annuity rules.	Same
	3. Same rules (A or B) apply if distribution because of death.	Same

any reason; that is, the money is vested in him entirely. The funds put in your account are available to you, without penalty, only upon your reaching 59½ years of age and thereafter. Table 13-II indicates the general features of the self-employed retirement plan. It is important to realize that once you start a plan, you can only terminate it before its objective is reached by showing an acute business necessity for termination (inability to continue your practice, etc.). But you can change from one investment group to another by simply freezing the old by making no further contributions. As the years go by, you have to realize that substantial funds belonging to you are locked into the plan until retirement. They cannot be borrowed by you in case of need, except by reason of permanent disability or death. There is a distinct possibility that the maximum contributions and percentage of contribution will be increased by new legislation in order to make self-employment retirement plans (S.E.R.P.) more liberal and attractive. See Table 13-III comparing the S.E.R.P. with the professional corporation (P.C.).

THE PROFESSIONAL CORPORATION (P.C.). The Professional corporation is a recent innovation. It allows you to incorporate your individual practice and for tax purposes at least to operate your practice like any one of the numerous corporate commercial businesses with you as an employee of the corporation drawing a salary. With incorporation, you have the right to introduce a tax-qualified pension plan, and you can do this even though you may be the only employee of the corporation. A corporate-approved pension plan has so many advantages that it may be worth the expense, tax difficulties, and extra paperwork that operating in corporate form entails. Through a professional corporation you can have so-called other "fringe benefits" like group life insurance, medical and disability insurance, and a medical expense payment plan, which are treated as business expenses.

Pension plans are generally formulated so as to provide each participant with a percentage of his present salary upon retirement. The higher the salary, the more the money required to be set aside in the plan. The older the individual, the greater the contribution to the plan because the time available before retiring is that much shorter. Since you, as the corporate owner, earn a greater salary than your employees and are usually older than other employees of the corporation, a higher contribution can be contributed to your retirement account without any taint of discrimination. Contributions to the retirement plan have the

TABLE 13-III

COMPARISON OF PROFESSIONAL CORPORATION PENSION
PLAN WITH THE SELF-EMPLOYMENT RETIREMENT PLAN (S.E.R.P.)

Item	Self-Employed Retirement Plan (Owner Employee)	Corporate Pension Plan
Participants	All full time employees with three years or more of service.	Maximum and minimum ages permitted; waiting period cannot exceed five years; can include full time employees only.
Contributions	Maximum—10 per cent of practice net income but not exceeding $2,500.	No dollar limit, except as needed by plan to provide specified retirement benefits.
Vesting (right to money in plan when employee leaves)	Immediate.	May be deferred to normal retirement age.
Distribution 1. General result	Penalty to owner except for death or disability, if distribution made before his age 59½, must distribute by age 70½.	Loans can be provided if reasonable.
2. Income tax result if lump sum	Taxed at ordinary income, tax rates subject to special five-year averaging.	Beginning January 1, 1970, only employer's contributions taxed at ordinary income tax rates; subject to seven-year averaging, but earnings and gains in the plan are taxed at favorable capital gain rates.
3. Taken as annuity over several years	Taxed as annuity.	Taxed at ordinary income rates.
Estate tax benefits	Subject to federal estate tax.	If you name beneficiary including trustee and not your estate, no federal estate tax to be paid on the amount going to the beneficiary or trustee.

effect of reducing your corporate taxable income. Unlike the self-employed retirement plan, there is no 2,500 dollar annual maximum that can be deducted as an expense. Whatever amount of money that is needed to meet the retirement objective can be contributed. If you employ others, reasonable conditions of entrance to the plan can be set up to limit participation, based on age, length of service, and whether they are full-time employees. Part time employees who customarily work no more than 20 hours a week and seasonal employees who do not work more than 5 months in a calendar year may be excluded as employees both under the self employed retirement plan or the corporate pension plan. Ownership to the funds can be restricted so that no employee owns any portion until he has been employed a number of years. This prevents immediate vesting of ownership. Upon retirement, only amounts contributed since 1970 by the corporation to the retirement fund for your benefit or that of your employee are subject to ordinary income tax rates if received in one lump sum on retirement. Any lump sum amounts so received are subject to a special seven-year averaging rule to cushion the tax effects. However, all earnings or gains earned by the fund as a result of investing the corporate contributions receive the more favorable capital gain tax rate. In case of death before retirement, if you name a beneficiary instead of your estate to receive the amounts contributed by the corporation for your benefit, these amounts are not subject to estate tax. If properly provided for in the plan agreement, money can be borrowed in case of need. These features of a corporate pension plan are superior to those provided by the self-employed retirement plan. The chart that accompanies this discussion indicates the principal distinction between the professional corporation and the self-employed retirement plan. But from a practical point of view, unless you are financially able to contribute to the pension plan more than 2,500 dollars a year for your account, the professional corporation will have little value.

Operating in Corporate Form. Only a regular professional corporation can introduce a pension plan that offers these benefits. The so called "small business corporation" (also called Sub-Chapter S Corporations), which elects not to be taxed as a regular corporation, is prohibited from making contributions beyond 2,500 dollars for any employee. While operating as a regular business corporation, you should be acquainted with some of the possible tax drawbacks associated with this form of corporate operation. These drawbacks pertain to improper accumulation of surplus, business expense disallowances, payroll taxes, and dissolution expenses, and the necessity of bona fide corporate operation.

Improper Accumulation of Surplus by the Corporation—Penalty Tax. When a regular corporation accumulates more than 100,000 dollars of retained earnings (the accumulation of net income), it may be subject under Section 531 of the Internal Revenue Code to a penalty tax because it has accumulated profits beyond the reasonable needs of the business. These funds, according to this section of the tax law, should have been paid to the stockholders in the form of dividends, where they would have been doubly taxed—once at the corporate level and once at the stockholder level. To avoid a penalty tax, your corporation would have to justify its earnings retention by showing a business need for keeping the money in the corporation.

Business Expense Disallowances. Another tax hazard for a regular corporation is the possibility of the disallowance of corporate expenses by the Internal Revenue Service on the grounds that the particular business expense is personal, a disguised dividend, and not a proper business disbursement. If successfully contended, two taxes would result: (a) the resulting increase in corporate profit would increase corporate tax because an expense has been reduced, (b) a taxable dividend to you since there has been a distribution from corporate profit to you. The following are some of the expenses that are prone to be scrutinized and possibly construed as dividends, in whole or part:

1. Meals and lodging on business trips.
2. Entertaining and promotion costs incurred for professional goodwill purposes, etc.
3. Convention expenses.
4. Home office and other home expenses deducted as business expense. Also, professional salaries may be construed as too high and unreasonable in part, and the disallowed portion of the salary can become subject to double tax as a dividend.

Other Uncertainties of Corporate Operation. Other drawbacks involved in corporate operations include additional payroll taxes, local taxes, and a tax upon dissolving the corporation. Also the Internal Revenue Service may contend that the operation of the corporation was not truly a corporate business but a bookkeeping device. Recently a professional corporation was disregarded as such when the actual activities of a group of doctors were carried on outside the corporation. Each professional maintained his distinct practice, without operational integration, except for common corporate bookkeeping, (Roubik 53 T.C. 36). The personal, one-man nature of a corporation may subject it to the personal holding company penalty tax.

There is no categorical answer to these problems in deciding whether to incorporate or not to incorporate. Each therapist must analyze his position as to the advantages and risks. It may be too early for the sole practitioner or partnership to make a definite changeover now. So much will depend upon the developing rules and prodedures of the Internal Revenue Service as they relate to professional corporations. However, it must be remembered that in the world of business, there are hundreds of thousands of business corporations operating under these restrictive tax rules and doing so quite successfully. It is difficult to see how the Internal Revenue Service can be tougher with the professional corporation than with its twin, the business corporation.

THE TAX-PREFERRED ANNUITY. Many psychotherapists are employed by tax-exempt educational, charitable, and religious organizations, either on a full- or part-time basis. Often this salary compensation is considered by the therapist as extra income, a supplement to his private practice. If you do not need a part of this compensation for your daily requirements, you can agree with your employer to accept less-direct salary which is fully taxable and to place part of your compensation before taxes are deducted in a tax-favored annuity. Let us suppose your salary is 1,000 dollars a month before income tax. You request your employer to purchase an insurance company annuity for 200 dollars a month to be taken from your salary and remitted directly to the insurance company. This entire 200 dollars is remitted free of income tax. Only the 800 dollars you receive now is taxable. Exempt organizations are not required to adopt a formal plan and receive Treasury Department approval. There is no discrimination if only certain employees are selected. This form of salary annuity agreement whereby you direct your employer to purchase an annuity while you are working, the proceeds of which are available to you in a lump sum or in periodic payments when you retire, is a practical method of retirement planning. This form of tax-sheltered retirement annuity is easily available to the therapist employed by most exempt organizations. Only a part of your salary can be excluded from current income. The amount that you can put away from current salary is dependent upon a formula based on years of employment multiplied by 20 percent of your includable compensation.

INVESTMENTS AND YOUR RETIREMENT CONTRIBUTIONS. Retirements plans provide that your contributions be invested in various ways, depending upon the plan and your investment preferences.

Annuities. When you select an insurance company to purchase an annuity, your eventual retirement benefits will be smaller than if you sought a moderately successful security investment, but the insurance company guarantees the benefit to be received. Stock market investments have no performance guarantee.

Mutual Funds. During your active working years, the monies placed in the Retirement Fund Plan can be used to invest in securities or mutual funds. You can never be guaranteed that the stocks you have selected will appreciate in value and upon retirement you will have what you hoped for. To overcome this disadvantage, many plans provide for split-funding—putting some of the money in a life insurance annuity for a return certainty and some in the more speculative security (equity) form of investment for possible rapid growth. Mutual funds have become a popular form of security investment for retirement. There are many kinds of mutual funds, with varying contracts, with or without a sales commission charge. The proponents of mutual funds point out that the merit of this form of investiment is that your share of the securities in the fund will be professionally managed, and because of mass purchasing power, a far wider spectrum of securities can be bought than you can buy as an individual. The wider the selection, they say, the better is the risk averaged. In practice, fund performance has been far from consistent. In general, mutual funds have not demonstrated any markedly superior performance because of stock diversification or expert management advisory service paid for by the mutual fund investor. Indeed over one-third of the over 300 funds in existence, commanding vast sums of money paid in by individual investor members and from retirement plans, have demonstrated only a moderate return in the last five years. Some of the more aggressive and speculative funds which have shown excellent results in a rising market (bull market) have in the present depressed situation (bear market) demonstrated poor results. The decision as to which mutual fund to select as an investment vehicle is as difficult as the selection of which group of securities will demonstrate a better performance.

ESTATE AND FAMILY FINANCIAL PLANNING

An Overall View

Estate and family financial planning concerns the transfer of your property or assets during your life, usually for tax-saving reasons and the final disposal of what you have at the time of your death.

Transfers during your life can be made by outright gift or by putting property into a trust under a trust agreement. The trustee holds the property for the benefit of a third person called the beneficiary.

Estate disposal at death, whether by will or by the laws of your state if you die without a will, subjects your estate to estate taxes for the value of the property and court costs for legal processing. The aim of estate and family planning is to fomulate plans that will minimize your federal and state taxes, reduce your court or probate expenses, and at the same time fulfill your intentions as to your heirs, the object of your bounty. Estate planning is a complicated subject since it is an interplay between your subjective desires and complex legal requirements dependent upon changing court interpretations, new laws, and regulations. Miscalculations and errors can be costly. They can erode your estate and frustrate your intentions.

Your Will

The will is a written instrument signed by you and witnessed. It gives instructions as to how and to whom your property is to go. When you do not have a will, your state probate court will do the property disposing for you in a manner prescribed by the state inheritance laws which may not be as you intended. It is also well to remember that your widow has special rights to your estate, and depending upon state law, she is entitled to at least one-third to one-half of your estate no matter what you decide to leave her by will.

Even when there is a will (testament), the passage of time can frustrate your testamentary intentions, for beneficiaries named in the will may have married or died. Those you thought incapable of handling money matters may now be competent to do so. New children and grandchildren may have been born. Property you once owned you may no longer have, and vice-versa. The executor you named in your will may not be able to perform his duties. New tax laws passed since the execution or signing of your will may have eliminated certain tax advantages utilized at the time in drafting the will. Revisions in the tax law may open up different approaches to estate-tax savings. Many new events may have occurred in your personal life requiring changes in your will. Wills once made need review with the passage of time for possible revision. For these reasons, estate and family planning requires skilled professional know-how on the part of your lawyer and accountant. What may be a proper provision in the will for one person's situation may be a costly recipe for someone else, although their income and financial circumstances may appear similar.

Probate

Property passing by will is subject to probate, the special court procedure of administrating estates. The probate court determines if your will is valid and that its provisions have been properly carried out. If you die without a will—that is, intestate—the court appoints an administrator whose duties consist in finding your property and disposing of it in a probate-like procedure. Probating your will or having an intestate estate administered is costly. On small estates of 10,000 dollars to 100,000 dollars, the cost can average 15 percent, representing legal fees, court costs, etc. The cost of probate is separate and aside from federal and state inheritance or estate taxes. Property that is held by you in the following manner can pass directly without a will to designated persons upon your death:

1. Any property jointly owned with right of survivorship, a method often used by a husband and wife as to the ownership of a bank account or home.
2. Life insurance on your life payable on your death to a designated person or beneficiary.
3. Property held in trust and passing on to someone else on your death but over which you have control during your life.

This form of disposal escapes probate costs but not estate taxes. But transferring property by joint means, through insurance or by trust, may create unexpected problems. For example,

1. If you hold property in joint name and then you and your wife die at the same time by accident, etc., leaving small children, the court will take charge of your affairs and appoint an administrator who may not be to your liking, and he will distribute the property as prescribed by law.
2. You may not be able to properly use the benefits of the marital deduction to save taxes, a subject explained later.

The probate-saving methods of transferring property should not be a substitute for a properly drawn will. Used with a will they can minimize probate and estate tax costs, provide for contingencies, and insure flexibility.

Estate Liquidity

Liquidity signifies the availability of cash on hand, as in a savings bank, or the ability to turn property quickly into cash. It is important in case of your death that your family is able to meet its daily obligations while your property is being transferred by will or otherwise. Be sure your wife has in her name sufficient cash or disposable assets that can be quickly reduced to cash if need be. In addition, your estate should have some measure of liquidity so as to have funds that can easily be given to your family or be available to pay expenses, including estate taxes and other costs. Life insurance and securities readily traded in the market are forms of property providing quick cash funds. An estate consisting mainly of real estate property or special business ventures may take a long time to dispose of while funds are currently needed for your family and to pay inheritance taxes.

Your Estate and the Marital Deduction

Estate taxes are taxes paid on the value of your property on death. It is, in effect, a tax on the transfer of property and has nothing to do with your income. The larger your taxable estate, the more progressive is the tax to pay, because the rate of tax, like income tax, is graduated upwards. A taxable estate of 50,000 dollars (after deducting a 60,000 dollar minimum exemption and a Federal allowance of a credit for state tax) will pay 6,920 dollars in Federal estate taxes. A taxable estate of 100,000 dollars pays 20,140 dollars, and one of 300,000 dollars pays 76,180 dollars. Your taxable estate consists of all your property: real estate, stocks and bonds, cash, life insurance, jointly owned property, etc., *less* debts (money you owe), the cost of settling your estate and a specific exemption allowed of 60,000 dollars. Life insurance enjoys no special Federal estate tax treatment, even if it passes outside of your will, as when it is payable directly to a named beneficiary. The proceeds of the policy go into your estate, even though it is not probated, and you save probate costs. Only when the ownership of the policy on your life is completely owned by someone else, like your wife, do the proceeds escape inclusion in your estate. Holding incidents of ownership, like having the right to change beneficiaries or borrow on the policies, will cause the policy proceeds to be included in your estate. What about the value of your practice at death? The value of the tangible material items like furniture and your car are part of your gross estate. Your reputation or prestige, roster of patients, and the so-called goodwill of your practice has no estate value unless it will survive your demise. It is not an estate value unless there is a buyer for your practice willing to pay for this goodwill. In that case, the amount to be paid becomes an estate property. It is surprising how quickly your estate may be liable for estate taxes. Although state inheritance tax rates are lower than Federal rates, there is a smaller exemption.

In these inflationary times, it is easy for the value of your property to amount to more than the 60,000 dollars which is the Federal exemption allowed before estate tax rates apply. The moderate estate of a successful therapist can easily consist of the following:

Life insurance proceeds	$50,000
Market value of home	60,000
Cash and securities	10,000
Gross assets	$120,000
Less debts and costs to settle	$10,000
Adjusted gross estate	$110,000
Specific exemption	60,000
Taxable estate	$50,000

If you are married, you get one more immediate advantage in addition to the 60,000 dollars exemption. You are entitled to a deduction called the marital deduction, of not more than one half of the value of the property passing to your surviving spouse. In effect, the estate of a married person on death is split for taxes —one half is taxed and one half passes to your wife without being taxed. In the above case, the husband's estate would be free of tax.

Adjusted gross estate (as above)	$110,000
Less marital deducation property (½ of $110,000)	55,000
	55,000
Specific exemption	60,000
Taxable Estate	—

The marital deduction is a very valuable right, and in general only property left outright to your wife or in a special marital deduction trust will qualify for the deduction. The property passing to your wife will be fully taxed on her death. At that time her estate will be taxed like a single person subject to the full impact of the estate tax without the benefit of the marital deduction.

SAVING THE SECOND TAX. Many a therapist has what he calls a simple will or other simple procedure that on his death transfers his property to his wife. In either case, he leaves it all to her. By doing so, his estate becomes liable to two estate taxes on the same property—one when he dies, and one at the time of his wife's death when she, for example, leaves the property to the children. Good estate planning avoids the double tax. If the marital deduction savings is combined with the use of a trust you can, in effect, split the estate that eventually will go to your children. To do this, the will is drawn so that one half of your estate goes to your wife outright. The other half is left in a trust giving her all the income from it during her lifetime. The trustee in addition may in his discretion use part or all of the principal of the Trust for her benefit. This nonmarital trust is not part of your wife's estate on her death, and the property in it on her death go directly to your children or anyone else you may designate. By means of this procedure, you avoid the piling up of assets in your wife's estate. The following example illustrates the difference between the simple will and the application of the nonmarital trust.

Assume you have a $200,000 estate. Here are the results with a simple will, leaving it all to your wife and then to your children:

At death of	Husband	Wife	Total
Adjusted gross estate	$200,000	$195,200	
Less marital deduction	100,000	0	
	100,000	195,200	
Personal exemption	60,000	60,000	
Taxable estate	40,000	135,200	
Tax	4,800	31,260	$36,060
Property transferred to wife	195,200	0	
Property transferred to children	0		$163,940

Here are the results using a nonmarital trust:

At death of	Husband	Wife	Total
Adjusted gross estate	$200,000	$100,000	
Less marital deduction	100,000	0	
	100,000	100,000	
Personal exemption	60,000	60,000	
Taxable estate	40,000	40,000	
Tax	4,800	4,800	$9,600
Property transferred directly to wife	100,000	0	
Property transferred to trust for wife's benefit while living	95,200	0	
Property that goes to children on wife's death	0	0	$190,400
Estate tax savings		($36,060-$9,600)	$ 26,460

The nonmarital trust ought not be used in every situation. If your wife owns considerable property in her own right, you will not be balancing out the estate by this method. A better plan might be to leave the 200,000 dollars in trust for your children with a life income from the trust to your wife.

The Short Term Trust

Suppose you wish to provide funds for your child's future when he reaches 21 years of age. Or suppose you have an elderly aunt whom you support. When you use funds that remain with you after paying income taxes, you are pursuing a costly approach. Fifteen thousand dollars paid for your child's education means that you have to earn 30,000 dollars if your tax bracket is 50 percent. But if you can put income-producing property like stocks, bonds, and savings accounts in a trust that earns 1,500 dollars a year, in ten years you can contribute about 14,000 dollars. Only a trust of ten years' duration or more qualifies. If you earn 6 percent on the property, you would have to place 25,000 dollars worth of property into the trust. At the end of ten years or more, the property would return to you intact in accordance with the trust agreement. While in the trust, the income on the property earned each year and distributed annually to a custodian account will belong to your child when he reaches majority, usually 21 years of age in most states. Income received each year on behalf of your child will be subject to a low bracket tax of 15-16%. Also, you do not lose your child as a dependent so long as he or she is under nineteen or a full-time student, and you furnish more than half of his or her support. One very important rule must be observed. The income that is earned must not be used in the discharge or satisfaction of your legal obligation as a parent or son to support the individual. When the income is being accumulated in a custodian account, it is not considered as used for this legal obligation of support.

Life Insurance and Disability Protection

No subject in family planning has as many differences of opinion as the role life insurance plays in family protection. The industry advocates are lined up against their critics. Questions such as how much insurance do you need and should you buy term insurance (pure-risk insurance) or ordinary life insurance (risk and savings plan insurance combined) can never be fully resolved, since the answer depends upon many other factors. For example, the return on the savings element in insurance is small —about 3 percent—but guaranteed. The proponents of term insurance have advocated the purchase of less-expensive term insurance while investing the difference saved in securities. Suppose you do this and thereafter the stock market declines. Would it not have been better to have purchased ordinary life insurance than shares in some mutual fund? Nevertheless, every therapist with dependents and a small personal estate should have all the protection he can afford. Unfortunately, it is too costly to purchase all you need at the initial higher premium rates of ordinary life insurance. Many ingenious plans to keep the cost of the term portion of ordinary life insurance down have been devised, utilizing the cash and dividend values of ordinary life policies. Term insurance also has problems, for over a period of time it becomes increasingly costlier to maintain. Some companies offer term policies with later conversion to ordinary life when you can afford the higher premium without taking a new medical examination. Usually it will be a number of years before a young therapist will have accumulated enough of an estate in the form of securities, real estate, and cash funds. Life insurance constitutes the most important form of initial protection against disaster. However, since life insurance is sold and not bought, care must be exercised not to carry a burdensome amount of insurance. At at time when inflation is long-term and persistent, the value of the investment portion of your life insurance is problematical. The options available in ordinary life policies that permit conversion to an annuity in later years may only provide a small portion of your retirement needs because of inflationary advances. Group life insurance can sometimes be brought through professional societies at a savings because of mass purchasing, etc. You should look into this kind of opportunity. The premiums paid for life insurance are not deductible for income tax purposes.

Disability and Office Expense Insurance

When a psychotherapist cannot work because of illness, his expenses continue to run. Disability insurance is the best safeguard against this occupational hazard by providing disability payments for current needs. Many professional societies sponsor disability insurance plans.

These plans pay for office expenses and income maintenance during your incapacity for a period you select. The greater the benefit period and the income provided, the more costly the premium. The premium paid on a standard personal disability insurance policy is not deductible as a business expense. The income received when you are disabled is tax free. It is best to provide separately for an office expense type policy. Its premium can be deducted as a business expense because it is not considered personal. Although the proceeds are business income they will be offset by your continuing office expenses.

INDEX